THE ANARCHISM OF JEAN GRAVE

THE ANARCHISM OF JEAN GRAVE

Editor, Journalist, and Militant

Louis Patsouras

Montréal/New York/London

Copyright © 2003 BLACK ROSE BOOKS

No part of this book may be reproduced or transmitted in any form, by any means electronic or mechanical including photocopying and recording, or by any information storage or retrieval system—without written permission from the publisher, or, in the case of photocopying or other reprographic copying, a license from the Canadian Reprography Collective, with the exception of brief passages quoted by a reviewer in a newspaper or magazine.

Black Rose Books No. FF313
Hardcover ISBN: 1-55164-185-2 (bound)
Paperback ISBN: 1-55164-184-4 (pbk.)

Canadian Cataloguing in Publication Data

Patsouras, Louis
The anarchism of Jean Grave : editor, journalist, and militant

Includes bibliographical references.
1. Grave, Jean   2. Anarchists--France--Biography.
3. Anarchism--France--History.   I. Title.

HX893.7G73P37 2001   320.5'7'092   C00-901404-7

Cover design: Associés libres

	BLACK ROSE BOOKS	
C.P. 1258	2250 Military Road	99 Wallis Road
Succ. Place du Parc	Tonawanda, NY	London, E9 5LN
Montréal, H2X 4A7	14150	England
Canada	USA	UK

To order books:
In Canada: (phone) 1-800-565-9523 (fax) 1-800-221-9985
email: utpbooks@utpress.utoronto.ca
In United States: (phone) 1-800-283-3572 (fax) 1-651-917-6406
In the UK & Europe: (phone) London 44 (0)20 8986-4854 (fax) 44 (0)20 8533-5821
email: order@centralbooks.com
Our Web Site address: http://www.web.net/blackrosebooks

A publication of the Institute of Policy Alternatives of Montréal (IPAM)

Printed in Canada

CONTENTS

1	Early Life, 1854-1869	1
2	War and the Commune, 1870-1871	13
3	Continuing Revolutionary Activity, 1872-1882	19
4	*Le Révolté* and into *La Révolte* Period, 1883-1890	34
5	The Trial of the Thirty Period, 1891-1894	46
6	*Les Temps Nouveaux* and Other Activity, 1895-1905	60
7	Between Syndicalism and Individualism, 1905-1913	73
8	In the World of Art	87
9	War and Social Revolution, 1914-1920	97
10	Twilight and Death, 1921-1939	110
11	Revolution and Utopia, Background	117
12	Road to Revolution	124
13	Utopia	139
14	Certain Common Views	151
15	Examples of the Anarchist Temperament	155
16	Postscript, 2002	173
Index		201

this work is dedicated to my parents
William and Helen (née Stratoudakis) Patsouras

1

EARLY LIFE, 1854-1869

JEAN GRAVE WAS BORN ON OCTOBER 16, 1854, in the village of Breuil-sur-Couze in the arrondissement of Issoire in the Puy-de-Dôme Department, which, with that of Cantal, comprises most of the old province of Auvergne, named after the Arvennis, an old Gallic tribe with a flourishing civilisation before being subdued by Julius Caesar. Very hilly, straddled by the Auvergne Mountains, a series of extinct volcanoes that run from north to south, Auvergne is largely agricultural: wheat and cattle are in abundance; good wine is made from its grapes; and, of course, it is justly renowned for its cheese. There is some industry, especially in Clermont-Ferrand.

Grave was born two generations after the French Revolution of 1789, a scant six years after the 1848 Revolution, and on the eve of accelerating industrialisation under Napoleon III. As this historical progression unfolded, the socialist tradition was in the process of leaving its utopian phase for its two main currents of anarchism and Marxism: Pierre-Joseph Proudhon, one of the founders of modern anarchism, had already written *What is Property?* (1840) with its answer of "theft," while the founders of Marxism, Karl Marx and Frederick Engels, soon followed with *The Communist Manifesto* (1848).

Grave's ancestors were from the peasantry. His father, also named Jean (1822-1875), was a miller when his son was born, but soon afterward moved to the nearby town of Saint-Germain-Lembron to farm near his parents' village after his business failed. Grave's paternal grandparents were small independent farmers who supplemented their income as part-time self-employed workers making such things as wooden shoes. His mother Elizabeth, née Crégut (1831-1874), came from the nearby town of Ardres-sur-Couze; both of her parents died from tuberculosis when she was young according to Grave. Her father was a court process-server.

As for the literacy of Grave's parents and grandparents (literacy became more prevalent in later generations of the nineteenth century), both his parents had a primary-school education, while his paternal grandparents were illiterate, and although there is no information on his maternal grandparents in this respect, his maternal grandfather may have been literate because of his occupation.

When Grave vividly recounted in his memoirs, *Quarante ans de propagande anarchiste*, the precious memories of early childhood, an especially touching one revealed his love of nature, entranced by the beauty of fields full of yellow flowers. Years later, when Grave was enclosed in a Paris attic as a newspaper editor, he always had a vase of fresh flowers near him.[1]

With the acceleration of the industrial revolution in France during the 1850s, the exodus of the peasantry to the cities increased. Obviously those involved in this, like Grave's parents, were anxious to escape an endemic rural poverty. Grave's family, as many others before and after, migrated to the urban areas in stages: In 1857 his father arrived in Paris as an unskilled worker, then his mother in 1858, after giving birth to a daughter, Anne, in March of that year, and, finally the children, who had been entrusted to the paternal grandparents and an aunt, in 1860.

It is an historical truism that Napoleon III's Second Empire (1852-70) is Saint-Simonian: industrial expansion and the rebuilding of Paris were expressions of economic dynamism and Louis Napoleon had genuine interest in the social problem. In this vein, he wrote *L'extinction du paupérisme*, which advocated that the unemployed work in agricultural colonies in a democratic setting electing their junior officers. The plan itself never materialised, but he introduced such reforms as universal primary education to age twelve, credit unions for workers, the subsidisation of workers' cooperatives, the establishment of honest government pawnshops, and, ultimately, the toleration of labour unions (article 1781 of the Civil Code allowed only employers to fix wages until 1868). If Saint-Simonianism, however, were equated with a higher standard of life for the proletariat, Louis Napolean could not qualify as its disciple.[2]

EARLY LIFE

What kind of Paris greeted the young Grave and his family? To begin, it was the revolutionary capital of the world (the centre of the 1789-94 French Revolution, the revolutions of 1830 and 1848) and was soon to be the scene of the greatest proletarian revolution of the nineteenth century, the Paris Commune of 1871.[3]

Economically, it was a Paris of small industry: approximately 31,500 manufacturing enterprises employed from two to nine workers, while only 7,500 employed ten or more. Of about 100,000 employers and 400,000 employees, two-thirds were in industry. (Inexorably, however, competition reduced the number of industrial enterprises from about 65,000 in 1847 to 39,000 in 1872.)[4] Small-industry was characteristic of France in the nineteenth and early twentieth centuries: for instance, toward the end of the nineteenth century, out of 575,000 industrial enterprises, 534,000 employed less than ten workers, while only 151 employed more than a thousand.[5] This pattern, reflecting the importance of small entrepreneurship, allowed workers a degree of social mobility in Paris, which coupled to an old revolutionary tradition, strengthened the bonds between the proletariat and the lower-middle class. There were certain tendencies, of course, that divided the working class, mainly provincialism and self-interest, but they were largely counterbalanced by much mutual aid and a revolutionary spirit.[6]

When Grave arrived in Paris in 1860, its population of more than one million had more than doubled since 1800. Of its 400,000 workers, 350,000 lived on the right bank, between Père Lachaise Cemetery and the rue de la Paix. Grave's family at first lived on the left bank (not far, however, from the main concentration) on rue Neuve-Sainte-Geneviève, now rue Tournefort in the fifth ward.[7] This section, dominated by the University of Paris, housed many students and workers. After a stay of about two-and-a-half years, Grave recalled that his family moved to an apartment at 140 rue Mouffetard (still in the fifth ward); later the building's attic served as his newspaper office. This was near the Jardin des Plantes and not far from the bustling Place d'Italie. Then, for a brief period of time, his family lived at the rue de l'Ecole Polytechnique and at the suburbs of Choisy-le-Roi and Vaugirard (the latter two locations were related to his father's unsuccessful attempts to become a small businessman) before returning to 138 rue Mouffetard, next door to his former address.[8]

The Paris of Grave's early life was pervaded by a strong sense of *la misère*, which was even much worse in the first half of the nineteenth century. For instance, from 1840 to 1851, indigence plagued between a fourth and a third of the population. Conditions undoubtedly improved during the Second Empire, but not significantly. Emile Zola's Rougon-Macquart series accurately depicted the horror and misery of proletarian life during this period; *L'Assommoir* is the best example.

Grave's memoirs vividly recounted the normal difficulties of a working-class life in the second half of the century: that his family lived in a one-room apartment, which was common for workers; that such a basic amenity as running water was scarcely available on rue Mouffetard, which had only a few water fountains,[9] and that crime, alcoholism, suicide, and violence were rife. Many anarchists whom he knew were criminals; Thirion, whom he was apprenticed to committed suicide;[10] a neighbour, invariably drunk would indiscriminately strike family members; and Grave himself was constantly abused by a brutal father.[11]

That the French proletariat had scant political influence in the councils of government during Grave's youth may readily be seen by the fact that there were only two laws concerning its protection: the first, of March 22, 1841, was on child labour in manufacturing establishments of more than twenty workers. To work, a child had to be eight years old and to age twelve could toil no more than eight hours a day, while from age twelve to sixteen the limit was twelve hours. For night work (two hours equivalent to three in the day), one had to be thirteen years old. The second, of February 22, 1851, was on apprentices. It stipulated a few hours of release time to attend school and no more than a ten-hour day to age fourteen. Yet, even these laws were scarcely observed.

A look at wages and prices during the Second Empire to ascertain whether the proletariat's living standards rose. Wages increased between a sixth and three-tenths, but the cost of living rose by half, food alone more than half and rents doubled. The steep increase in rents was linked to the rebuilding of Paris, which demolished much of the old housing; this began

EARLY LIFE

the exodus of workers to the suburbs that later formed the Red or Communist Belt around Paris in the twentieth century. Prior to this, workers and bourgeoisie often lived in the same buildings, the former occupying the higher floors, the latter the lower; this before the introduction of elevators.

What was the family income of the Graves? Grave himself did not present any information on this. With the birth of Jeanne in 1869, the younger of the two daughters, there were five family members. Grave's father, a shoemaker from the late sixties to his death, was obviously the main breadwinner. Weill in *Histoire du mouvement social* presented a typical yearly budget of 1875 francs for a proletarian family of four in the sixties: 1100 francs for food, 300 for rent, 100 for laundry, 75 for heat and light, and 300 for miscellaneous expenses. As for wages, he stated that an average shoemaker during this period earned about a thousand francs a year. Thus, in order to supplement the family's income, the young Grave had to work at various jobs, while his mother and older sister toiled in the garment trades.[12] Indeed, not only were wages inadequate, but the hours of work were many, a twelve-hour day, six-day week the norm.[13] Not surprisingly, an important battle cry of labour in the nineteenth and twentieth centuries was for an eight-hour day.

Although from a traditional Catholic peasant background, Grave's parents were not religious in the accepted sense of the term. His father was a free thinker, while his mother believed that undoubtedly there was "something out there above us." Despite doubts, Grave's parents baptised their children, had them attend religious classes to receive confirmation, and sent the young Grave to Catholic school. The skeptical religious views of Grave's parents prevailed, however, over the traditional practices. Even as a youngster, Grave was a rabid anticlerical and a convinced atheist. His religious views were tested just before the death of his sister Anne in early November 1874 when a nun from the Saint-Vincent de Paul Order wished to see her. When Grave engaged the nun in a philosophical debate, he shocked her by stating that he did not believe in God who, if He existed, was responsible for the evil in the world, something that He could prevent. Because Grave's sister evidently shared his views, having no wish for the church's consolations, the nun seldom returned.[14]

THE ANARCHISM OF JEAN GRAVE

Although Grave's formal education was unquestionably scanty by twentieth-century French standards, it was about average for that of the Second Empire. Of 2.5 million male children in primary schools, most were enrolled in public schools. About twenty percent, however, attended schools run by two Catholic Orders (the Brothers of the Christian Doctrine that played a major role in the industrial areas, and the Brothers of Mary). Although children of poorer workers did not receive much education, if any, by now two-thirds of the workers were literate, most semi-literate.

Despite the fact that most children in Paris attended public school, Grave received his education from 1860-65 at the religious school run by the Brothers of the Christian Doctrine in the rue des Fossés-Saint-Jacques, as his parents believed that a Catholic school would better aid him to procure work. Grave endured a narrow and restrictive religious working-class education, featuring the lives of saints and the Catechism to make him a good Catholic and, at the same time, allow for the difficulties and sorrows of a proletarian existence to be stoically borne for the promise of heavenly bliss. To confirm the hardships of this world, Grave's school days were characterised by a strong sense of discipline, obedience, and punishment; recalcitrant students were punished by having their outstretched hands struck with leather thongs. In this harsh milieu, he enjoyed one activity, singing. In 1865, he graduated with a certificat d'études, thus completing his primary schooling.[15]

Reading and other recreation relieved the dreary round of proletarian life. After the age of ten, Grave became an omnivorous reader of fiction, history, and science; he particularly enjoyed the first as his family had quite a few books, including the novels of Alexandre Dumas (the elder), the Comtesse Dash, James Fenimore Cooper, and Mayne Reid (an English author). In addition, the family possessed Augustin Thierry's *Histoire de France* and the *Dictionnaire* of Décembre and Allonier, an illustrated encyclopedia.[16] Family activities consisted of walks in the nearby Jardin des Plantes, eating at the popular Richefeu restaurant while being entertained by magicians, and in attending popular plays.[17] The reading undoubtedly aided Grave's becoming an outstanding intellectual.[18]

EARLY LIFE

Grave's memoirs are a rich source for understanding the various forces which molded him; his relations with his parents are fundamental in this respect. To be sure, Grave's family was patriarchal, but his mother enjoyed considerable authority as she shared in making decisions (her earning to supplement the family's income played a role in this) over the children who were expected to obey their parents promptly. Parental control was often enforced by corporal punishment, Grave beaten by both parents, often and severely by his father, seldom and lightly by his mother.

In the interplay between Grave and his parents, his mother, whom he dearly loved, was pictured as tender-hearted and understanding, often intervening to protect him from an authoritarian and abusive father who, for no apparent reason, would beat him, even as a teenager. This harsh treatment probably led to Grave's severe stuttering in public, which humiliated him and eroded his self-confidence. Grave's intense hatred and guilt toward his father led to his contemplating suicide when his father died. This emotional instability continued in his later life in the form of a quarrelsome nature and certainty of always being right, justly called the "Pope of Mouffetard Street." Grave's stuttering forced him to conduct his revolutionary activity exclusively through writing or with comrades in informal egalitarian settings, formally organised groups being too stressful and painful.

As an adult, Grave recalled that he fought against the authoritarian environment of his childhood. What he recounted may not be exactly true since adults often have a distorted picture of their early years. He saw himself as quiet and reasonable, only complying to rational demands of parents and adults, an opponent of authority and injustice: "All injustice, even if it did not personally affect me, irked me. I could not suffer authority." At bottom, Grave had an ambivalent attitude toward his father: On the one hand, he feared and hated him; on the other, he sympathised with his difficult lot in life and even admired his advanced socialist views.

A brief commentary is needed on Grave's psychological state and its bearing on class and class struggle. That Grave was quite severely impaired psychologically and had authoritarian features of a social-psychological nature, as enunciated by T. W. Adorno *et al.* in *The Authoritarian Personal-*

ity, is obvious. Of interest is that in making a comparison between the revolutionary Grave and revolutionary Luther of Erik Erikson's *Young Man Luther*, which amply reveals Luther's psychological disturbances, one is left with the distinct impression that both largely fulfilled their fathers' ambitions. Luther's successful entrepreneur father desired that his son become a prosperous lawyer and was angered when he became a Catholic monk from fear. At the end, however, Luther's religious revolution transformed him into a successful bourgeois in every sense of the term. Grave's father, a politicised worker who failed in business, was a bona fide revolutionary socialist. Grave's rebellion against him led him to extend his father's socialism to anarcho-communism. Certainly, Grave is the antithesis of Erich Fromm's lower-middle class authoritarian in *Escape from Freedom*, who embraced Nazism—who admired the superior bourgeoisie and nobility, but despised the inferior workers.[19]

The economic environment of small business in Paris with its corollary qualities of "initiative" and "enterprise" clearly influenced Grave's father. When he first came to Paris, he was an unskilled worker in a company of used rags, packing rags into balls for transport. But he became self-employed in this business, borrowing money from a friend to establish himself at Choisy-le-Roi. The venture failed. Undaunted, he opened a second-hand store at Vaugirard, but it also foundered. Apparently, sometime near 1866, when the family lived at 138 rue Mouffetard, his father turned to shoemaking with a neighbour whose shop was nearby.

Soon after graduating from primary school, Grave began a series of apprenticeships with master workmen in their home workshops who were often subcontractors of more successful entrepreneurs. Thus, exploited artisans would in turn exploit apprentices. Despite this harsh condition, which could not but exacerbate social relations between masters and apprentices, Grave had generally good relations with them. His first apprenticeship, however, to a mechanic, Delompré, was the exception as it was characterised by acrimonious arguments. Indeed, one became so heated that Grave attempted to strike Delompré with a hammer, who deflected the blow. Grave understood his violent temper, stating that he was as "timid as a young bird, but when necessary, I know how to overcome my diffidence, and like all shy people I easily resort to extremes."[20] Grave's parents soon removed him from this unpleasant tutelage. The next apprenticeship to Thirion, a shoemaker from Lorraine, proved to be pleasant as he would entertain Grave while working with stories and songs. Grave described him as an exceedingly gentle and charming individual "who would not even hurt a fly." At times, ever generous, Thirion would take him to see popular plays. There was, however, a tragic side to Thirion's life because he was alcoholic and suicide-prone; he would disappear for days at a time while drunk and attempt suicide. Finally, Grave's parents had him leave this gentle but troubled man because of his long drinking bouts—he committed suicide.

Grave continued his shoemaker's apprenticeship, principally with Vergnolles, a competent teacher whom he respected. Grave's father, however forced Grave to leave Vergnolles in order to work with him. The two worked "independently" for other shoemaker-entrepreneurs who contracted work with them. Not unexpectedly, relations between Grave and his father were in a constant state of turmoil because his father blamed him for all faulty workmanship. Grave did remember, however, one redeeming paternal quality, singing in the native patois of Auvergne. (Grave, incidentally, was well aware of the regional differences among workers; he invariably mentioned, in describing his employers, their native provinces; a large part of the Parisian proletariat was from the provinces.) The "partnership" of father and son soon foundered economically. His father briefly became a railroad worker, while Grave returned to Vergnolles. Soon, however, father and son were again working together as shoemakers.[21]

Sometime before 1868, Grave recalled going with Vergnolles to the Préfecture de Police to procure his *livret*, a "notebook" that workers were forced to carry, which indicated their work record, including remarks by employers concerning behaviour and performance; an unsatisfactory *livret* would invariably lead to unemployment. The *livret* was introduced in the middle of the eighteenth century, abolished in 1792, reintroduced by Napoleon in 1803, abrogated by Louis Napoleon in 1868, reinstated after the Paris Commune of 1871, and finally terminated by the Third Republic in 1890. For Grave, the *livret*, which he compared to the official card carried by prostitutes, clearly indicated the lowly position of the proletariat. He was, thus, well aware of what R.H. Tawney, the well-known British historian and socialist, called the "moral humiliation" experienced by workers in their dealings with the bourgeoisie.[22]

In delving into Grave's background, mention has been made of his father's socialism. Although Grave's paternal grandfather supported Louis Napoleon, as did most of the peasantry, his father, even at Breuil-sur-Couze, was a republican and an anticlerical, and once in Paris became associated with the left current of French socialism as a member of a Blanquist group.[23]

The Blanquists were led by Louis-Auguste Blanqui (1805-1881), the foremost French revolutionary of the nineteenth century. Born into an upper-middle-class family (his father was a high government official under Napoleon I), he not only received an excellent lycée education, but university training in law and medicine. As a teenager he joined the *Charbonnerie* (a secret revolutionary society whose aim was to destroy the monarchy), and then participated in the July 1830 Revolution in Paris. Later, he was one of the principal founders of The Society of the Seasons, formed in Paris in 1837, that tried an unsuccessful uprising there in 1839. He then took part in the 1848 Revolution in Paris, and in the 1870-71 events by leading an unsuccessful revolt in Paris on October 31, 1870. He paid a steep price for his activities since more than half of his adult life was spent in prison. His grand design envisaged a small and tightly knit revolutionary socialist group overthrowing the bourgeoisie in order to install a proletarian dictatorship organising work along cooperative lines.[24]

That Grave's highly politicised family was cognisant of international developments was indicated by the young Grave's daydreams to liberate oppressed people at the head of an army. Indeed, while still a youngster, Grave wrote a play, never finished, of a Polish hero fighting to overthrow the Russian yoke. Polish uprisings against the Russians, as is well known, were sympathetically greeted in France.[25]

EARLY LIFE

Notes

1. Jean Grave's birth certificate is deposited at Breuil-sur-Couze in the Puy-de-Dôme Department. On Grave's family and early life, see Jean Grave, *Quarante ans de propagande anarchiste*, préface de Jean Maitron, présenté et annoté par Mireille Delfau (Paris: Flammarion, 1973), pp 36ff. To be cited as *Quarante ans*. This work represents Grave's unabridged memoirs. The preface by Dr. Maitron is excellent. The abridged version of the preceding work is *Le Mouvement libertaire sous le 3e République* (Paris: Les Oeuvres Répresentatives, 1930). To be cited as *Mouvement libertaire*.

2. On Saint-Simon, see Frank E. Manuel, *The New World of Henri Saint-Simon* (Cambridge, Mass.: Harvard University Press, 1956). See, for example, Alfred Cobban, *A History of Modern France*, Vol. II: *From First Empire to the Fourth Republic* (Baltimore: Penguin Books, 1961), pp 152–63. Gordon Wright, *France in Modern Times; 1760 to the Present*, (Chicago: Rand McNally, 1960), pp 219–21, saw Napoleon III as Saint-Simonian but acknowledged that it was moot whether the proletariat received higher living standards during his reign. Favorable to Napoleon III: Albert Guérard, *Napoleon III* (Cambridge, Mass.: Harvard University Press, 1943). Critical toward Napoleon III: J. M. Thompson, *Louis Napoleon and the Second Empire* (Oxford: Blackwell, 1954). Also see Marcel Blanchard, *Le Second Empire* (Paris: Collin, 1950), which is an excellent synthesis.

3. For an excellent account of the early French revolutionary movement, see C. E. Labrousse, *Le mouvement ouvrier et les théories sociales en France de 1815 à 1848* (Paris: C.D.U., 1954).

4. Georges Weill, *Histoire du mouvement social en France, 1852–1902* (Paris: Félix Alcan, 1904), p 15. Georges Duveau, *La Vie ouvrière en France sous le Second Empire* (Paris: Gallimard, 1946), pp 321–27. Of the 400,000 workers, 300,000 were men, and 100,000 were women. A. Audiganne, *Mémoires d'un ouvrier de Paris, 1871–72* (Paris: Charpentier, 1873), p 109, stated that by 1870, there were about 600,000 workers in the Paris area. On the fact of less employers in Paris between 1847 and 1862, see Jean Bruhat, Jean Dautry, Emile Tersen, *et al*, *La Commune de 1871* (Paris: Editions Sociales, 1970), p 26.

5. John H. Clapham, *The Economic Development of France and Germany, 1815–1914*, (Cambridge: Cambridge University Press, 1921), p 258.

6. A. Audiganne, *Les populations ouvriers et les industries de la France* (Paris: Capelle, 1860), I, 283.

7. Duveau, *La vie ouvrière*, pp 321ff and pp 345–47. *Quarante ans*, p 49.

8. *Ibid.*, pp 49ff.

9. *Ibid.*, p 85 on housing; p 84 on running water.

10. *Ibid.*, p 72.

11. On Parisian working-class life in the first half of the nineteenth century, see Louis Chevalier, *Laboring Classes and Dangerous Classes; In Paris in the First Half of the Nineteenth Century* (New York: Howard Fertig, 1973).

12. Grave's largely autobiographical novel—he is Caragut—is *La Grande famille, roman militaire* (Paris: P. V. Stock, 1907), p 103.

13. On socioeconomic conditions in the Second Empire, see Bruhaut, *La Commune de 1871*, pp 27–37; and Duveau, *La Vie ouvrière*, pp 233–35, who saw the average working day of the period at almost twelve hours; in pp 321–22, he stated that the higher-paid workers in the eighteen-sixties earned between 1,100 to 1,500 francs per year (women's wages were about half those of the men). Weill, *Histoire du mouvement social*, pp 116–7.

14. On Grave's family and religion, see *Quarante ans*, pp 46ff and 127–8.

15. On Grave and education, see some statistics in Duveau, *La vie ouvrière*, pp 449–50. *Quarante ans*, p 45, p55.

16. *Quarante ans*, pp 65–6, and p 126.

17. *Ibid.*, pp 47–9, 70. Grave writes much about the plays that he saw as a teenager; they include Eugene Sue's *Le Juif Errant* (the play was adapted from the book) and Dumanoir's and Dennery's *Don César de Bazan*.

18. Most of the socialist leaders came from bourgeois backgrounds: Robert Michels, *Political Parties: A Sociological Study of the Oligarchian Tendencies of Modern Democracy* (New York: Collier Books, 1962), pp 107ff. This work was first published in 1911.

19. On Grave's relations with his parents see his *La Grande famille*, pp 84–85; the quote is from p 84; also, see *Quarante ans*, pp 55–58, p 74; and p 241 on his not being able to talk in public due to a severe stutter. The psychological appraisal of Grave has been influenced by these works: Erik. H. Erikson, *Childhood and Society* (New York: W. W. Norton, 1963), pp 48–108, for example. Erik H. Erikson, *Youth and Crisis* (New York, W. W. Norton, 1968), pp 91ff. Erik H. Erikson, *Young Man Luther: A Study of Psychoanalysis and History* (New York: W. W. Norton, 1962), pp13–97. E. Victor Wolfenstein, *The Revolutionary Personality: Lenin, Trotsky, Gandhi* (Princeton, N. J.: Princeton Univ. Press, 1971), pp 3–32 and pp 292ff. Barrington Moore Jr., *Injustice: The Social Bases of Obedience and Revolt* (White Plains, N. Y.: M. E. Sharpe, 1978), pp 89–109. Also see T. W. Adorno, Else Frankel-Brunswik, Daniel J. Brothers, and R. Nevitt Sanford, *The Authoritarian Personality* (New York: Harper and Brothers, 1950), pp 759ff on "The Authoritarian Personality." Erich Fromm, *Escape from Freedom* (New York: Rinehart, 1941), pp 141–206.

20. *Quarante ans*, p 63.

21. *Ibid.*, pp 62–8.

22. On the *livret* and other social matters, see Duveau, *La Vie ouvrière*, pp 233–5; and Weill, *Histoire du mouvement sociale*, pp 5ff. *Quarante ans*, p 81. R. H. Tawney, *Equality* (London: George Allen and Unwin, 1931), p 37.

23. *Quarante ans*, p 87.

24. On Blanqui, see Alan B. Spitzer, *The Revolutionary Theories of Louis-Auguste Blanqui* (New York: Columbia University Press, 1957).

25. *Quarante ans*, p 56.

2

WAR AND THE COMMUNE, 1870-1871

BASICALLY, THE FRANCO-PRUSSIAN WAR of 1870-1871 was caused by the rival imperialism of France under Napoleon III and of Prussia under its wily Chancellor, Otto Von Bismarck. Napoleon III's hubris, which tried to emulate the exploits of his legendary uncle, was decisive in unleashing the war. On July 14 (Bastille Day), 1870, without negotiating, and without allies, France declared war on Prussia to redress an alleged insult cleverly engineered by Bismarck.

From the beginning, the war went badly for France; by September 1870, Napoleon III had been taken prisoner and Paris was encircled. A new government of national defense was then formed under Léon Gambetta, a Radical Republican. He attempted to resurrect the old Jacobin, nationalist-revolutionary spirit, but losses already suffered were inordinately severe. The siege of Paris (from September 19, 1870, to January 28, 1871) could not be broken, necessitating a three-month truce with the Prussians.[1]

During this tempestuous period, Grave and his father followed the political and military events in the left-wing press and his father participated in some key revolutionary happenings. They read the Blanquist *La Patrie en Danger*, Jules Vallès' *Cri du Peuple*, Félix Pyat's *Le Vengeur*, and Vermersch's *Père Duchêne*.[2] The father joined the unsuccessful Blanquist attempt to procure arms in August 1870,[3] and with Paris in danger enrolled in the National Guard. Grave also wished to join, but was rejected because of his small size.[4]

Grave well recalled the hardships of the siege, especially rationing of bread and meat with accompanying long lines of people patiently waiting to purchase their share. When meat became scarce, family cats were butchered for food, and finally rats were sold at the rate of one franc each. When the German bombardment of the city began in early January 1871, the Graves, along with others, moved to a nearby large underground basement for refuge.[5]

After the conclusion of an armistice with Prussia in late January 1871, elections were held in early February for a National Assembly. For various reasons (one was that in times of peril the people followed the local conservative elite), universal male suffrage elected a body dominated by Royalists who repudiated Gambetta's leadership and made peace with the Prussians on February 19. To make matters worse, the Assembly elected Louis Adolphe Thiers as provisional executive. Not only did radical Paris dislike him for his part in suppressing the workers' revolt in Lyons in 1834 and reactionary role in the 1848 revolution, but it was outraged by the Assembly's Law of Maturities, ordering that debts (many incurred by the lower-middle class and workers who manned the walls of Paris against German attack) be paid within a brief period. But this was not all. On March 18, 1871, Thiers sent troops to remove the artillery of the National Guard, provoking the proletariat and lower-middle class of the city to revolt and to establish the Paris Commune in which the people were determined to rule themselves. Paris thereupon became a revolutionary island in a conservative sea.[6]

These events undoubtedly influenced Grave's later political outlook: that the state was basically in the hands of economically dominant groups bent on perpetuating their interests, economic and political, was corroborated by the Law of Maturities;[7] and that state authority was basically irresponsible and rested ultimately on force and deceit was confirmed by the government's surprise attempt to remove the artillery from Montmartre.[8]

Within a few days, elections for a municipal government (the Commune) were held: of the ninety-two elected representatives, ten were Blanquists, seventeen were in the First International, about forty were left-wing Jacobins basically aligned with the working class, and the remainder were Republican moderates and radicals. The last group quickly resigned. Supplementary elections held on April 16 further increased socialist representation.⁹ The strong Blanquist contingent reflected the fact that Blanqui was the chief inspirer of the Commune, although he was arrested by Thiers a few days before its beginning. Blanqui's importance may be measured by the Commune's offering to exchange all of its hostages for him alone.¹⁰

The Commune had a strong anarchist element. Proudhonian Mutualists included such well-know figures as Eugène Varlin, the outstanding leader of the French union movement in the 1860s; Gustave Courbet, the famous painter; and Charles Longuet, a prominent socialist who later married one of Marx's daughters. The Bakuninist strain had such stalwarts as Elie Reclus, the director of the Bibliothèque Nationale during the Commune; his brother, Elisée Reclus who was captured in the early fighting; and Louise Michel, the Commune's great heroine who fought to the bitter end.¹¹

In examining the Commune's decrees, we find that anarchism was significant. The Commune opposed centralisation, its aim being a federation of communes. It favoured a people's government in which distinctions between governors and governed would be largely erased. Representatives of the people were to receive the wages of average workers, be popularly elected, and be subject to immediate recall. It opposed a military caste as all were to bear arms. It was militantly anti-religious, its aim to liberate humanity from the machinations and superstitions of clerics. Finally, it would destroy bourgeois property and administration for one based on co-operative ownership and democratic management of production.¹²

All of the measures and principles enunciated by the Commune were deeply imbedded in Grave's thought: his antimilitarism, antireligious sentiments, opposition to centralisation, and stress on equality and fraternity tied to liberty. Years later, in an article, "Les Anarchistes sont les seuls socialistes," Grave evoked the traditions of the Commune to rebuke other socialists for compromising with the present, for wishing to come to terms with the bourgeois state by accepting its public offices, and for assuming that hierarchy would continue even under socialism.¹³

Grave *experienced* the Commune. He closely followed the various events and shared its hopes and struggles to survive. He recalled that, as others, he was affected by a general revolutionary euphoria, which he described as a "revolutionary virus."[14] When the fighting began, he wished to enroll in a Commune battalion, but was overruled by his father. But he accompanied his father to the various training exercises of his National Guard battalion at the Place du Panthéon.[15] He reminisced that the rank and file had wished to march immediately on Versailles to make short shrift of its conservative government, but orders never came, and the opportunity for victory, however slight, was lost. From this experience, he drew the tactical lesson that the masses should act in a revolutionary situation without waiting for directions from any leadership.[16]

When in the final "Bloody Week," May 22-28, 1871, the Versailles army had broken into the city and the last desperate fighting occurred, Grave was active in building a street barricade where the rue Mouffetard intersected with other streets. He wished to defend it, but was prevented from doing so by his father.[17] Although Grave himself did not see the horrible repression inflicted on the Communards, he was acutely aware of its intensity from eyewitness friends.[18] In Grave's novel, *La Grande famille*, the hero Caragut (notice the similarity to Crégut) witnessed the Commune's dead littering the streets in the last desperate fighting and declared that for him all that was most despicable, "discipline, obedience, and oppression," triumphed with the Commune's fall.[19] The last of the fighting occurred at Père Lachaise cemetery where on May 28, at the Wall of the Federals, 147 Communards who survived the fighting were executed. (More than twenty thousand Communards were shot by on-the-spot courts-martial in the final week; another five thousand were put to death after court trials.)[20]

Grave often referred to the Commune because it was the most significant revolutionary experience that provided the yardstick for his socialism. In *La Société future*, he stated that an important lesson learned by the proletariat during the Commune was that capital was its main enemy.[21] Then, too, as a result of the Commune's failure, he saw the revolution not as a single act, but as a series of struggles over a period of time.[22] Indeed, the nondoctrinaire nature of the Commune was also consonant with anarchist principles and paralleled his assertion of the impracticability to prescribe precise and exact details for a future society.[23]

WAR AND THE COMMUNE

In attempting to understand Grave's revolutionary élan during his long lifetime, his Commune experiences were decisive. Indeed, for the revolutionary socialist generation of Grave's youth and maturity (until the 1917 Bolshevik Revolution), it was the Commune which symbolised the hopes and aspirations of revolutionary socialists.[24]

Notes
1. On the siege of Paris, see Robert Baldick, *The Siege of Paris* (New York: Macmillan, 1964).
2. *Quarante ans*, p 98. Jules Vallès is perhaps the best remembered of the newspaper editors mentioned; a militant Communard, his newspaper personified the spirit of the Commune. On his life, see Jean Maitron, *Dictionnaire biographique du mouvement ouvrier français*; Part III: *De la Commune à la Grande Guerre* (vols. 10-15; Paris: Les Editions Ouvrières, 1973-7), XV, 279-81. To be cited as *DB*. On the press of the period, see A. Dupuy, *1870-1871, La Guerre, la Commune, et la presse* (Paris: A. Colin, 1959).
3. *Quarante ans*, p 91.
4. *Ibid.*, p 93.
5. *Ibid.*, pp 95-103.
6. For information on the National Assembly see Frank H. Brabant, *The Beginning of the Third Republic in France; A History of the National Assembly (February-September 1871)* (London: Macmillan and Co., 1940), pp 61-73. Edward S. Mason, *The Paris Commune; An Episode in the History of the Socialist Movement* (New York: Macmillan Co., 1930), chap 2, on the founding of the Paris Commune. On the Paris Commune of 1871, see also G. D. H. Cole, *A History of Socialist Thought*, Vol. II: *Marxism and Anarchism, 1850-1890* (London: Macmillan Co., 1957) to be cited as Cole II; R. W. Postgate, *Revolution from 1789 to 1906* (New York: Harper Torchbooks, 1962); Franck Jellinek, *The Paris Commune of 1871* (New York: Grosset and Dunlap, 1965); Charles Rihs, *La Commune de Paris; sa structure et ses doctrines* (Paris: Seuil, 1973); Bruhat, La Commune; Stewart Edwards, *The Paris Commune, 1871* (Eyre and Spottiswoode, 1971); and André Decouflé, *La Commune de Paris (1871); révolution populaire et pouvoir révolutionnaire* (Paris: Cujas, 1969).
7. Jean Grave, *La société mourante et l'anarchie*, preface Octave Mirabeau (Paris: Tresse et Stock, 1893), pp 199-212.
8. *Ibid.*
9. Rihs, *La Commune*, pp 87-94.
10. Alain Sergent and Claude Harmel, *Histoire de l'anarchie* (Paris: Le Portulan, 1949), pp 400-407; and Rihs, *La Commune*, stated that the Commune was a combination of leftist tendencies.

11. For short biographical sketches of well-known Communards, see Bruhaut, *La Commune*, pp 421–46.
12. Postgate, *Revolution from 1789 to 1906*, pp 298ff.
13. Jean Grave, "Les Anarchistes sont les seuls socialistes," *Les Temps Nouveaux*, Sept. 28-Oct. 4, 1895, p 1.
14. Jean Grave, "Nos Fautes; la foule et les minorités révolutionnaires," *La Bataille*, Oct. 14, 1918, p 2; Grave, *La Grande famille*, p 87, has Caragut opting for a "just republic, giving to all the good life, liberty and equality."
15. *Quarante ans*, p 109 and p 115.
16. *Quarante ans*, p 109; Cole II, 137 agreed with Grave's view that the Commune's only hope was to have struck quickly. Also see Jean Grave, "Ne nous illusionnons pas," *Publications de "La Révolte" et "Temps Nouveaux,"* No. 12 (April 1, 1922), p 13. To be cited as *Publications*.
17. *Quarante ans*, p 118.
18. *Ibid.*, p 121.
19. Grave, *La Grande famille*, p 89.
20. Bruhaut *et al.*, *La Commune*, pp 255–97.
21. Jean Grave, *La Société future* (Paris: P. V. Stock, 1895) p 3.
22. *Ibid.*, p 8.
23. Jean Grave, *La société au lendemain de la révolution* (Paris: Au Bureau de *La Révolte*, 1893), p 4.
24. Cole, II, 163-73 on the Commune's significance on anarchism and Marxism.

3

CONTINUING REVOLUTIONARY ACTIVITY, 1872-1882

ALTHOUGH THE DEFEAT OF THE PARIS COMMUNE considerably diminished socialist activity for a spell in Paris, it would soon resume its vibrancy. Indeed, significant theoretical changes in socialist thinking occurred just before and after the Commune.

Already by the 1860s, the advanced sections of the French proletariat were greatly influenced by Mutualism, which formed the central thrust of the social ideas of Proudhon (1809-1865), the principal founder of modern anarchism and the single most important personage of French socialism. Along with Grave and Robert Owen, he was one of the few prominent socialist thinkers born into a working-class family. Like Grave, Proudhon was a printer, and as a worker, he did not view the proletariat as an abstraction, but as a living and vibrant social reality. He early became involved in working-class activity by joining a clandestine workers' organisation in Lyons during the early forties. In 1844, he met Michael Bakunin and Marx, forming a lifelong friendship with the former, but soon breaking with the latter, presaging the acrimonious debates between anarchists and Marxists in the First International in the sixties.[1]

Proudhon's Mutualism envisioned a society largely based on the economic activity of self-employed farmers and artisans. Although the existence of private property allowed for socio-economic inequality (intensity and longevity of work would vary according to individual effort), there was nonetheless a general equality in that one could not exploit the labour of others. Economic activity among individuals and/or groups would be legitimised through contracts.[2] Formal government was minimal since local autonomous communes would federate only under a common constitution.³ Two important buttresses of this system were a strong family, in which the wife was clearly subordinate to the husband,⁴ and the national bank operating on the national level. The peaceful change from capitalism to anarchism would come as workers and farmers gaining political power would impose a levy on the bourgeoisie by having a national bank make low-term or interest-free loans to them, as individuals or associations, to begin their self-managed enterprises.⁵ Proudhon was confident that the people had the requisite capacity to run everything; this optimism was based primarily on the fact that as a worker, he knew them as capable, not caricatures of stupidity.

Although Proudhon at times urged cooperation between the proletariat and the bourgeoisie, his last work, *De la capacité politique des classes ouvrières* (1865), focusing on class struggle, urged workers to separate themselves from the bourgeois power structure by developing a countersociety and accompanying counterculture to usher in anarchism.

The influence of Proudhon on Grave's thought is not inconsiderable. Although Grave at first rejected Proudhon's essentially peaceful and evolutionary pattern for change and repudiated his stress on privately owned non-exploitative property, he agreed with him that economic activity should be governed by contractual agreements among individuals and workers' associations, thus individual autonomy would be maintained.⁶

With the demise of the Paris Commune, Mutualism in anarchist circles gave way to the revolutionary collectivism of Bakunin (1814-1876). Born into a noble Russian family that was Westernised (his father had a Ph.D. from the University of Padua), he became a revolutionary while a young Hegelian in Berlin in the early forties, and soon afterward met and was influenced by Proudhon. He participated in the February 1848 Revolution in Paris, and in the 1849 Dresden Revolution with Richard Wagner. Bakunin's involvement in the latter adventure led to his forcible return to Russia and consequent imprisonment and banishment to Siberia, from where he escaped.⁷

Bakunin's ideas differed from Proudhon's in several key respects. Whereas Proudhon emphatically rejected the revolutionary overturn of the State in one fell swoop, Bakunin envisaged a cataclysmic revolution from the activities of a small, secret, and highly disciplined organisation to create the necessary conditions through propaganda by deed—terroristic acts, like bombings and assassinations, to be launched against the power structure to ignite revolt among the people.[8] To this end, he founded the International Social Democratic Alliance in 1868.[9] In the economic sphere, in contradiction to Proudhon's stress on small and privately owned property, Bakunin foresaw the importance of agricultural and industrial collectives,[10] probably influenced by the increasing industrialisation of Europe which Proudhon had not sufficiently anticipated. Despite the differences noted between them, they agreed on the importance and necessity of the local autonomous commune as the bedrock of a future anarchist society. The communes obviously would federate.[11]

While anarchist ideas were spreading among the proletariat, so too were those of Marxism. Marx (1818-1883), along with Proudhon, is the foremost socialist thinker of the nineteenth century. An upper-middle-class German-Jew (his father was a lawyer), he received an excellent university education, procuring a Ph.D. in philosophy from the University of Jena. Because of his involvement in the 1848 Revolution, when he urged German workers to revolt against the government, he was ultimately expelled from Germany, living in London from 1849 to his death. Marx's critique of capitalism was the most cogent ever written by a socialist. Although Marx emphasized revolution in his early years, he later tempered it by advocating the creation of working-class parties to engage in electoral and reformist politics. Indeed, he and his collaborator, Engels, envisaged the possible peaceful acceptance of socialism in such advanced capitalist nations moving toward democracy as Great Britain, France, and the United States.[12]

The conflicting currents of anarchism and Marxism collided in the First International (1864-1876), which was formed to promote greater working-class activity in both national and international levels.[13] Although in the earlier congresses, the differences between Proudhonian Mutualists, Marxists, and others did not lead to any appreciable disunity, in later ones a bitter struggle erupted between the Bakuninist-inspired anarchists and the Marxists.[14] The former, rejecting reformism, desired immediate revolutionary action by small and clandestine groups, advocated complete group autonomy within the International, and resolutely opposed the state. The latter, however, were rapidly becoming cautious and reformist in strategy: They downplayed revolutionary action for the present, accepted bourgeois cooperation for social reform, insisted on centralisation within the International, and envisaged the state to slowly wither away, even with the advent of socialism.[15] These basic differences led to the eventual split between anarchists and Marxists in the eventful Hague Congress of 1872. The anarchists left to found a rival Saint-Imier International that lasted to 1877, while the weakened First International expired a year earlier.[16] The failure of the Paris Commune and the internecine bickering within socialism, coupled to a general economic slump which weakened unions, saw the eighteen-seventies as the nadir of European socialism.

Despite the setbacks in the seventies, from a theoretical perspective, anarchism progressed when Bakuninist collectivism was refined by a further advance, anarcho-communism. Its first consistent modern advocates, Elisée Reclus (1830-1905), his brother Elie (1827-1904), and a Genevan worker François Dumartheray added the free distribution of goods and elimination of wage labour to Bakunin's views.[17] These anarcho-communist ideas were similar to the Marxian second phase of socialism or "com - munism," earlier foreseen by such philosophers as Pythagoras and More in his *Utopia*.[18] The Reclus brothers, born into a Huguenot family, were Fourierists in their youth before becoming followers of Proudhon, then Bakunin. Elie, after studying theology, worked for the Crédit Mobilier founded by the Perière brothers, while Elisée was interested in geography. Both were exiled for their activity in the Commune. Elie returned to become an ethnologist; Elisée taught geography at the Free University of Brussels from 1894 to 1905, to become one of the most distinguished geographers of the nineteenth century. Both, especially Elisée, were friends of Grave.

The most prominent thinker of anarcho-communism, a member of the Russian nobility, was Peter Kropotkin (1842-1921). This sensitive but forceful idealist was acutely aware of the social injustice which permitted the nobility to enjoy great privileges at the expense of social misery for the masses. After graduating in 1857 from the exclusive Corps of Pages attached to the Czar, he enrolled in an army regiment spending five years in

CONTINUING REVOLUTIONARY ACTIVITY

Siberia. There, in numerous expeditions, he was thoroughly impressed by the fact that their success depended more on voluntaristic cooperation than on authoritarian discipline.

In 1872, Kropotkin made his first trip to Western Europe. While in Switzerland, he noticed a striking difference between anarchists and other socialists: in the formally organised socialist groups, socioeconomic and intellectual differences between leaders of middle-class origin with few exceptions, and followers, usually blue-collar workers (some of whom, however, were skilled), were so marked that a truly egalitarian spirit did not exist between them. In the Swiss Jura Federation, however, among Bakuninist anarchists, of generally economically independent and educated craftsmen, a spirit of general equality prevailed.[19] After returning to Russia, Kropotkin joined a revolutionary circle whose aim was to propagate revolutionary socialist ideas among the people. In 1874, Kropotkin was imprisoned for his role in this activity, but soon afterward escaped and went to London.[20] In 1877, after a brief stay in Paris, he arrived in Geneva, the centre of the important anarchist Jura Federation,[21] to write for *L'Avant Garde*, the leading anarchist newspaper of the period, in the course of which he effectively developed his anarcho-communism.[22]

Anarchism, including anarcho-syndicalism, played an important role in French intellectual/artistic life and trade union movement, was a strong element in Italian labour, developed a powerful mass base in Spain, formed a significant segment of the Russian revolutionary tradition, well-ensconced in the Socialist Revolutionary Party, and had modest success in the United States among pockets of German, Jewish, and Italian immigrants, in addition to being involved in its labour movement, principally in the Industrial Workers of the World.

Anarchist influence in these nations was tied to certain socioeconomic and cultural patterns. In France, the persistence of small enterprise, coupled with a puissant revolutionary tradition, inevitably fostered among workers a desire to control industry. In Italy, Spain, and Russia, which had traditional rural societies characterised by deep class division and endemic social oppression, anarchist revolutionary fervor attracted many workers and peasants. In the United States, the alienation experienced by politicised immigrants and the normal labour violence of a tempestuous frontier nation, strongly individualistic, formed the requisite crucible for anarchist penetration.

Anarchist success in these nations and social settings, however, did not equal that of democratic socialism, including its Marxist component, especially as industrialisation became more widespread, with its increased labour differentiation and heirarchy dividing the proletariat into various status groups, thus diminishing its solidarity: industrialisation also pacified the proletariat by raising living standards. The advent of representative democracy also aided in deflecting proletarian revolution as its very essence is gradualism. These developments favoured democratic socialists, including Marxists, at the expense of anarchists. The former were in mass electoral parties which basically advocated piecemeal reform, whereas the latter were in relatively small and informally organised groups that stressed immediate revolution. Even so, with the passage of time, such anarchists as Grave had to accept the impact of reformism in devising a revolutionary strategy.[23]

Soon after the fall of the Commune, Grave's family moved to the Avenue des Gobelins, installing themselves in more spacious quarters; the family's improved economic position (Grave and his father, still shoemakers, earned more) and the birth of a second daughter allowed this.

This improvement of fortune was to be short-lived because Grave's mother and sister Anne contracted tuberculosis: The former died after a long period of debility in March 1874; the latter in November of the same year, Grave and his father nursing them to the end. The tragedy of illness resulting in early death was not uncommon in the nineteenth century, but more prevalent among the workers than the bourgeoisie.[24]

More tragedy and change soon followed. In early 1875, Grave's father was hospitalised with a high fever but after release from the hospital, left with his daughter Jeanne to stay with his sister and her husband in Saint-Germain-Lembron. Grave, now alone, was soon drafted by the marines, but although he contemplated desertion, he entered the service in October of the same year. His stay at Brest and Pontanezen was of brief duration, because on his father's death in 1876, he secured a discharge late in the year on the basis of being the oldest surviving member of his family.[25]

CONTINUING REVOLUTIONARY ACTIVITY

Grave's military experiences as a marine were vividly recounted in his largely autobiographical novel, *La Grande famille*. In a well-written realistic novel replete with drama, the reader was invited to empathise with the young recruits in various situations: at inspection, observing the infantile temper tantrums of officers; in the barracks and on arduous field maneuvers; and in the houses of prostitution where the frustrations of the hapless and dazed recruits were taken out on lowly prostitutes.

Grave graphically described the psychological dehumanisation of military life, which moulded its subjects into disciplined robot-killers. Perceptively, he linked the brutality of military life to society at large, in which to survive, one must either accept the alienation of the status quo or rebel and still suffer. The denouement saw Caragut, the protagonist, commit suicide after killing a tyrannical noncommissioned officer.[26] Here, Grave drew from self-experience: the trauma of knowing that his father's death was rather imminent and an attack of yellow jaundice brought about a generally depressed psychological condition that led to contemplating suicide.[27] Grave's novel is indicative of his coming to grips with the intense pain of misfortune in a repressive bourgeois society.

After his military discharge, Grave returned to Paris, finding a room in the apartment building where his family lived after the Commune. He continued his shoemaking with a former neighbour and, after a brief respite, plunged into socialist activity.[28] In 1877, he voted for a republican in the general elections; the first and only time he ever voted.[29]

In 1879, Grave became involved in a significant socialist current when drawn to the meetings of the Parti des Travailleurs Socialistes de France from reading their newspaper, *Le Prolétaire*.[30] An unstable mixture of anarchists, Marxists, and other socialists, it was founded in 1879 at the Marseilles Labour Congress in which the socialist faction decisively defeated those favourable to capitalism.[31] At party meetings, Grave gravitated to the anarchist side in which his closest friends were Pierre Jeallot and Minville, both workers and participants in the Commune. The former had already been imprisoned six months for radical activity in 1878-79; the latter had been an officer in the Commune.[32] Grave fondly recalled that after meetings the three would talk until dawn four or so times a week. Unfortunately, this interfered with his shoemaker's work, so he bravely took the remedy of less talk and more sleep.[33]

The anarchist group which Grave joined in 1879 had been greatly influenced by Kropotkin and Andrea Costa (an Italian follower of Bakunin, later a Marxist and a founder of the Italian Socialist Party) who were in Paris in 1878. The movement was temporarily weakened when both were convicted for associating with an international organisation, the Anarchist International. Costa was imprisoned for one year, but Kropotkin escaped to Switzerland.[34]

Grave's activity in 1879 included belonging to a proletarian group formed to aid the amnestied Communards, The Committee to Aid the Amnestied, which collected a few thousand francs, and in serving on a committee soliciting aid for striking workers.[35]

In early 1880, Grave with Jeallot and Minville, founded the Social Study Group of the Fifth and Thirteenth Wards of Paris, the first significant anarchist group in Paris since the Commune's fall. It was at this time that Grave, as its secretary, began his writer's apprenticeship.[36] (An example of his early writing is in *Le Droit Social*, a Lyons anarchist newspaper.)[37] The meetings of the Social Study Group, in typical anarchist fashion, did not have a chairperson. Many well-known anarchists attended the meetings. They included Errico Malatesta, one of anarchism's most inspiring figures who had come to France after leading an unsuccessful anarchist insurrection in the 1870s near Naples;[38] Carlo Cafiero, an Italian disciple of Bakunin who also participated in that insurrection; Warlaan Tcherkesoff, a revolutionary Georgian Prince who became a militant anarchist; and Jules Guesde, a Communard of anarchist leanings and undisputed leader of the Parti des Travailleurs Socialistes de France.

The meetings were of more than esoteric importance as they aided in formulating the program of Guesde's newspaper, *L'Egalité*,[39] whose basically anarchist position affirmed that the proletariat could free itself only through revolution, voting allowed only as a form of protest since elected candidates could not accept public office.[40] In the spring of 1880, however, Guesde became a Marxist, conferring with Marx in London on a minimum program, which permitted socialists to hold public office.[41] The new

CONTINUING REVOLUTIONARY ACTIVITY

Guesdist position, which essentially consisted of reformism in practice and revolution in theory, was rejected by Grave and other anarchists.[42]

The meetings of the Social Study Group were well documented because of the indefatigable work of police spies. A typical police report would reveal the location of the meeting, Fournier Hall, 19 Pascal Street; the approximate number attending, along with some names, twenty-five, including Grave and Jeallot; and the problem discussed, voting, a fraud.[43] Grave's anarchist group even ventured into journalism in 1881 when it issued *Le Bulletin des Groupes Anarchistes*, but only one number was published because of financial difficulties and lack of communication with other anarchist groups.[44]

It was during this period that Grave also became involved in the art of producing propaganda placards. One of his principal partners was Emile Gautier, a brilliant lawyer and noted anarchist militant with a penchant for conducting innumerable conferences. Grave's contribution was *Mort aux voleurs*, the thieves representing the bourgeoisie.[45]

Grave's anarchist activity involved him in a quixotic event on March 18, 1880, when the Social Study Group decided to lay a wreath at the Wall of the Federals in Père Lachaise cemetery to pay homage to martyrs of the 1871 Commune. The wreath was carried by Malatesta and one of his followers, a young Greek, Apostol Paolidès. When the police tried to wrest the wreath from the two, both resisted this untoward police incursion and were promptly arrested and expelled from France.[46]

The differences between Marxists and anarchists within the party were inexorably exacerbated by the Guesdist minimum program. This was shown at the July 1880 Regional Congress of the Centre. Grave, a delegate from the Social Study Group, drafted its report which focused on electoral participation, the most controversial problem.[47] In speaking before the congress, Grave made clear the anarchist position: that it would be more appropriate to purchase dynamite from funds than to squander them on electoral activity; that voting, especially when leading to serving in public office, was counterrevolutionary; and that the aim of militants should be to awaken the people to revolution, not be elected as representatives. The speech, which had wide press coverage, gave Grave some notoriety.[48] Basically, Grave and his comrades, the minority group, opposed the minimum program on the basis that it would sink revolutionary fervor on the shoals of reformism.[49]

The final split between Guesdists and anarchists came in 1881 at the Regional Congress of the Centre in Paris on May 22. The anarchists had instructed their delegates not to use their own names for voting purposes, but those of the groups they represented; the Guesdists majority insisted otherwise. The anarchists then walked out. While the issue causing the break might seem minor, it underscored anarchist antipathy to and distrust of reformist "representation."[50]

The anarchists then held their own congress, attended by two hundred delegates in Paris between May 25 and 29, 1881. Among the principal groups represented were the Social Study Group of Paris, the Sixth Section Group of Paris, and the Social Revolutionary Group of Lyons. In addition, many anarchists who could not attend sent letters of interest. The congress endorsed propaganda by deed, condemned the salary system, and called for the elimination of private property.[51]

In 1881, anarchists also held their London International Congress from July 14 to 20, with thirty delegates, including such stalwarts as Kropotkin and Malatesta, representing thirteen nations with many thousands of activists. A vigorous militancy was demonstrated in passing resolutions upholding propaganda by deed, rejecting voting, and authorising establishment of a Correspondence Bureau in London to better inform the various groups of common activity. The last never materialised.[52]

In the early eighties, basically reflecting the mood of Bakuninism so prevalent of the London International Congress, French anarchists embarked on propaganda by deed. Grave recalled that almost everyone, including himself, was thinking of "committing unusual acts that would be capable of undermining bourgeois society."[53] In a letter to *Le Droit Social*, Grave typified this temper:

> So, comrades, it is time to free ourselves from this situation [exploitation under capitalism] which can be done only if we wish to. We must, once for all, discard bourgeois ideas in the press and novel,

CONTINUING REVOLUTIONARY ACTIVITY

and begin to study the real causes of our misery, to bring about the proper remedy. [54]

Articles in *Le Droit Social* gave detailed directions for preparing nitroglycerine and other dangerous explosives.[55] Anarchism was to make use of modern technology to destroy such visible objects of authority as state buildings and thus to prove that state power was impotent against the will of determined anarchists. Grave himself, intoxicated by it all, manufactured nitroglycerine, but apparently did not use any. An obvious question presents itself at this juncture: does not violence beget violence, does it not then lead to a continuation of oppression and authority? Grave is not a Tolstoyean pacifist (neither is Christ at times for that matter); for him, violence to free oneself is an "act of liberty."[56]

Even the police aided the cause by subsidising the only anarchist newspaper in the early phase of propaganda by deed, *La Révolution Sociale*. Louis Andrieux, a police commissioner, supplied money to Serraux (Egide Spilleux), a police agent posing as an anarchist addicted to violence who was able to induce Louise Michel and Emile Pouget, noted anarchist militants, to edit the newspaper, despite a warning by Grave that he was a spy. Certainly, the two were aware of the risk, but decided that priority be given to the written word. Grave thought that Michel, whom he knew well enough to visit, was simply too trusting.[57] Earlier, Spilleux had approached Grave and Malatesta in 1880 at one of the meetings of the Social Study Group with the same proposal, of money to come from a wealthy woman in London. But when Grave checked the source with friends there, wealth was lacking. Not deterred, Spilleux then offered Grave the editorship and three thousand francs from unknown sources, he agreed only if Spilleux would only be the business manager. Spilleux refused.[58]

By 1882, Grave was already venturing deeply into anarcho-communist theory in *La Société au lendemain de la révolution*, which appeared in serial form in *Le Droit Social*. Grave, particularly interested in the problem of authority, stated that the most important consideration after the revolution was to prevent socialists from forming a government, thus to preserve the revolution and thus to ensure success for anarchism.[59]

THE ANARCHISM OF JEAN GRAVE

This anarchist activity coincided with a rising combative spirit among the proletariat in the eighties. The slashing of wages in coal mines within a background of general social misery produced the well-known outbreaks in 1882 at Montceau-les-Mines (part of an industrial area near Le Creusot, about fifty miles north of Lyon). Miners there fought the local power structure by launching a series of raids against religious houses. While anarchists at first were not involved, they joined the actions of 1883 and 1884 when a new series of attacks were undertaken against churches and houses of mine management.[60] Grave, at this time, along with others, was arrested and interrogated by the police for possible connection to these outbreaks, but promptly released for lack of evidence.[61]

Many individual acts of propaganda by deed were committed during this period. Perhaps the most publicised was the bombing of the restaurant of the Bellecour Theater in Lyons in October 1882, killing one. An anarchist journalist, Antoine Cyvoct, was arrested for this crime, tried, and sentenced to life imprisonment. In 1898, he was freed for lack of evidence presented at his trial. When released, Cyvoct reaffirmed his innocence, even after Grave confronted him with the fact that a comrade had supplied him with the dynamite to commit the bombing. Grave opined that Cyvoct ultimately believed his own lie.[62]

Notes

1. On Proudhon, see George Woodcock, *Pierre-Joseph Proudhon* (New York: Macmillan Co., 1956); George Woodcock, *Anarchism: A History of Libertarian Ideas and Movements* (Cleveland: Meridian Books, 1962), pp 106-44; Alain Sergent and Claude Harmel, *Histoire de l'anarchie*, pp 117-48; Robert L. Hoffman, *Revolutionary Justice: The Social and Political Theory of P-J. Proudhon* (Urbana, Ill.: University of Illinois Press, 1972); Edward Hyams, *Pierre-Joseph Proudhon; His Revolutionary Life, Mind and Works* (New York: Taplinger Publishing Co., 1979).

2. Pierre-Joseph Proudhon, *Idée générale de la Révolution au XIX siècle* as cited in *Oeuvres complètes de P-J. Proudhon*, eds. C. Bouglé and H Moysset (Paris: Marcel Rivière, 1923), III, 269ff.

3. Pierre-Joseph Proudhon, *De la capacité des classes ouvrières* as cited in *ibid.* (Paris: Marcel Rivière, 1924), IV, 197ff.

4. Pierre-Jospeh Proudhon, *La Pornocratie ou les femmes dans les temps modernes* as cited in *ibid.* (Paris: Marcel Rivière, 1929) XV, 407ff.

5. Proudhon, *Idée générale de la Révolution*, pp 241ff.

6. See chapter on utopia.
7. On Bakunin, see E. H. Carr, *Michael Bakunin* (New York: Vintage Books, 1961) and Anthony Masters, *Bakunin; The Father of Anarchism* (New York: Saturday Review Press/E. P. Dutton, 1974); Arthur P. Mendel, *Michael Bakunin* (NY: Praeger, 1981).
8. G. P. Maximoff, *The Political Philosophy of Bakunin: Scientific Anarchism* (Glencoe, Illinois: The Free Press, 1953) pp 372-79. Aileen Kelly, *Mikhail Bakunin: A Study in Psychology and Politics of Utopianism* (Oxford: Clarendon Press, 1982), pp 227-56 on "Absolute Dictatorship."
9. Carr, *Bakunin*, pp 359-74.
10. Maximoff, *The Political Philosophy of Bakunin*, p 298.
11. Carr, *Bakunin*, pp 271ff.
12. On Marx, see Maximilien Rubel and Margaret Manale, *Marx Without Myth; A Chronological Study of His Life and Work* (New York: Harper Torchbooks, 1976); pp 272ff on Marx versus Bakunin. Also, David McLellan, *Karl Marx; His Life and Thought* (New York: Harper and Row, 1973). Saul K. Padover, *Karl Marx; An Intimate Biography* (New York: McGraw-Hill, 1978). Melvin Rader, *Marx's Interpretation of History* (New York: Oxford University Press, 1979).
13. On the First International, see Centre de la Recherche Scientifique, *La Première Internationale* (Paris: Centre de la Recherche Scientifique, 1964).
14. Cole, II, 88ff and Sergent and Harmel, *Histoire de l'anarchie*, pp 313-4.
15. On differences between anarchists and Marxists, see James Joll, *The Anarchists* (New York: Universal Library, 1966), pp 102-14; Cole II, 173-212; Masters, *Bakunin*, pp 184ff.
16. Cole II, 198ff.
17. Ernest Victor Zenker, *Anarchism: A Criticism and History of Anarchist Theory*, trans. from German (London: Methuen and Co., 1899), pp 142ff. On the Reclus brothers, see Paul Reclus, *Les frères Elie et Elisée Reclus, ou du protestantisme à l'anarchisme* (Paris: Les Amis d'Elisée Reclus, 1964). On Elisée Reclus, see also Marie Fleming, *The Anarchist Way to Socialism: Elisée Reclus and Nineteenth-Century European Anarchism* (London, Croon Helm, 1979); pp 137-39 on his importance as the originator of anarcho-communism.
18. On Pythagoras' life and ideas, see Martin A. Larson, *The Religion of the Occident* (Patterson, New Jersey: Littlefield, Adams and Co., 1961), pp 155ff. On Sir Thomas More's utopia, including the absence of wage labor, see Glenn Negley and J. Max Patrick, *The Quest for Utopia: An Anthology of Imaginary Societies* (Garden City, N. Y.: Anchor Books, 1962), pp 258ff.
19. Peter Kropotkin, *Memoirs of a Revolutionist*, ed. James Allen Rogers (New York: Anchor Books, 1962), pp 183-88.
20. On Kropotkin, see two excellent biographies: George Woodcock and Ivan Avakumovik, *The Anarchist Prince: A Biographical Study of Peter Kropotkin* (London: V. Boardman, 1950) and Martin A. Miller, *Kropotkin* (Chicago: Chicago University Press, 1976).

THE ANARCHISM OF JEAN GRAVE

21. On the Jura Federation, see Jean Maitron, *Histoire du mouvement anarchiste en France, 1880-1914* (Paris: Société Universitaire d'Editions et de Librairie, 1955), pp 56-65. Hereinafter cited as *HMA*.
22. Woodcock, *Anarchism*, p 198.
23. On general development of anarchism during this period, see appropriate sections in Woodcock, *Anarchism*; Joll, *The Anarchists*.
24. *Quarante ans*, p 127; Grave, *La Grande famille*, pp 94-104. On disease especially ravaging the working class, see Chevalier, *Laboring Classes and Dangerous Classes*, pp 12-17, for example.
25. *Quarante ans*, pp 132-45.
26. Grave, *La Grande famille*, pp 330ff.
27. Interview with Madame Paul Delasalle, August 9, 1964. *Quarante ans*, p 131.
28. *Quarante ans*, pp 147-8.
29. *Ibid.*, p 147.
30. *Ibid.*, p 148. *HMA*, p 99.
31. On the early French Socialist movement, see Aaron Noland, *The Founding of the French Socialist Party, 1893-1905* (Cambridge, Mass: Harvard University Press, 1956); Claude Willard, *Le Mouvement socialiste en France (1893-1905); Les Guesdists* (Paris: Editions Sociales, 1965). On the Marseilles Labor Congress, see Léon Blum, *Les Congrès ouvriers et socialistes français, 1876-1900* as cited in *L'Oeuvre de Léon Blum, 1891-1905* (Paris: Albin Michel, 1954) I, 392-97.
32. *Mouvement libertaire*, p 3; and International Institute for Social History at Amsterdam, letter, Grave to Nettlau, Nov 6, 1925. Material from this source will be cited AM. On Jeallot, see *Quarante ans*, p 150,153, pp 156-9; on Minville see *ibid.*, pp 150ff.
33. *Mouvement libertaire*, p 3.
34. *HMA*, p 97; Woodcock, *Anarchism*, p 293. On Kropotkin's activity here, see his *Memoirs of a Revolutionist*, pp 406-07.
35. *Mouvement libertaire*, p 4.
36. *Ibid.*, pp 5-6; AM, letter, Grave to Nettlau, November 6, 1925.
37. *Le Droit Social*, February 12, 1882, p 3.
38. *Mouvement libertaire*, pp 5-8. On Malatesta, see V. Richard ed., *Malatesta; His Life and Ideas* (London: Freedom Press, 1965). Malatesta wrote quite a bit; see his theoretical work on anarchism, *L'Anarchie* (Geneva: Groupe D'Etudiants Révolutionnaires de Genève, 1902).
39. *Quarante ans*, pp 148-9; two papers associated with the French Socialist Workers' Party, Paul Brousse's *Le Prolétaire* and Jules Guesde's *L'Egalité*—Grave read both.
40. *L'Egalité*, February 21, 1880.
41. On Guesde, see Willard, *Le mouvement socialiste en France*.
42. *Mouvement libertaire*, p 14.
43. *Police Archives*, Box 13/1505, Dossier No. 293839, July 6, 1881.

CONTINUING REVOLUTIONARY ACTIVITY

44. *Mouvement libertaire*, p 6-7.
45. On Gautier, see *Quarante ans*, pp 159-60; Alfred Vizetelly, *The Anarchists: Their Faith and Their Record including Sidelights on the Royal Personages Who Have Been Assassinated* (New York: John Lance Co., 1911), p 65.
46. *Quarante ans*, p 156.
47. *Mouvement libertaire*, pp 11-15; and Blum I, *Les Congrès ouvriers*, pp 416-18.
48. Jacques Prolo, *Les Anarchistes*, Vol. X of *Histoire des partis socialistes en France*, ed. A Zavaès (Paris: Marcel Rivière, 1912), pp18-19. *Le Citoyen de Paris, Supplément*, July 25, 1880, p 3.
49. *HMA*, pp 101-2. Only seven of about thirty groups in this congress were anarchist.
50. *Ibid.*, p 107; *Le Révolté*, May 28, 1881.
51. On this congress, see the good account in *Le Révolté*, July 11, 1881.
52. On the London International Congress, see *HMA*, pp109-10.
53. *Mouvement libertaire*, p 15.
54. *Le Droit Social*, February 12, 1882.
55. *Ibid.*, May 28, 1882.
56. *Mouvement libertaire*, p 15. On the quotation see Grave, *L'Anarchie, son but, ses moyens* (Paris: P. V. Stock, 1899), p 130. On Christ and violence: Matthew 10:34ff, Luke 22:36ff.
57. Louis Andrieux, *Souvenirs d'un préfet de police* (Paris, Jules Rouff, 1885), I, 337-41. *La Révolution Sociale* lasted from December 1880 to September 1881. On Grave and Michel, see *Quarante ans*, pp 524-26. He attended her funeral in 1905 and wrote in *Les Temps Nouveaux*, Jan 14-20, 1905, a touching eulogy. Among the following remarks was: she was "one of the purest figures of the revolutionary party." On her life, see Edith Thomas, *Louise Michel ou la velléda de l'anarchie* (Paris: Gallimard, 1971).
58. *Mouvement libertaire*, pp 191-94.
59. Jean Grave, *La Société au lendemain de la révolution* (Paris: Publications de 5e et 13e Arrondissements, n.d.), pp 3-31. Also, Cole, II, 328. *Le Droit Social* was published from February 12 to July 23, 1882. It was closed down by the government for advocating propaganda by deed.
60. *HMA*, pp 148-51. *Le Révolté*, September 16, October 28, November 11, and December 9 and 23, 1882.
61. *Quarante ans*, pp 176-88.
62. On Cyvoct, see *Le Révolté*, Dec. 22, 1883 on his life and trial; *Les Temps Nouveaux*, March 26-April 1, 1898 on his being freed. *Quarante ans*, pp 191-93 and *HMA*, p 162.

4

LE RÉVOLTÉ AND INTO LA RÉVOLTE PERIOD, 1883-1890

THE CONTINUING MOOD FOR REVOLUTION was reflected in 1883 by anarchist activity at Montceau-les-Mines and by Grave's *Organisation de la propagande révolutionnaire* which called for combat against the bourgeoisie through the formation of small, clandestine, and spontaneously organised groups to commit such acts of terrorism as the assassination of notorious exploiters and the destruction of factories during strikes. The revolutionaries were to be publicly defended by the anarchist press, further exacerbating the spirit of revolt. In addition, it advocated the establishment of study groups to propagate anarchism among the general public.[1] An example of this was the well-publicised event of March 1883 in Paris in which Michel and Pouget led a group of hungry people to attack bakeries. For this very serious crime in the government's eyes, Michel received a six-year term of imprisonment and Pouget one of eight years. Both were pardoned in 1886.[2]

Rising anarchist activity was met by expected government repression. In January 1883, sixty-five anarchists were tried in Lyons for being members and officers of the First International and other charges. For belonging to a defunct organisation, Kropotkin and others received prison sentences for up to five years. Kropotkin, the best-known of the defendants, was pardoned in 1886 and soon left for London.[3]

Anarchism, like other movements, not only had its average militants but also its major figures. Its criteria for status, however, were somewhat different from those of socialist parties whose aim was to participate in electoral politics. The well-known anarchist, rejecting the "political" path of electoral socialists, was either a newspaper editor, theoretician, or terrorist;

LE RÉVOLTÉ AND INTO LA RÉVOLTE PERIOD

seldom, if ever, all three, but a few were in the first and second categories simultaneously, like Grave.

Grave became editor in 1883 of *Le Révolté*, anarchism's most influential newspaper, after its founding editor, Kropotkin, who had begun publication in 1879 in Geneva, was expelled in 1882 through pressure exerted by the Russian government. When the search for a new editor was launched, Elisée Reclus, on the advice of Peter Kropotkin's wife, Sophia, asked Grave to accept the position. Hesitant at first, Grave finally agreed when assurance was given for an option to leave after six months. The following reasons importantly influenced Grave's selection as editor: Elisée Reclus did not wish the editorship for himself; Grave by now was well known in anarchist circles as a pamphleteer and as a correspondence secretary of his Paris group, and was friendly with the Kropotkins whom he had met in early 1881 in Paris.[4] A sense of excitement gripped Grave concerning the new challenges and surroundings. But one drawback, however, remained; he had fallen in love with a beautiful young seamstress, Clotilde Thérèse Benoît, and there would be a temporary separation.[5]

Grave arrived in Geneva toward the end of 1883, living at first with Finet, a former Parisian friend whom he found unemployed. Ever generous, he contributed a portion of his eighty-franc monthly salary to support Finet's family until he found employment.[6] Life in Geneva was rather pleasant: Grave's fiancée joined him and he made friends with many local anarchists, often spending his leisure time with them in recreation. In looking at Grave's long and tempestuous life, this period was certainly one of his most enjoyable.[7]

Grave's most pressing problems at this time obviously had to do with various aspects of his work, which he successfully resolved; learning the intricacies of editorship, including the typographical end (it was at this time that he donned the printer's blouse), overcoming resentment of co-workers to an outsider, and increasing circulation.[8] On the last aspect, Grave through his many Parisian contacts, augmented it from fifteen hundred to three thousand copies.[9] A problem arose with sending the newspaper to France which refused admission to revolutionary journals. After bribery of customs officials proved too expensive and smuggling the newspaper across the border resulted in the arrest of many comrades, simply mailing it in sealed envelopes proved effective.[10]

The comparative calm which Grave and his fiancée enjoyed was shattered when police raided anarchist lodgings, including Grave's, on suspicion that Anarchists might blow up the Federal Palace in Berne. Grave himself was held for questioning, but soon released. After this unpleasant experience, he decided with Elisée Reclus to move the newspaper to Paris since most of the readers were in France.[11] The last issue of Le Révolté in Geneva was published on March 14, 1885.[12]

Thus it was that Grave and his common-law wife left Geneva in late March 1885 for Paris to live at the home of her brother, Joseph Benoît at 140 Mouffetard Street.[13] Again, tragedy soon struck Grave: In October 1885, just after his wife gave birth to a son, Jean-Paul, both died. Grave mourned their deaths for many months but resolved to continue his work.[14] During this difficult period, he received a letter from the Kropotkins expressing sympathy.[15]

Grave stayed near his in-laws, in the attic of the apartment building in which they lived, for the next seventeen years;[16] it not only served as his living quarters, but also as a newspaper office for Le Révolté, La Révolte, and early years of Les Temps Nouveaux. His life was Spartan with the exception of one luxury, a vase of fresh flowers next to his books.[17] A noted journalist, Félix Dubois, drew an interesting picture of Grave and his attic in 1894:

> Jean Grave is the real manager of La Révolte if one can say that it has one. His place of residence, situated in a narrow house at the very end of Mouffetard Street, is the legal address of the newspaper. We have walked up five floors; yet, we must still go up another flight of unequal steps at the end of which we find ourselves facing an attic door. We see a sign on it; we know that this is the entrance to the newspaper's office.
>
> There is no bell. We knock. A dog barks. A voice tells us to come in and we turn the doorknob to enter. Once in, we see that the desks merely serve as places to dry clothing and to put things on.
>
> In a narrow attic, piles of newspapers and shelves overcharged with pamphlets fight over space left by a slanting roof. The room

contains two chairs. What passes for a table is merely a few boards set over some boxes. It is here that *La Révolte* is put together. Near the attic window, to better utilise the little light which enters, comrade Grave has installed his place of work.

Grave has not always been a writer. Previously, he had been a shoemaker and then a printer whose distinctively long black apron he still wears. About thirty to thirty-five years old, with large head and ample brow, he has at once both a resolute and gentle air. His simple manner has nothing in common with the fanatics of public meetings. His voice is so tranquil and soft that it is sympathetic. We ask ourselves if it is possible that in the deep crevices of his mind, he has something in common with Ravachol, Pini, and other thieves?[18]

Le Révolté was a weekly four-page tabloid (before the 9-15 May 1886 issue, it was a semi-monthly) with a circulation of 4,000 copies, selling first at ten centimes a copy, then at five in order to increase circulation.[19] In September 1887, the newspaper's name was unexpectedly changed to *La Révolte*. A local antimilitarist league was conducting an extensive campaign for military desertion, which Grave aided by inserting the winning numbers of one of its raffles in the newspaper. The government quickly charged the newspaper's legal publisher, Emile Méreaux, Grave's long-time collaborator and friend, with being involved in an illegal raffle since newspapers at this time could not legally participate with other groups in lotteries. When Méreaux was tried and received fifteen days' imprisonment and a fine of five hundred francs,[20] Grave, erroneously thinking that the fine would be charged against the newspaper, quickly changed its name.[21]

Although *La Révolte* by 1889 had a circulation of only about 6,000,[22] it was important in the artistic and intellectual communities. Subscribers included such leading anarchists as Kropotkin, Pouget, Paul and Elisée Reclus and such anarchist-inclined painters and writers as Octave Mirbeau, Paul Adam, Jean Richepin, Bernard Lazare, Maximilien Luce, and Paul Signac along with progressive writers not tied to anarchism, notably Anatole France and Stephane Mallarmé. Even a few conservative intellectuals subscribed, like Edouard Drumont, the anti-Semitic editor of *La Libre Parole*, and Maurice Barrès, who represented a feudalistic social conservatism, one antithetical to bourgeois values, toying with vague socialist notions to improve the deplorable social conditions of the masses through *noblesse oblige*.[23] Several of the leading literary magazines, strongly influenced by anarchism, also subscribed, notably *La Revue Blanche* and *La Plume*.

But the overwhelming majority of subscribers and readers were workers, miners, barbers, and so forth. Of the 1,057 subscribers, 767 resided in France. Of those in other nations, the United States led with 61, a third in the New York City area, Italy followed with 33, England with 29, some of whom represented political exiles like Kropotkin, then Switzerland with 27, Belgium with 24, and Holland with 20; in Latin America, Brasil led with 6, while in Eastern Europe, Rumania was first with 12.[24]

In November 1887, Grave introduced a *Supplément Littéraire* of four pages, at first appearing every second issue, then weekly by August 1890.[25] It included a book review section to which Grave often contributed. The reason for this endeavour was succinctly and cogently spelled out in its first issue:

> To show that ideas which we defend have not come about just recently and that we are only continuing in all modesty the work of thinkers that bourgeois tradition pretends to follow.[26]

This, indeed, was more than fulfilled in a rich intellectual harvest. Articles, often continuing for months, emphasizing social criticism and socialist alternatives to capitalism, were divided into four categories. First, works by three rather obscure early French anarchists who flourished in the 1850s: (1) Joseph Dejacque, a worker who participated in the workers' revolt of June 1848 in Paris, best known for his *L'Humanisphère*, a utopia free of social coercion.[27] (2) Anselme Bellegarrigue, close to the individualist strain of anarchism.[28] (3) Ernest Coeurderoy, a physician involved in the February 1848 Revolution in Paris and in the abortive revolt there of June 1849 against Louis Napoleon.[29]

Second, expositions on utopia and social criticism of those literary and philosophical giants whose influence spanned the ages: classic utopias (Sir Thomas More's *Utopia*[30] and François Rabelais' *Gargantua and Pantagruel*[31]) and the mordant social criticism of the Enlightenment whose progressive heritage was greatly appreciated (Grave's favourite among the *philosophes* was Denis Diderot, a most audacious exponent of freedom).[32] Even the New World was not neglected, with Henry David Thoreau whose anarchism was amply revealed in such works as *Civil Disobedience* and *Walden*, both critical of the state and bourgeois society.[33] Also in this section were Leo Tolstoy, Russian novelist and Christian anarchist,[34] and Emile Zola whose outstanding naturalistic novels recounted the difficulties of working-class life in France.[35]

Third, essays by mostly contemporary anarchist thinkers and anarchist-inclined writers: Portions of the yet unpublished *Mutual Aid* by Kropotkin ran for many issues;[36] the Reclus brothers, Elie and Elisée,[37] and, of course Proudhon[38] and Bakunin;[39] and novelists like Paul Adam,[40] Jean Richepin,[41] Zo d'Axa,[42] Lucien Descaves,[43] and Mirbeau.[44] The popular poet, Eugène Pottier, who wrote the verses of the *Internationale*, the anthem of the international working class, was also included.[45] At times Grave would even insert excerpts from his own literary effort: *La Grand famille*, for example, was published under its original title, *Sous l'uniforme*.[46]

And fourth, writings of such non-socialists as Drumont and Herbert Spencer, who favoured Social Darwinism and Classical Economics, but only elements of their work with an anarchist bias, like fear of government bureaucracy and majority opinion.[47]

About a year after his return from Geneva, Grave went to see Severine, a well-known woman journalist and unattached socialist deeply committed to feminism and pacifism. When Severine, who assumed the editorship of *Le Cri du Peuple* after Vallès death, broke with Guesde, her anarchist sympathies led her to seek Grave's aid to enlist the services of Kropotkin for her newspaper. Kropotkin, however, declined to write for her because of other commitments. Severine and Grave soon became friends and collaborated on various projects.[48]

In July 1890, the *Supplément* involved Grave in litigation with the La Société des Gens de Lettres, a literary organisation led by Zola that protected members from unauthorised use of their work, and with Guy de Maupassant, the magnificent short-story writer. Grave was told by the Société either to pay monies for inserting excerpts of member authors in the *Supplément* or face a court suit.[49] Grave replied that there should be exemption since his paper was not of a commercial nature, but of general enlightenment. But since he did not want any litigation, he asked for their fee. The Société replied that it was a hundred francs quarterly. Then, it indicated that a mistake had been made: that two hundred francs were owed, eighty to be paid immediately. The irate Grave firmly refused to pay anything.[50]

In this quarrel both sides had valid claims: Grave's desire for a meaningful newspaper on scanty economic resources as opposed to the Société's normal concern to protect its members. Grave was especially resentful of Zola, who before joining the Société had allowed him to publish portions of his work without payment.[51] Maupassant, who had joined the fray as an independent, also informed Grave that permission was needed to publish excerpts of his work.[52] Grave's reply to him was a theoretical exposition of the underlying relationship that linked artist to society. Because society nourished the artist (the very nature of art made it as much social as private), no artist in good faith should ever prevent dissemination of his work.[53] Many writers supported Grave's stand in the two controversies, basically reiterating his views.[54] For the legal aspects in the two cases, Grave was represented by Jean Ajalbert, a noted lawyer often involved in defending leftists. As late as 1911, Grave had difficulties with the Société: A letter to Grave in January of that year from Henri Barbusse, the author of *Le Feu* (a realistic World War I novel), forbade his inserting one of his works in the *Supplément*. Ultimately, Grave was forced to pay the protesting writers whose works he used.[55]

As a small revolutionary movement, with scathing criticism of society, it should not be surprising that anarchism attracted criminals who at times identified with it as victims in revolt against society. In fact, in the early nineties, the position that anarchism should take with respect to criminals was of some significance. Before delving deeper into the problem, it must be pointed out that most criminals close to anarchism were of the petty variety; but some were major, like bank robbers.[56]

Grave was acquainted with many of these criminals since they would come to his office to purchase the paper and pamphlets. He was even sympathetic to a few. One was Clément Duval, a notorious robber who justified his profession as redress to social oppression. Grave saw this anarchist-criminal as an idealist, a characteristic which he liked.[57] After being sentenced to French Guyana for life in 1887, Duval endured many hellish years of prison before escaping in 1901 to the New York City area where he stayed permanently.[58] Another well-known one, Léon Ortiz, who led a gang of thieves, often visited Grave's office for anarchist publications and regularly contributed funds for propaganda by deed. Grave suspected that some of the spectacular bombings, including the one of the Café Terminus in Paris' Saint-Lazare railroad station, were financed by Ortiz's gang. In a moment of weakness, Grave had allowed Ortiz to settle money problems with another gang member in *La Révolte*'s office. The police later questioned Grave about this matter, but he denied any knowledge of it.[59]

Those for and against criminality at once admitted that bourgeois society was unjustly based on the exploitation of labour. The disagreement was whether exploitation justified theft. In 1891, a long and heated controversy erupted in *La Révolte* when Paul Reclus, an engineer and son of Elie Reclus, administered the paper during Grave's six-month imprisonment at Sainte-Pélagie in Paris. He wrote an unsigned article whose basic thesis was that in bourgeois society, theft was as morally defensible as work.[60] Grave was so perturbed that he asked Elisée Reclus to restrain his nephew's exuberance. The nephew, however, was backed by the uncle:

> We are like furious wolves, disputing with one another our daily existence at the expense of the weak; each loaf of bread that we eat is taken from the poor and leaves in its wake its own particular drop of blood.[61]

Grave's rejoinder was "Encore la morale," in which he asked whether theft would regenerate humans to make revolution. In the first installment, Grave equated property with theft, and theft with property. A thief would then only be a mere bourgeois, not a revolutionary.[62] In the second installment, he amplified his attack by clearly pointing out that theft was a factor working against revolutionary energy:

> Since the days of the Pharaohs in Egypt, the masters have stolen the labour of their slaves, and the slaves instead of revolting have stolen from their masters.[63]

THE ANARCHISM OF JEAN GRAVE

In the third installment, the principal point was that theft was indicative of social passivity:

> Theft is property. It is appropriation not expropriation. Only the weak steal, while only force expropriates.[64]

The debate continued for years. A letter from Elisée Reclus to Grave on May 21, 1893, especially defended robbery committed by a revolutionary to aid his friends.[65] Again Grave disagreed and was backed by Kropotkin, who himself was against all theft, informing Grave of the great damage it caused to the Populists in Russia.[66] Ultimately, Grave was against theft because:

> To practice theft is to diminish one's self as one must lie and deceive. This does not enhance character. Many who at first only stole for propaganda funds have then made it their livelihood.... This was inevitable. Money corrupts, especially when to have it we risk our liberty by using equivocal ends.[67]

The arguments between Grave and anarchists who excused or committed criminal acts have many dimensions. For example, the oppressive and sharp class divisions so characteristic of nineteenth-century Europe led to the rise of many peasant rebels, especially in Southern Italy, whom the peasants regarded as their champions against the wealthy and the state.[68] Bakunin himself extolled the virtues of the "bandit...the hero, the defender, the avenger of the people...against the civilisation of State, aristocracy, bureaucracy and clergy."[69] Indeed, the connection between crime and poverty does not make it unlikely that social protest and crime may at times be intertwined.[70]

Notes

1. Jehan Le Vagre [Jean Grave], *Organisation de la propagande révolutionnaire* (Paris: Publications de Groupe des 5e et 13e Arrondissements, 1883). The Police Archives has this pamphlet, BA/1505. The police were obviously aware of this pseudonym. Grave's stress on small groups fomenting revolution is Bakuninist and Blanquist.
2. *HMA*, pp 150-51.
3. *Ibid.*, pp 163-65 on the Lyons trial.
4. On the founding of *Le Révolté*, see Pierre Kropotkine, "Comment fut fondé *Le Révolté*," *Les Temps Nouveaux*, February 20-26, 1904, pp 1-2 and March 19-25, 1904,

LE RÉVOLTÉ AND INTO LA RÉVOLTE PERIOD

  p 3. *Mouvement libertaire*, pp 19 and 39; Woodcock and Avakumovic, *The Anarchist Prince*, pp 183ff; Kropotkin, *Memoirs of a Revolutionist*, p 279.
5. *Quarante ans*, p 246.
6. *Ibid.*, p 197.
7. *Mouvement libertaire*, p 41.
8. *Ibid.*, pp 39-40.
9. Jean Grave, "Du Révolté aux Temps Nouveaux," *Les Temps Nouveaux*, March 5-11, 1904, pp 2-3. *Mouvement libertaire*, p 41, estimated circulation at 2,500.
10. *Les Temps Nouveaux*, March 5-11, 1904, pp 2-3. *Mouvement libertaire*, p 42.
11. *Mouvement libertaire*, pp 44-46.
12. *Le Révolté*, March 14, 1885.
13. *Mouvement libertaire*, pp 47-48.
14. *Quarante ans*, p 569.
15. *Institut Français d'Histoire Sociale, Grave Archives*, letter Kropotkin to Grave, November 7, 1885. To be cited as GA.
16. *Mouvement libertaire*, p 48.
17. Victor Serge, Alexandre Croix, and Jean Bernier, "L'Anarchie," *Crapouillet*, (January 1938), p 16, shows a drawing of Grave with his flowers and books in the attic. The same drawing is in *Mouvement libertaire*.
18. Félix Dubois, "Le Péril anarchiste," *Le Figaro, Supplément littéraire*, January 13, 1894, p 6. This description is also quoted in Alain Sergent, *Les Anarchistes: scènes et portraits recueillis et présentés* (Paris: Frederic Chambriand, 1951), pp 32-34. On p 15 of *ibid.*, there is a drawing of three men in the office of *The Revolt* titled "La salle de rédaction de *La Révolte*." Grave is the man whose back is turned. In Barbara W. Tuchman, *The Proud Tower: A Portrait of the World Before the War: 1890-1914* (New York: Macmillan Co., 1966), we have the same drawing following p 80. Her description of Grave on pp 74-75 is good. Also, see the description of a very disorderly office in Emile Darnaud (ed.), *140 rue Mouffetard Paris* (Paris: Foix, 1889), pp7-8. For a drawing of the house at 140 Mouffetard Street (five stories and an attic), see *L'Illustration*, March 2, 1889, p 176.
19. *Le Révolté*, February 12-18, 1887.
20. *Mouvement libertaire*, pp 63-64 and Grave, *Les Temps Nouveaux*, March 5-11, 1904, pp 2-3.
21. Grave, *Les Temps Nouveaux*, March 5-11, 1904, pp 2-3.
22. *La Révolte*, June 30-July 6, 1889 and Félix Dubois, "Le Péril Anarchiste," *Figaro, Supplément Littéraire*, January 13, 1894, p 6.
23. On Maurice Barrès, for example, see Edouard Berth, *La fin d'une culture* (Paris: Marcel Rivière, 1927), pp 105-49. On Drumont's activity and philosophy, see his *Le Testament d'un antisémite* (Paris: E. Dentu, 1891); see especially pp 1-56 on anti-Semitism.

24. On subscribers, see *Archives Nationales*, F⁷ 12506 (1894).
25. *La Révolte, Supplément Littéraire*, 19-25 November 1887. Henceforth cited as *RSL*.
26. *Ibid.*
27. On Dejacque, see Woodcock, *Anarchism*, p 278ff and Sergent and Harmel, *Histoire de l'anarchie*, pp 263-67. *RSL*, No. 44 (1st year), 1888, one example. Grave reprinted *L'Humanisphere* in 1899.
28. On Bellegarrigue, see Woodcock, *Anarchism*, pp 276-78 and Sergent and Harmel, *Histoire de l'anarchie*, pp 230-38. *RSL*, No. 36 (7th year), 1893, one example.
29. On Coeurderoy, see Sergent and Harmel, *Histoire de l'anarchie*, pp 255-63. *RSL*, No. 9 (7th year) 1893, one example.
30. *RSL*, No. 1 (5th year), 1891.
31. *Ibid.*, No. 20 (7th year), 1894.
32. *Ibid.*, No. 21 (3rd year), 1889, for example.
33. *Ibid.*, Nos. 29 and 31 (2nd year), 1889. On Thoreau, see, for example, Carl Bode (ed.), *The Portable Thoreau* (New York: Viking Press, 1964).
34. *RSL*, No. 16 (1st year) 1888, for example. On Tolstoy and anarchism, see Woodcock, *Anarchism*, pp 222-35.
35. *RSL*, No. 12 (1st year). On Zola, see Matthew Josephson, *Zola and His Time* (Garden City, New York: Garden City Publishing Co., 1928).
36. *RSL*, Nos. 21-26 (7th year), 1894.
37. *Ibid.*, Nos. 38-41 (6th year), 1893.
38. *Ibid.*, Nos. 28 and 32.
39. *Ibid.*, No. 38 (5th year), 1892.
40. *Ibid.*, No. 34 (4th year), 1891.
41. *Ibid.*, No. 36 (4th year), 1891.
42. *Ibid.*, No. 38 (4th year), 1891.
43. *Ibid.*, No. 20 (3rd year), 1890.
44. *Ibid.*, No. 8 (3rd year), 1889.
45. *Ibid.*, December 24-30, 1889. GA, letter Pottier to Grave, 23 May of 1887, allowing for use of poetry. On Pottier and his works, see Eugène Pottier, *Chants Révolutionnaires*, preface Lucien Descaves (Paris: Editions Sociales Internationales, 1937).
46. *RSL*, Nos. 30-31 (5th year), 1892.
47. *Ibid.*, No. 28 (4th year), 1891 on Drumont, and *Ibid.*, No. 43 (4th year) 1891. On Spencer, see Richard Hofstadter, *Social Darwinism in American Thought* (Boston: Beacon Press, 1955).
48. On Severine's life and activity, see Bernard Lecacche, *Severine* (Paris: Gallimard, 1930). On Grave and Severine, see *Quarante ans*, p 218, p 230, p 241, and p 275, for example.

LE RÉVOLTÉ AND INTO LA RÉVOLTE PERIOD

49. *Mouvement libertaire*, pp 86-87. La Société des Gens de Lettres is hereinafter Société.
50. *Bibliothèque Nationale, New Acquisitions*, 24, 272, letter, Grave to Félix Nadar, n.d. From internal evidence the letter was probably written in November-December, 1891, while Grave was still in Sainte-Pélagie prison. In *Mouvement libertaire*, p 86ff, Grave does not do himself justice in the Société controversy; he did not indicate there the reasonableness shown in the Nadar letter. Nadar was a communard and a photographer.
51. *Mouvement libertaire*, pp 87-88; and GA, Grave to Mirbeau, July 21, 1891.
52. *Mouvement libertaire*, p 91; letter Maupassant to Grave.
53. *Ibid.*, pp 91-92.
54. Octave Mirabeau, *L'Echo de Paris*, August 4, 1891, one example.
55. *Mouvement libertaire*, pp 94-95; and GA, letter, Ajalbert to Grave, n.d. Also, *Quarante ans*, p 275. GA, letter Henri Barbusse to Grave, January 23, 1921.
56. *Quarante ans*, pp 217-19.
57. *La Révolte*, January 29-February 4, 1887. *Mouvement libertaire*, p 57.
58. HMA, p 177. Prolo, *Les Anarchistes*, pp 29-37.
59. *Mouvement libertaire*, pp 215-16. For more information on Ortiz, see A. Bataille, *Causes criminelles et mondaines de 1894: les procès anarchistes* (Paris: E. Dentu, 1895), pp 156-58.
60. Elisée Reclus, *Correspondance*, III (Paris: Alfred Costes, 1925), pp 96-98. On Paul Reclus, see Reclus, *Les frères Elie et Elisée Reclus*, p 203, and Paul Reclus, "Vol et Travail," *La Révolte*, November 21-27, 1891.
61. Paul Reclus, "Vol et Travail," *La Révolte*, November 28-December 4, 1891.
62. Jean Grave, "Encore la Morale," *ibid.*, December 5-11, 1891, pp 1-2.
63. *Ibid.*, December 12-17, 1891, pp 1-2.
64. *Ibid.*, December 19-24, 1891, pp 1-2.
65. Reclus, *Correspondance*, III, p 140. Fleming, *The Anarchist Way*, pp 198-202 on Elisée Reclus' justifying theft by a revoltuionary.
66. *Mouvement libertaire*, pp 61-62. Miller, *Kropotkin*, p 212.
67. *Mouvement libertaire*, p 197.
68. On this phenomenon, see Eric J. Hobsbawm, *Primitve Rebels: Studies in Archaic Forms of Social Movement in the 19th and 20th Centuries* (New York: W. W. Norton, 1959), especially pp 1-125.
69. Kropotkin's quotation is in *ibid.*, p 28.
70. Chevalier, *Laboring Classes and Dangerous Classes*, p 72ff, among others, states that the great French novelists—Balzac, Hugo, and Zola, among others—tied urban poverty to crime.

5

THE TRIAL OF THE THIRTY PERIOD, 1891-1894

ON MAY DAY 1891, TWO INCIDENTS occurred which touched off a train of events leading to national hysteria, during which time Grave was not only imprisoned three times, but also involved as a principal figure in the Trial of the Thirty, one of the more celebrated political trials in French history. Simultaneously, a workers' demonstration at the small town of Fourmies (in Northeastern France) was dispersed by troops who killed ten workers, while at the Paris suburb of Clichy an anarchist group exchanged shots with police.[1]

The riposte of *La Révolte* to the two incidents, particularly the Fourmies massacre, was a series of articles condemning the government. An especially critical one (unsigned), "Viande à Mitraille," not only decried the army's role at Fourmies, but also called on soldiers to disobey their superiors and to desert.[2] The government reacted swiftly to the article, viewing it as criminal and demanding of Grave as editor to reveal the writer. When Grave refused to divulge that it was written by Méreaux, he was promptly arrested.[3]

In early June 1891, Grave was tried in the Criminal Court of Paris for urging mutiny and desertion in the army.[4] Throughout the trial he was Promethean: "No one has the right to judge me nor to prevent my saying what I think."[5] His unyielding posture did not endear him to judge and jury. The obvious mistake that Grave made in his trial was to refuse the services of a lawyer (he admitted this years later), which undoubtedly hampered his defence. Not surprisingly, given the prevalent public fear of anarchism, he was sentenced by jury to six months' imprisonment and a hundred-franc fine.[6]

THE TRIAL OF THE THIRTY PERIOD

Grave was incarcerated in Sainte-Pélagie in Paris where he settled down to perform serious mental labour. Not only did he finish the first draft of the largely autobiographical, *La Grande famille*,[7] but he also completed his most popular theoretical work, *La Société mourante et l'anarchie*. (Much of the latter work consisted of previous articles in *La Révolte*; Elisée Reclus suggested the title,[8] while Mirbeau, a leading literary figure sympathetic to anarchism, wrote the preface.)[9] The imprisonment itself did not noticeably hamper Grave's editorial responsibilities at the newspaper since his sister-in-law, Madame Joseph Benoît, served as his almost-daily courier.[10] The incarceration was enlivened by talking daily with a fellow anarchist, Charles Malato, a well-known militant of the period who later wrote a book about his prison experiences, cell doors were opened during the day allowing prisoners to visit one another. Like Grave, Malato had been convicted (he served a fifteen-month sentence) in April 1890, for provoking "murder, pillage and arson" in the anarchist journal *l'Attaque*. At first, Grave was rather cool to Malato who had earlier called him "the Pope of Mouffetard Street" when he had objected to Malato's acceptance of leadership for anarchism to effect revolution, but the prison milieu was conducive to forgetting past disagreement.[11] (Soon after Grave's discharge from prison, after being harassed by the police—the guilt was not expiated—he was again jailed for three weeks.)[12]

The events at Clichy and Fourmies were part of a general pattern of intensified struggle between anarchists and state. The unusually stiff prison sentences meted out to anarchists involved at Clichy (one received five years) so incensed some of them that they began a campaign of propaganda by deed.[13]

The most notorious of the terrorists was François Koeningstein, better known by his mother's maiden name of Ravachol.[14] After Ravachol committed a series of dastardly acts which did not endear him to anarchists (he murdered a miser and searched the tomb of a wealthy countess for jewelry), probably to justify himself to them, including Grave, who thought that he was a police spy bent on discrediting anarchism, he embarked on propaganda by deed.[15] In March 1892, he blew up the houses of the judge and prosecutor who had tried the Clichy anarchists, injuring no one. He was soon apprehended, tried for the murder of the miser, and executed in July 1892. The anarchists applauded Ravachol's later acts and came to regard him as one of their martyrs.[16] Grave, for example, blamed Ravachol for murder, but at the same time respected his sincerity and courage.[17]

Auguste Vaillant fulfilled the next chapter of propaganda by deed when he threw a bomb full of nails in the Chamber of Deputies from one of its galleries on December 9, 1893, injuring a few deputies. Although defended by a brilliant lawyer, Fernand Labori, he was sentenced to death and executed in February 1894.[18]

The mounting wave of terror led to the government's passage of the first two of the three Exceptional Laws. The First, on the press, passed the Chamber of Deputies and Senate on December 11 and 12, 1893, respectively. For provoking or calling for such acts as "murder, pillage and arson," a journalist might receive from one to five years of imprisonment and be fined from one hundred to three thousand francs.[19] The Second, on criminal association, passed both houses a week later. It was so worded that even knowing an anarchist or merely talking about anarchism in a group could be considered criminal. A key article read:

> All formal or informal associations of no matter how many members or how long in existence, and all understandings, which prepare or commit crimes against persons and property, constitute a crime against public peace.[20]

The next significant propaganda by deed took place soon afterward. On 12 February 1894, a week after Vaillant's execution, Emile Henry, from a working class Communard family, threw a bomb in the Terminus Café located in the Saint-Lazare railroad station in Paris, killing one and injuring twenty. This senseless and indiscriminate act was extremely damaging to anarchism, equating it with untoward violence. Henry was soon apprehended, convicted and executed.[21]

Under the mounting wave of anti-anarchist hysteria, Grave was arrested for violating the First of the Exceptional Laws and incarcerated in the Mazas prison in Paris in early January 1894. The specific charge against him was that *La Société mourante et l'anarchie* was instrumental in provoking such propaganda by deed as robbery, mutiny, and murder. Some background should be presented here: Grave had been influenced by a Mirbeau letter in late 1893 to negotiate with P.V. Stock, the publisher of the book, for the publication of an inexpensive one-franc edition issued in January 1894, which contained another chapter, "La Méthode Expérimentale." This addition, apparently permitting the government to view the second edition as legally a new work, led to the confiscation of copies from various bookstores and the publisher's warehouse.[22]

So it was that Grave was tried before the Criminal Court of the Seine Department on February 24. To say the least, the prosecutor's charges concerning the nature of the work were untrue because even a cursory reading would amply indicate that Grave did not now advocate propaganda by deed. He did, however, condemn the morality of contemporary society, one engaged in imperialism and allowing for stock manipulation, which simultaneously severely punished a poor man who filched bread for his children.[23] Not surprisingly, many civil-rights advocates came to Grave's defence.

Grave was ably defended by Emile de Saint-Auban, a noted leftist lawyer and intellectual, whose defence included four distinguished character witnesses—brief comments from whom are quoted. The first, from Elisée Reclus:

> I have known Jean Grave for twenty-five years. I have great affection for him. He has educated himself splendidly. He has followed his studies in a meritorious manner. His intelligence is of the highest order. Jean Grave is especially concerned with anthropology. Knowing the character and habits of Jean Grave, I can say that he never favoured or counselled any criminal act.[24]

The second, from Mirbeau, a leading novelist, affirmed that, although he only knew Grave through correspondence, he had written the preface of *La Société mourante et l'anarchie* because of his great admiration for him and their mutual philosophical preoccupations.[25] He added: "I consider him an apostle. As a very superior logician who has pushed reasoning to its uttermost limits."[26] He also opined that the literary world had high regard for Grave, who in fact enjoyed "great authority" among them.[27]

The third, from Paul Adam, a noted author:

THE ANARCHISM OF JEAN GRAVE

> I do not personally know Jean Grave. I see him here for the first time. But I can say that it would have been very much to my credit to have written this book.[28]

The fourth, from Bernard Lazare, a well-known journalist and anarchist sympathiser:

> I have known Jean Grave for four years. His loyalty and integrity are above reproach. He is writer of great talent whose work is among the best that I know.[29]

The character witnesses were an integral part of De Saint-Auban's basic strategy: Grave's ideas, not Grave the criminal, were on trial. In this light, he compared Grave to such famous social critics as Victor Hugo and Gustave Flaubert, both of whom had also written about the oppressive nature of bourgeois society, including the wish for its demise, without having had to endure imprisonment.[30]

Grave himself had been unusually nervous during the proceedings, especially under the cross-examination of the prosecutor, and when asked to say a few words on his behalf at the end of the trial, his only words were: "I accept the responsibility of what I have written."[31]

The prosecutor asked the jury that Grave be imprisoned for five years, reminding them of the prior six-month prison term - obviously attempting to reinforce his case.[32] The jury, however, probably swayed by the outstanding defence, returned to declare Grave guilty with extenuating circumstances and imposed a sentence of a two-year imprisonment and a thousand franc fine.[33] It seemed incredible that Grave was imprisoned for writing a book. An additional dimension concerning the case, not known to the public at the time, were reports of police agents stating that Grave and Pouget, among others, were possible organisers of an anarchist European Information Bureau.[34]

Two well-known individuals should be particularly noted for aiding Grave during this trying period—Mirbeau and Georges Clémenceau. The former, an anarchist sympathiser (as already noted, a character witness for Grave), wrote an apology of Grave the week before the trial, "Pour Jean Grave" in *Le Journal* (a daily that dealt with politics, literature, and art), which castigated anarchist terrorists such as Henry, while praising Grave for his struggle to learn and to create, his acute sense of social justice, and the social sweep of *La Société mourante et l'anarchie*.[35] The latter, a leading Radical politician of the period, defended Grave's work as "cogent and logical" and right to criticise existing social institutions, although disagreeing with anarchist solutions.[36]

That Grave was found guilty angered a large part of the artistic/intellectual community. Mirbeau, again in the forefront, expressed shock and dismay at the turn of events. Even reactionaries like Drumont supported Grave's freedom to write. Indeed, within a week, a petition by more than a hundred and twenty artists and intellectuals, including Lucien Descaves, Jean Richepin, Adolphe Retté, Laurent Tailhade, Stuart Merrill and Paul Gaugin appeared in the prestigious daily, *L'Echo de Paris*, protesting against Grave's imprisonment. Notably absent was Zola who regarded Grave's work as replete with inflammatory propaganda.[37] Thanks to the efforts of Mirbeau and Clémenceau and the wide appeal of the petition, Grave now became known to the general public. Obviously touched by the avid concern, he thanked his supporters afterward, including Drumont.[38]

Soon after Grave's imprisonment, the government inexorably continued its drive against anarchism that by end of winter the anarchist press was closed and approximately four hundred anarchists were arrested. Two important events in the repression were the closing of Pouget's *Père Peinard* on February 21 and of *La Révolte*, run by Julien Ledot after Grave's arrest, on March 10.[39]

Soon after Henry's execution, an Italian anarchist, Santo Caserio, assassinated President Sadi Carnot at Lyons in late June 1894, for which he was tried and executed in August 1894, dying as bravely as the others. His was the last of the classic acts of propaganda by deed in France.[40]

Caserio's act led to the passage of the Third of the Exceptional Laws on July 26 and 27, 1894 by the Chamber of Deputies and Senate respectively. Now, even to apologise for or to excuse any propaganda by deed or such an unlawful act as mutiny, for example, could lead to imprisonment from three months to two years and a fine from a hundred to two thousand francs.[41] The socialist parties joined the anarchists in fighting this law, fearing that its provisions might be used to prevent any meaningful criticism of government.[42]

It was in this atmosphere of tension and hysteria that approximately thirty leading anarchist of the four hundred arrested were placed on trial in Paris before the Criminal Court of the Seine Department from August 6 to 14, 1894. This trial, one of the more noted in French history, is known as the Trial of the Thirty. In addition to Grave (although in prison he would be tried again), other prominent anarchists involved included Sébastien Faure, a brilliant journalist and formidable orator; Pouget, an old acquaintance of Grave's who was involved in labour-union activity; Paul Reclus; Félix Fénéon, an outstanding literary critic; and Charles Chatel, the former editor of *L'En Dehors*. Eleven of the Thirty were criminals, Ortiz the most notorious.[43]

The accused were charged by the prosecutor, Bulot, of belonging to a criminal conspiracy whose aim was to overthrow the government through such means as arson and assassination and that even those who advocated propaganda by deed in speech or writing were just as responsible as those committing such acts.[44]

Grave by then the best known of anarchist theoreticians in France and a leading journalist, inevitably became one of the primary defendants. At his peak intellectually, he was not too impressive physically when described as a "corpulent anarchist with a protruding forehead and pale complexion."[45] Grave was charged principally for developing the basic strategy of French anarchism in the 1883 pamphlet, *Organisation de la propagande révolutionnaire*, with *La Révolte* serving as a dangerous revolutionary organ supporting propaganda by deed and serving as liaison for various anarchist groups in its "Petite Correspondance" column.[46]

The cross-examination of the two most important defendants, Grave and Faure, was not conducted openly, perhaps in order to forestall favourable publicity in the event of a vigorous defence. For Faure this was a wise precautionary move, but for Grave the prosecutor need not have been cautious because under verbal fire he invariably became flustered.

THE TRIAL OF THE THIRTY PERIOD

Bulot's summation attempted to link Grave's pamphlet with the propaganda by deed committed by Ravachol, Henry and others for the purpose of making Grave appear not only sympathetic to them but also as one of their intellectual mentors. To reinforce this tack, he read a letter from Elisée Reclus to Grave during the Pini trial (an 1889 trial of an anarchist who stole for propaganda funds), in which theft by a worker was justified on the basis of retribution for bourgeois expropriation of labour.[47] (Although Grave was against theft, the prosecutor, nevertheless, tried the guilt-by-association ploy.)

Grave's defence was delivered on August 9 by De Saint-Auban, again his lawyer. He began by chiding the prosecutor for comparing a brilliant thinker like Grave to common criminals, the jury reminded that a man of such unimpeachable character as Frantz-Jourdain, a prominent architect and socialist, had already testified about Grave's sterling qualities. A testimonial letter was then presented from Professor Manouvrier, an eminent anthropologist at the School of Medicine of the University of Paris, that alluded to Grave's great intelligence and essentially peaceful nature.[48] (Not only had Manouvrier maintained extensive correspondence concerning anthropological problems with the imprisoned Grave at Saint-Pélagie, but he visited him there.)

De Saint-Auban's main argument was to show the unreasonable nature of the Exceptional Laws as applied to anarchists, specifically directed against the Second, which provided stiff penalties for criminal "associations" and "understandings"; the former term applied to a group having a definite aim in mind, while the latter signified a concrete action by two or more persons.[49] He indicated that both terms as applied to anarchists were logically absurd because: (1) Anarchists usually disagreed with one another concerning the essentials of their belief; (2) the very nature of anarchism with its emphasis on individual autonomy precluded any such combinations.[50] Then he pointed out that the Grave who advocated propaganda by deed in *Organisation de la propagande révolutionnaire* and in "Lutte et Théorie"[51] had now become a man of peace. Finally, with respect to *La Révolte* as a centre of criminal conspiracy, he argued that it should be regarded as simply another newspaper.[52]

THE ANARCHISM OF JEAN GRAVE

After the defence lawyers had completed their final summations, the defendants were allowed to make final statements. Although Grave was visibly nervous before making his presentation (so much so that de Saint-Auban and others offered to read it), he courageously persevered. He began by picturing himself a martyr:

> Gentlemen, forgive this speech of twenty or so lines. I have not previously taken your attention. I am not an orator. I have always avoided talking. I have been silent all my life. Silent have I remained during this trial and in silence will I succumb under the weight of injustice.[53]

But then Grave defended himself vigorously: Not only had he always opposed theft and anarchist organisation, but he viewed violence as unimportant in bringing about change since his "communism" was that of the Proudhonian variety. Grave then contended that he was in court not for criminal actions, but for opinion, which in any case, was not concerned with antisocial acts.[54] After final statements by many other defendants, the jury retired to deliberate and returned two hours later with the verdict: exoneration of Grave, Faure, Pouget, and others as leaders of a criminal conspiracy, but guilt and long-term imprisonment for Ortiz and the criminal group for theft.[55]

The trial of the Thirty may be regarded as marking the general end of anarchist propaganda by deed. Regrettably, most of these acts of wanton violence by the terrorists did incalculable damage to anarchism by equating it with violence and irrationality, elements better suited to those in positions of authority. Most anarchists after this time saw the promise of revolution, not in sterile acts of individual terrorism, but in *syndicale* or other mass collective action. Grave himself continued to defend propaganda by deed on principle, while being cognizant of its limitations. In his *L'Anarchie, son but, ses moyens*, he observed that it was both a result of and a protest against social oppression, but that it could not by itself overturn the state. Indeed, he indicated that peaceful methods of dissent were just as efficacious.[56]

After his acquittal, Grave continued to serve his prior prison sentence at the Mazas facility until early September when he was transferred

THE TRIAL OF THE THIRTY PERIOD

to Clairvaux Prison, a former Cistercian monastery in Eastern France. He was housed in the area reserved for political prisoners which he shared with two others: Fortuné Henry, an anarchist militant whose brother Emile had been involved in the bombing of the Terminus Café, and Jules L. Breton, a socialist also tried under the Exceptional Laws who later became a prominent socialist politician. Housing and food provided in this prison were not too disagreeable; the cell was spacious enough and rather comfortable, while the menu of steak, vegetables, and wine was supplemented by the generosity of the wealthy Breton who was amply provisioned. Since Grave was a political prisoner, he was allowed such privileges as access to books and newspapers, which, as in the Sainte-Pélagie period, led to intense intellectual activity that resulted in completing *La Société future*. Loneliness was further fended off by extensive correspondence with his in-laws, nephews and nieces; letters to the youngsters particularly charming. Prison life was also made more bearable by the timely provision of pocket money and many letters from Elisée Reclus.[57]

Grave endured prison with remarkable stoicism but was indignant that Paris prisons did not segregate the very young from adults. In a letter to Mirbeau which appeared in the *Supplément* of *La Révolte*, he averred that "six, eight and ten year old" children were thrown together with older inmates already "corrupted." He wondered whether society, in allowing for this condition, should be exonerated for begetting future criminals.[58]

Following the resignation of Casimir-Perier as president on 15 January, 1895 and his replacement by Félix Faure, a general amnesty for political prisoners was declared to mark the new term. Within a week, Grave received a pardon and returned to 140 Mouffetard Street.[59]

Notes
1. *La Révolte*, May 9, 1891, p 1; May 23-29, 1891; and September 5-11, 1891, pp1-3.
2. [Emile Méreaux], "Viande à Mitraille," *ibid.*, May 16-22, 1891, p 1.
3. *Mouvement libertaire*, pp 75-76.
4. *La Révolte*, June 6-12, 1891, p 1; June 13-19, 1891, p 1.
5. *Ibid.*, June 13-19, 1891.
6. *Mouvement libertaire*, p 76.
7. *Ibid.*, p 85 and p 146. Its original title of *Sous l'uniforme* was changed just before publication in 1895.
8. *Mouvement libertaire*, p 83.

9. *Ibid.* On Mirbeau and anarchism, se Reg Carr, *Anarchism in France: The Case of Octave Mirbeau* (Montreal: McGill-Queen's University Press, 1978).
10. *Mouvement libertaire*, p 80.
11. *Quarante ans*, pp 245-6. Charles Malato, *Philosophie de l'anarchie* (Paris: P. V. Stock, 1897), advocated anarchist organisation and acceptance of leaders for revolution. The first edition of this work was published in 1889. Malato's prison experiences were recounted in *Prison fin-de-siècle: Souvenirs de Pélagie* (1891). On his life, see *DB*, XIII, 334-35.
12. *Mouvement libertaire*, pp 105-08.
13. *Ibid.*, p 102. Miller, *Kropotkin*, p 212; Kropotkin objected to terrorism.
14. On Ravachol, see Jean Maitron, *Ravachol et les anarchistes* (Paris: René Julliard, 1964), pp 39-76; Vizetelly, *The Anarchists*, pp102-26; Henri Varennes, *De Ravachol à Caserio (Notes d'audience)* (Paris: Garnier, n.d.), pp 1-78; and Gilbert Guilleminault and André Mahé, *L'Epopée de la Révolte* (Paris: Denoël, 1963), pp57-92.
15. *La Révolte*, January 16-22, 1892.
16. On anarchist press reaction to Ravachol, see *HMA*, p 208.
17. *Mouvement libertaire*, p 102. A. Hamon, *Les Hommes et les théories de l'anarchie* (Paris: Aux Bureaux de la Révolte, 1893), pp 4-11, pointed out that the press was mute concerning the French army's desecration of the graves of the Indochinese.
18. On Vaillant, see *HMA*, pp 218-25.
19. For the specific texts of these laws, see Varennes, *De Ravachol à Caserio*, pp 351-56.
20. *Ibid.*, p 353. For an anarchist crticism of the Exceptional Laws, which, for example, could imprison one for merely attending an anarchist meeting, see Emile Pouget, "L'Application des lois d'exception de 1893 et 1894," *La Revue Blanche*, XVI (15 July 1898), pp 426-43. On the fact that the Third Republic was indeed repressive towards anarchism, see Jean-Pierre Machelon, *La République contre les libertés?* (Paris: Presses de la Fondation Nationale des Science Politiques, 1976), pp 399-446.
21. *Mouvement libertaire*, p 139, stated that Henry was despondent due to an unfortunate love affair. On Henry, see Varennes, *De Ravachol à Caserio*, pp 208-45.
22. On events leading to the trial, see Emile de Saint-Auban, *L'Histoire sociale au Palais de Justice: plaidoyers philosophiques* (Paris: A. Pedone, 1895), pp 20-43; *Mouvement libertaire*, pp 118-25; *HMA*, p 232; and, Varennes, *De Ravachol à Caserio*, pp 153-63; *Quarante ans*, p 304; Carr, *Mirbeau*, pp 72-73.
23. Grave, *La Société mourante et l'anarchie*, p 111.
24. Varennes, *De Ravachol à Caserio*, p 159.
25. *Ibid.*, p 160.
26. *Ibid.*
27. *Ibid.*
28. De Saint-Auban, *L'Histoire sociale*, p 204.
29. *Ibid.*
30. *Ibid.*, pp 205-43, on De Saint-Auban's defense.
31. *Mouvement libertaire*, pp 120-21.

THE TRIAL OF THE THIRTY PERIOD

32. Varennes, *de Ravachol à Caserio*, p 158; *Mouvement libertaire*, pp 120-21.
33. De Saint-Auban, *L'Histoire sociale*, p 204-05; *Mouvement libertaire*, p 120.
34. *Archives Nationales*, Box F[7] 12504. *HMA*, p 106, stated the Bureau was a police hoax.
35. Carr, *Mirbeau*, pp 73-75; pp 174-77 for all of "Pour Jean Grave."
36. *Mouvement libertaire*, pp 97-99; and, De Saint-Auban, *L'Histoire sociale*, pp 207-08.
37. On Mirbeau's shock at the guilty verdict, Carr, *Mirbeau*, pp 76-77. On the petition, see *L'Echo de Paris*, March 4, 1894, p 3, and Carr, *Mirbeau*, p 76. On Zola and the guilty verdict, see Josephson, *Zola and his Times*, pp 377-78.
38. On Drumont, see *Quarante ans*, p 338.
39. *HMA*, p 237; Varennes, *De Ravachol à Caserio*, p 286; *Mouvement libertaire*, p 115.
40. On Casario, see *HMA*, pp 234-35.
41. For the text of the Third Exceptional Law, see Varennes, *De Ravachol à Casario*, pp 355-56.
42. Harvey Goldberg, *The Life of Jean Jaurès*, (Madison: University of Wisconsin Press, 1952), pp 126-28.
43. For a complete list of defendants, see Varennes, *De Ravachol à Casario*, pp 280-88. On the fact that Pouget, Paul Reclus, and other anarchists (tried in absentia) had evaded the police dragnet, see De Saint-Auban, *L'Histoire sociale*, pp 245-46.
44. On the Trial of the Thirty, see A. Bataille, *Causes criminelles et mondaines de 1894* (Paris: Dentu, 1895), pp 146-203; Varennes, *De Ravachol à Casario*, pp 287-345; De Saint-Auban, *L'Histoire sociale*, pp 245-97; and *Gazette des Tribunaux*, Aug 6-14, 1894.
45. Bataille, *Causes criminelles et mondaines de 1894*, pp 188-93.
46. *Gazette des Tribunaux*, August 6 and 7, 1894, pp 1-2; and Varennes, *De Ravachol à Casario*, pp 296-97.
47. On Bulot's speech, see Bataille, *Causes criminelles et mondaines de 1894*, pp 188-93.
48. De Saint-Auban, *L'Histoire sociale*, pp 247-96, on his defence of Grave.
49. On the Law of December 18, 1893, see Varennes, *De Ravachol à Casario*, pp 353-55.
50. De Saint-Auban, *L'Histoire sociale*, p 252.
51. Jean Grave, "Lutte et Théorie," *La Révolte*, February 17, 1888.
52. De Saint-Auban, *L'Histoire sociale*, p 270.
53. Varennes, *De Ravachol à Casario*, p 342; and Bataille, *Causes criminelles et mondaines de 1894*, pp 202-03.
54. Bataille, *Causes criminelles et mondaines de 1894*, pp 202-03; and *Mouvement libertaire*, pp 134-35.
55. Bataille, *Causes criminelles et mondaines de 1894*, p 203.
56. See *HMA*, pp 244ff. On propaganda by deed and Grave, see his *L'Anarchie, son but, ses moyens*, pp 129-45.
57. On the incarceration at Clairvaux, see *Quarante ans*, pp 327-36. GA letters from Elisée Reclus to Grave, Sept. 12 and November 26, 1894; and letter from Grave to a nephew, November 19, 1894.
58. *RSL*, May 28 to June 2, 1892.
59. *Quarante ans*, pp 335-36.

DORMER-WINDOW OF JEAN GRAVE'S WORKSHOP

Office of "Les Temps Nouveaux," in the rue Mouffetard

JEAN GRAVE at *"Les Temps Nouveaux"*

6

LES TEMPS NOUVEAUX AND OTHER ACTIVITY, 1895-1905

GRAVE'S MOST IMMEDIATE AND PRESSING concern after returning from prison was to found a weekly. To this end, he saw Elisée Reclus in Brussels, then Kropotkin in London;[1] the former committed financial aid, while the latter promised articles.[2] With Grave's royalties from *La Société mourante et l'anarchie* and the generous aid of many friends, publication was assured.[3] Thus there sprang into being *Les Temps Nouveaux*, published from May 4, 1895 to August 1, 1914, during which time it was one of the four leading anarchist newspapers in France.[4]

That the weekly lasted twenty years is indeed eloquent testimony not only of Grave's, but also of others' economic sacrifices. Grave himself donated at least 12,000 francs from book royalties, an 800-franc stamp collection, and the larger part of his 200-franc monthly salary.[5] An example of generous outside aid was that of Stuart Merrill, a noted Symbolist poet, who time and again contributed money.[6]

The raffle was also employed to secure needed monies; the first one, held in May 1899, collected 1,000 francs, the winners being treated to such artistic delights as paintings by Paul Signac and Camille and Lucien Pissarro.[7]

There were, however, a few disappointments in raising funds. A noteworthy example was a speech to be given by Kropotkin in May 1896 in Paris to better publicise the weekly; French authorities prevented his coming to France from London, but something was salvaged as the speech was transformed into a series of brilliant articles.[8]

As in any new start, there were optimistic expectations for a high circulation; the first printing was of 18,000 copies, but within a brief period the number was reduced to 8,000, of which only 2,700 were sold.[9] By 1902, readership increased to 5,200: 4,100 to non-subscribers and 1,100 to subscribers, later declining to 5,000.[10] The newspaper was a weekly, except for a period in 1909-1910 when it appeared every fifteen days because of economic difficulties. It was a tabloid of four pages with a *Supplément Littéraire* of eight pages which, in October 1903 was reduced to four. The price per copy was ten centimes inside France, fifteen outside.[11]

There were three other important anarchist newspapers in France before World War I. The first, *La Guerre Sociale*, virtually although not strictly anarchist, founded by Gustave Hervé, a staunch antimilitarist and revolutionary socialist, invited many anarchist contributors, notably Faure and Pouget.[12] The second, Faure's anarcho-communist *Le Libertaire* (1885-1914), had about the same circulation as *Les Temps Nouveaux*. Faure effectively publicised his newspaper by conducting many conferences and presenting innumerable speeches.[13] The third, Pouget's anarcho-communist *Le Père Peinard*, published intermittently from 1889 to 1900, was written in the vernacular of the proletariat.[14]

The group of writers that Grave was associated with in the newspaper may be favourably compared with any other in general intellectual ability in France, if not the world. General theory and comment by Kropotkin and Elisée Reclus alone would have made for a first-rate staff, but Grave also enlisted many of the ideologues and activists of *anarcho-syndicalisme*, such as Fernand Pelloutier and Paul Delesalle. Grave himself, as chief editor and leading spirit, was recognised by many artists and intellectuals as a significant social thinker.

There was also another group of writers, generally not as well known as those mentioned, who, indeed, did most of the writing. Of high intellectual calibre, they included André Girard, Charles Benoît Charles Albert, René Chaugi, the physician Marc Pierrot, Tscherkesoff and Adolphe Retté. Girard, born into an upper middle-class family of considerable culture, was a long-time collaborator from *La Révolte* period. As the weekly's chief administrator, he coped ably with vexing daily problems and found time to cover "France" under the "Mouvement Social" column. His work was partially curtailed when he left the administration for a position in a publishing house to please his wife.¹⁵ Even afterward, he still was one of the more important contributors, writing many *Les Temps Nouveaux* pamphlets and articles in such areas as education, strike activity, brutality in the army, and general anarchist theory.¹⁶ Girard's place in administration was taken by Benoît whose mother ran a small café in Rouen. From an early age he was involved in anarchist activity, notably in a series of strikes in Rouen in the late nineties and writing antimilitaristic propaganda. He was especially concerned with the dissemination of anarchist ideas through *Les Temps Nouveaux* pamphlets.¹⁷ Charles Albert was not an atypical figure to be found in anarchist intellectual circles, wealthy and cultured, a friend of many artists, especially Signac. His articles on various subjects amply indicated not only broad erudition, but also deep concern for the social problem. He left the staff in 1910 after arguing with Grave over a trivial matter, the newspaper's appearance.¹⁸ Chaugi, another long-time collaborator from *La Révolte*, was also wealthy. An unusually charming individual, perhaps because of an excessive shyness probably caused by stuttering, he was one of the more effective staff writers. His articles, which revealed an unusually complex style of writing and great mastery of subject matter, were those of an outstanding intellectual. He also wrote pamphlets for the newspaper.¹⁹ Doctor Pierrot, another of the old faithful, assisted in daily operations, contributed money and wrote articles which combined extensive reading in the social and physical sciences.²⁰ Tcherkesoff, whom Grave knew from the days of the Social Study Group in the 1880s, wrote on many subjects, but his forte was in describing Turkish atrocities perpetrated on subject peoples. Grave was much impressed by this friend with a "soft voice", who in order to earn a living became a worker.²¹ Retté, a prominent anarchist novelist from the bourgeoisie (he used Grave as a leading character in one of his works), wrote many articles on the social problem.²²

Besides Grave, the two best-known contributors were Kropotkin and Elisée Reclus. Kropotkin, a scholar with a worldwide reputation by the first decade of the twentieth century, wrote extensively on theoretical issues and contemporary events; many articles ran in serial form for months. Perhaps the most notable was *L'Etat; son rôle historique*, a masterful exposition

LES TEMPS NOUVEAUX AND OTHER ACTIVITY

on the rise of the oppressive state.[23] Reclus did not write many articles since his other commitments, especially his teaching, took much time, but what he did present was of a uniformly high quality.[24]

In enlisting the services of well-known writers for articles, Grave experienced some disappointment. Two leading examples were Lazare and Adam, both character witnesses for Grave in his February 1894 trial. Both indicated a willingness to write and were listed as contributing editors in the first issue of May 4, 1895. Lazare had stipulated a fee for his services that Grave apparently overlooked. Although this misunderstanding strained relations between them, Grave eulogised Lazare's character and work.[25] As for Adam, not fulfilling a promise angered Grave, but only after Adam became a conservative were relations severed between them.[26]

The importance of Les *Temps Nouveaux* must not only be measured by its weekly circulation, but also by pamphlets from its press - at least eighty-eight from 1895 to 1914 with a combined circulation in the many thousands. Among the most noteworthy were Grave's *La Colonisation* and *Organisation, initiative, cohésion*, Malatesta's *Entre Paysans*, and Kropotkin's *Aux jeunes gens*. They provided an excellent example of fusing the word to graphic art through covers drawn by such outstanding painters as Luce, Steinlen, and Hermann-Paul, which featured such social themes as the dignity of labour and social misery of the people.[27]

The weekly obviously reflected Grave's and the staff's daily concerns, not only with the ongoing social struggle in France, but as seen in the "Mouvement International" column with that in other nations.[28] An important example of the latter was its publicity on the *Mano Negra*, a name invented by Spanish authorities to indicate a non-existent anarchist organisation, which they used as an excuse to crackdown on anarchists who occasionally committed propaganda by deed against reactionary and brutal landlords. In late 1883, hundreds of Spanish anarchists were imprisoned, many sentenced to death. Years later, taking the cue from Spanish anarchists, the weekly ran a series of articles, appealing for assistance to finally free the survivors. Many responded, including Anatole France and Clémenceau. Within a short time, even some of the leading newspapers, *L'Aurore* principally, joined the chorus urging that the victims be freed. By March 1903, prisoners still alive were released.[29]

THE ANARCHISM OF JEAN GRAVE

As anarchist journalist and propagandist, Grave had to endure much harassment at the hands of the police, who acted on the assumption that merely being an anarchist in itself was criminal, and who, in order to justify this, attempted frame-ups. On the night of May 31, 1905 in Paris, a Spanish anarchist, Aviño, threw two bombs, injuring no one, at the carriage of President Emile Loubet who was riding with Alphonso XIII of Spain from the Opera to the Foreign Ministry building. The attempted assassination horrified the bourgeois press which launched its usual campaign of anti-anarchist hysteria. The police responded with a roundup of anarchists, including Grave and Malato.[30] In the Clamart Woods, just outside Paris, some of Grave's correspondence, torn and scattered about, was conveniently found by police. Grave was arrested on the basis that this evidence in some manner tied him to the attempted assassination. He denied the allegation and was released for lack of evidence.[31] Who placed Grave's letters in the woods? No one definitely knows; I have already given my opinion. During the trial of Malato and others accused of the attempted assassination, Grave and other anarchists were called by the prosecution to testify as to the probable culprit, but the ploy did not succeed for the defendants were acquitted.[32] Aviño himself escaped capture.

In 1896, Grave apparently attended one of the historic congresses of the Second International, held in London, leading to the final split between anarchist and other socialists. Grave was entered as a representative of a metal workers' union at Amiens in which anarchist influence was strong, anarchists comprised a large part of the French delegation.[33] A great debate centered on whether anarchist delegates should be seated since, unlike Marxists and other socialists, they opposed participation in electoral reformist politics.[34] In a historically significant vote that formalised the final break between "revolutionary" anarchists and "reformist" socialists, anarchists not directly involved in union activity (this was the surface manifestation of the split) were expelled. Thus, the ruling did not apply to anarchist union militants of long standing, like Delesalle and Pelloutier.[35]

After their ouster, the anarchists then held a meeting in London which included Kropotkin, Pouget, Malatesta and Michel: Grave probably did not attend. After the socialists were condemned for expelling anarchists, a round of discussions reaffirmed the almost-traditional anarchist position: revolution, not reform.[36]

While visiting Kropotkin in 1895 in London, Grave was introduced by him to Miss Mabel Holland Thomas, an Englishwoman of wealth and culture interested in anarchism. By 1897 she was writing articles of great literary merit for the newspaper: In "Le Message," a vignette, the hero urged the rebirth of humanity through the ideals of anarchism;[37] in "L'Excentrique," she praised the eccentric as one most concerned with social misery.[38] Within a brief period, the friendship of Miss Thomas and Grave developed to where he would daily write to her.[39]

A significant project in 1897-1898 had Grave participating on an education committee, which included Leo Tolstoy, Kropotkin and Elisée Reclus.[40] The problem which faced them was how to teach children in a society under the impress of authoritarian and class-ridden relations that inculcated them with submission and obedience, on the one hand, and of personal aggrandisement on the other, both linked to the grading system. The teacher, an authority figure, enforced a regimented learning reflecting the competition so characteristic of the middle-class spirit, in which joy in learning was purely accidental.[41]

In contradiction to this educational pattern was the anarchist one, greatly influenced by Rousseau's *Emile or On Education*, which outlined the essentials of modern progressive education, emphasizing the importance of respecting children's individuality in learning in the context of mutual aid. The teacher would be a guide, not a judge. The school would also insist on coeducation in order to foster equality and mutual respect between the sexes. As in all other areas, the educational system was to be locally controlled.[42]

The hope of Grave and of others was that, despite generations of social oppression, anarchist mutual aid might still make it possible to establish such social complexes as schools in order to instil anarchist ideals. A school was duly established, but quickly foundered on the petty squabbles of the teachers. Grave later returned his attention to education by editing a children storybook that featured an anarchist perspective.[43]

It has already been noted that Grave was involved in an educational project with Tolstoy who, although obviously known for his novels, is not

THE ANARCHISM OF JEAN GRAVE

well recognised as a Christian anarchist. Grave, an admirer of Tolstoy's works, inserted excerpts from *War and Peace*, *Resurrection*, and *Kreutzer Sonata* in the *Supplément*. Tolstoy, in turn, was conversant with portions of Grave's work: his diary of 5 February, 1898, wrestled with Grave's *L'Individu et la société*, only to reject its atheistic anarchism for one based on the life and ideals of Christ. For Tolstoy, God exists and thus man is not just "an accidental chain of atoms." Although Grave differed with Tolstoy concerning God's existence and insistence on non-violence (Grave would not turn the other cheek to social oppression), he could certainly agree with much of the following Tolstoyan views: (1) universal brotherhood and equality based on self-sacrificing love; (2) cooperative living under communist arrangements that repudiated all exploitation. Moreover, Tolstoy viewed the state as representing organised violence and social oppression and considered the Russian Orthodox Church as a worldly force which made a mockery of Christ's ideals. Despite differences between Grave and Tolstoy, their common anarchism allowed Tolstoy to send Grave an autographed photograph (it is between pages fifty and fifty-one in *Le Mouvement Libertaire*) on which is inscribed: "A mon estimé collaborateur et confrère Jean Grave—Léon Tolstoi 1902, 15 Mai."[44]

Although France by the late nineteenth century was well on its way to becoming a modern industrial nation, the medieval element of anti-Semitism still claimed its due, indeed involved in the most celebrated court case in French history, in which anarchism played a part.

In January 1895, Captain Alfred Dreyfus, born into a wealthy Alsatian-Jewish family, was sentenced to life imprisonment on Devil's Island for spying. The basic inconsistency in the case was motive: Why should he sell military secrets to the Germans? (Dreyfus' family moved from Alsace-Lorraine, when annexed by Germany in 1871, to France for patriotic reasons). Questions were therefore raised as to whether the injustice was due to anti-Semitism.[45]

Dreyfus was caught in a large historical net in which the France of the French Revolution was engaged in a power struggle with the Royalist-clerical complex whose *Weltanschauung* still resided in the Old Regime. The heavily royalist and clerically influenced army officer corps was an important power centre of the reactionaries.

LES TEMPS NOUVEAUX AND OTHER ACTIVITY

From the beginning, anarchism was involved in the case, although there was a division between anarchists who were Dreyfusards and those only marginally concerned. It was Lazare, a prominent anarchist writer hired by the Dreyfus family, who renewed interest in the case by thorough investigative work exposing its many inconsistencies.

In the 1898-1899 period the case reached a period of high intensity. On one side were the Dreyfusards, mainly liberal and left-wing intellectuals, who saw Dreyfus as a victim of injustice and anti-Semitism; on the other were the nationalist and royalist-clerical groups that defended the army's justice and pictured their opponents as subverters of French tradition.[46] When in January 1898, Zola wrote *J'Accuse!* in the Dreyfusard *L'Aurore*, charging the army of wrongly condemning Dreyfus, the political climate was electrified.[47]

Grave and *Les Temps Nouveaux* were not at first actively engaged in Dreyfus' defence. It was difficult for Grave to accept that a member of an elite group could be falsely accused of treason, but he soon admitted of being unaware of the intense anti-Semitism among army officers.[48] But he was angry that many liberal and left-wing intellectuals were now so concerned with a member of the governing class, while previously ignoring the fate of many obscure anarchists unjustly imprisoned. After the frustration and bitterness welling up from defending so many lost causes, Grave intimated that perhaps there was, after all, a higher type of justice in having one of the privileged becoming a victim.[49]

But Grave was not hostile to Dreyfus since he wrote a letter to Zola in *L'Aurore* in February 1898, praising his courageous stand on behalf of Dreyfus and urging review of the case, especially as it was conducted in secret.[50] Indeed, Grave wrote about half-a-dozen articles in *L'Aurore* in early 1898 on justice for Dreyfus and would have written more if not denied a request to insert articles on anarchism and antimilitarism.[51] Furthermore, by November 1898, Grave realised that the case had transcended the guilt or innocence of Dreyfus, and that in defending him the anarchists were attacking reactionary army-clerical-royalist groups all the more effectively.[52]

In the meantime, anarchist Dreyfusards, most notably Faure and Pouget, played a leading role in founding the anarchist Dreyfusard daily,

THE ANARCHISM OF JEAN GRAVE

Le Journal du Peuple, which appeared in 1899. Although Faure desired Grave's participation in this journal, insisting that there were less differences between him and Grave than Clémenceau's *L'Aurore* to which Grave contributed, Grave refused.[53] Literary anarchists had already joined the Dreyfusards and were well represented in *La Revue Blanche* by such authors as Mirbeau and Laurent Tailhade.[54]

The climactic period in the political atmosphere which the case inspired occurred in early June 1899 when civil disturbances seemed possible between left and right. On June 4, President Loubet was attacked by a reactionary baron at the Longchamps race track in Paris. To protest this provocation and to show their readiness to defend the Republic, various socialist and republican groups held a mass show of force at the same racetrack on June 11. Many anarchists joined the socialists in forming the Committee of Vigilance that participated. But Grave and other anarchists assembled in the nearby Meudon Woods, on alert to join the larger group if assaulted by the forces of reaction. No attack took place and tensions subsided rapidly. Dreyfus received a pardon in September 1899.[55]

On balance, anarchist participation in the Dreyfus Case proved to be tactically correct as it not only provided a larger platform for their ideas, but also led to a renewed interest in the fortunes of obscure anarchists languishing in prison; Grave, whose relations with Zola had improved dramatically during the case, enlisted his aid on their behalf.[56] As a result of this and other work, a few anarchists were freed.[57]

In 1900, Grave wrote a report on organisation that was to have been submitted before an international anarchist congress to be held in Paris then. At the time, there was a concerted drive in anarchist circles for the formation of a political party. Although not against it, Grave resolutely opposed any official organs, such as a newspaper or a central committee claiming to speak for anarchism as a whole, lest it make anarchism no different from other socialist groups. The congress itself was never held as the French government refused permission. Grave's report was published as a pamphlet under the title of *Organisation, initiative, cohésion*.[58]

An important event occurred at the end of the period, the 1905 Russian Revolution. Just after "Red Sunday" on January 22, 1905 in St. Petersburg (it marked the beginning of the revolution), Charles Albert and Grave organised a political meeting to commemorate the anniversary of the death of Peter Lavrov, a well-known Russian socialist who had died in 1900, to show support for the revolutionaries. Anatole France, Jean Jaurès, Descaves, Steinlen, Mirbeau and Severine, among others, promised to attend. The meeting, unfortunately, was never held since France, Mirbeau and others did not attend for fear that the French government, not to embarrass the Russian one, would not only prohibit the gathering, but expel Russian political exiles. In an unforgiving stance, Grave blamed Mirbeau and others for cowardly behaviour.[59]

Notes

1. *Mouvement libertaire*, p 147.
2. *Ibid.*, p 148.
3. *Ibid.*
4. *Ibid.* The name of the journal was suggested by Elisée Reclus.
5. *Mouvement libertaire*, pp 293-98.
6. *Ibid.*, pp 153-54; and GA, letter, Merrill to Grave, October 1, 1896.
7. *Les Temps Nouveaux*, April 15-21, April 22-28, and May 6-12, 1899.
8. Woodcock and Avakumovic, *The Anarchist Prince*, pp 271-73.
9. *Mouvement libertaire*, p 300.
10. *Les Temps Nouveaux*, September 12, 1908, p 1.
11. At times the *Literary Supplement* did not appear. For a period in 1907, the price of the newspaper was fifteen centimes.
12. On Hervé, see *Quarante ans*, p 90.
13. On Faure, see Flax [Victor Meric], "Sébastien Faure," *Les Hommes du Jour*, No. 18, 1908 (month not given), pp 2-4.
14. See Roger Langlois (ed.), *Emile Pouget; Le Père Peinard, Textes choisies et présentés* (Paris: Editions Galilée, 1976).
15. *Mouvement libertaire*, pp 155-58. On Girard's background, I am indebted to Monsieur Léon Ancely, one long involved in anarchist circles, a good friend of Madame Paul Delesalle and Madame Charles Benoît: letter, Ancely to Patsouras, June 2, 1965.
16. Some articles chosen at random: André Girard, "Biribi et autres lieux," *Les Temps Nouveaux*, May 16-22, 1896, pp 1-2; André Girard, "La Grève Nouvelle," *ibid.*, October 15-21, 1898, p 1.

17. See his obituary by Maurice Chambelland, "Charles Benoît," *La Révolution Prolétarienne*, March 1950, pp 29-30.

18. On Charles Albert [Charles Albert Daudet], see *Mouvement libertaire*, pp 228-29. Interview with madame Paul Delesalle, August 9, 1964, who knew him. One of his articles in nine installments: "Le Préjugé politique," *Les Temps Nouveaux*, November 1901, to February, 1902. Also, see *DB*, XI, 172-73.

19. On Chaugi [Henri Louis Auguste Gauche], see *DB*, XII, 254; interview I had with Madame Paul Delesalle, August 9, 1964. A few of his articles in *Les Temps Nouveaux*: "Domestiques," December 15-21, 1901, p 1; "Sur la religion," April 1-7, 1899, pp 1-2.

20. On Pierrot, see *HMA*, pp 253-54; *DB*, XIV, 267-68. For an article by him in *Les Temps Nouveaux*, see "La Grève des cheminots," October 15, 1910, pp 1-2.

21. On Tcherkesoff, see *Quarante ans*, pp 156-57, p 500, p 503, p 516, and pp 519-20; *DB*, XV, 202-03. On theory, see William Tcherkesoff, "Pages d'histoire socialiste," *Les Temps Nouveaux*, January 11-17, 1896 to April 29-May 5, 1899.

22. On Retté, see William Kenneth Cornell, *Adolphe Retté, 1863-1930* (New Haven, Yale University Press, 1942). On Grave as a character in Retté's *Au pays des lys noir*, see *ibid.*, p 179. A good article: Adolphe Retté, "Les Mineurs," *Les Temps Nouveaux*, October 19-25 and October 26-November 1, 1895, pp 3-4 respectively.

23. Pierre Kropotkine, "L'Etât: son rôle historique," *Les Temps Nouveaux*, December 19-25, 1896 to July 3-9, 1897 (ten installments).

24. Reclus, *Les Frères Elie et Elisée Reclus*, pp 141ff. Elisée Reclus, "L'Anarchie," *Les Temps Nouveaux*, May-June 1895.

25. *Mouvement libertaire*, pp 141 and 153. Grave's tribute to Lazare is in *Les Temps Nouveaux*, December 5-11, 1903. GA, two letters from Lazare to Grave, 1891, concerning the wish for a copy of *La Révolte*.

26. *Mouvement libertaire*, pp 151-52. On his life, see Camille Mauclair, *Paul Adam, 1862-1920* (Paris: Flammarion, 1921). Letter 1466 in GA, 1891, Adam to Grave, gave permission to Grave to reproduce excerpts of *Robes Rouges* in *La Révolte* in addition to praising Grave for his social concern.

27. For a comprehensive list of these brochures, see *Les Temps Nouveaux*, October 18, 1913, p 8. In *Mouvement libertaire*, pp 302ff, there was much information on the subject.

28. See any issue of *Les Temps Nouveaux*.

29. See for example two articles by Jean Grave, "Pour ceux qui blessent les injustices," *Les Temps Nouveaux*, December 6-12, 1902, p 2; and "Où en est la presse," *ibid.*, December 27-January 2, 1903, pp 1-2. Two long articles by Georges Clemenceau for *La Dépêche de Toulouse* in December, 1902, are included in *La Mano Negra: La main noire* (Paris: Imprimerie Charles Blot, n.d.), pp 1-7. Also, see Murray Bookchin, *The Spanish Anarchists: The Heroic Years 1868-1936* (New York, Free Life Editions, 1977), pp 106-08.

LES TEMPS NOUVEAUX AND OTHER ACTIVITY

30. *HMA*, p 386.
31. *Mouvement libertaire*, pp 222-24. *Les Temps Nouveaux*, July 1, 1905, p 2.
32. *Mouvement libertaire*, p 223. A. Dunois, "Le Procès," *Les Temps Nouveaux*, December 9, 1905, p 2.
33. On the London Congress, see Augustin Hamon, *Le Socialisme et le congrès de Londres* (Paris: P. V. Stock, 1899), pp 99-180.
34. For an excellent article by Grave against voting and parliamentary activity, which are seen as essentially counterrevolutionary: "Questions des tactiques," *Les Temps Nouveaux*, August 22-28, 1896, pp 1-2.
35. Jean Grave, in *Les Temps Nouveaux*, September 12-18, 1896, p 2, defended the right of anarchists to attend the conference on the basis that they too were socialists. Grave does not mention that he actually attended the conference.
36. See Paul Delesalle, "Les Conférences anarchistes de Londres," *Les Temps Nouveaux*, August 22-28, 1896, p 2.
37. Mabel Holland Thomas, "Le Message," *ibid.*, September 4-10, 1897, p 1.
38. Mabel Holland Thomas, "L'Excentrique," *ibid.*, November 20-26, 1897, p 7.
39. Interview with Madame Paul Delesalle, June 27 and August 9, 1964.
40. See Groupe d'initiative pour l'école libertaire, *La Liberté par l'enseignement; l'école libertaire* (Paris: *Les Temps Nouveaux*, 1898), pp 1ff. Jean Grave, "L'Ecole Libertaire," *Les Temps Nouveaux*, October 22-28, 1898, p 2. *Mouvement libertaire*, pp 175-78.
41. Grave, *La Société future*, pp 240ff. Jean Grave, *Enseignement bourgeois et enseignement libertaire* (Paris: *Les Temps Nouveaux*, 1900), pp 1ff. André Girard, *Education: autorité paternelle* (Paris: *Les Temps Nouveaux*, 1898), pp 5ff.
42. On anarchist educational theory, see Grave, *La Société au lendemain de la révolution*, pp 68-69; Grave, *La Société future*, pp 340ff ; Grave, *Terre libre*, pp 229-39. For Tolstoy the great work on education was Rousseau's *Emile*: Isaiah Berlin, *The Hedgehog and the Fox; An Essay on Tolstoy's View of History* (New York, Oxford University Press, 1963), p 67. Also, see Leonard I. Krimerman and Lewis Perry, *Patterns of Anarchy* (Garden City, N.Y.: Doubleday Anchor Books, 1966), pp 436-88, on the views of Tolstoy, Paul Goodman and others on education.
43. William Morris, Leo Tolstoy and others, *Le Coin des enfants; recueil de contes* preface by Jean Grave, illustrated by Mabel Holland Thomas, Hermann-Paul and others, 3 vols., (Paris: Librairie des *Temps Nouveaux*, 1905-07) I, pp 7-13.
44. See Leo Tolstoy, *The Journal of Leo Tolstoy, 1895-1899*, I, trans. Rose Sturmsky (New York: Alfred A. Knopf, 1907), 206. On his life, see Alexandra Tolstoy, *Tolstoy; A Life of my Father*, trans. Elizabeth Reynolds Hapgood (New York: Harper and Bros., 1953). On Tolstoy's anarchism, see Paul Eltzbacher, *Anarchism; Exponents of the Anarchist Philosophy*, trans. Steven T. Byington (New York: Libertarian Book Club, 1960), pp 149-81.

45. On the Dreyfus case, see Louis L. Snyder, *The Dreyfus Case; A Documentary History* (New Brunswick, N. J.: Rutgers University Press, 1973). Also see Léon Blum, *Souvenirs sur l'Affaire* (Paris: Gallimard, 1935). Bernard Lazare, *Une erreur judiciare; la verité sur l'Affaire Dreyfus* (Brussels: [no publisher], 1898) pp 1-24 (24 pp).
46. On left-wing intellectuals, see Blum, *Souvenirs de l'Affaire*, chapter 4. On Jaurès and the socialists, see Goldberg, *The Life of Jean Jaurès*, pp 271ff. The Guesdist-Marxists had a position similar to Grave's—unconcern over the personal fate of Dreyfus: see Noland, *The Founding of the French Socialist Party*, pp 86-88. Blum, *Souvenirs sur l'Affaire*, pp 85ff recounted the termination of the friendship between himself and Maurice Barrès as a result of the case. Blum (1872-1950) was the principal leader of French Socialism from after World War I to his death. On Blum's life, see Jean Lacouture, *Léon Blum* (Paris: Seuil, 1977).
47. *L'Aurore*, January 13, 1898. This newspaper was founded in 1897 to defend Dreyfus. Its editor was Georges Clemenceau (1841-1929), a Radical and Dreyfusard whose ministry in World War I symbolized French determination. On his life, see J. Hampden Jackson, *Clemenceau and the Third Republic* (London: The English Universities Press Ltd., 1959) pp 110-32, on the Dreyfus episode.
48. *Quarante ans*, p 361.
49. Jean Grave, "Purulences," *Les Temps Nouveaux*, January 22-28, 1898, pp 1-2; Jean Grave, "Pour ceux qui sont au bagne," *ibid.*, March 12-18, 1898, p 1.
50. *L'Aurore*, Feb. 17, 1898.
51. *Quarante ans*, p 364.
52. Jean Grave, "L'Agitation et les anarchistes," *Les Temps Nouveaux*, November 5-11, 1898, p 1.
53. *Le Journal du Peuple*, February-December 1899. Sébastien Faure, *Les Anarchistes et l'Affaire Dreyfus* (Paris: Imprimerie Lafont, 1898), pp 6-19, stated that the anarchists in defending Dreyfus were fighting clericalism and chauvinism. GA, letter Faure to Grave, Jan. 9, 1899.
54. Blum, *Souvenirs de l'Affaire*, p 93. Carr, *Mirbeau*, pp 99-110. Fernand Kolny (ed.), *Laurent Tailhade (1854-1919); Au Pays de mufle: suivi de nombreux poèmes inedits et précédés de la vie de l'auteur* (Paris: François Bernouard, 1929), pp xxxxiv ff. *Quarante ans*, p 33, on Severine.
55. *Mouvement libertaire*, p 164. Jean Grave, "Kif'Kif bourriquet," *Les Temps Nouveaux*, June 17-23, 1899, p 1. Flax, *Les Hommes du Jour*, No. 27, 1908.
56. *Mouvement libertaire*, pp 168-70. Included are two letters from Zola to Grave. One is dated December 6, 1900; the other has no date, but is presumably of the same period. Josephson, *Zola and His Time*, p 506, included Grave among those at Zola's funeral.
57. *Mouvement libertaire*, pp 170-71. HMA, pp 320-22.
58. Jean Grave, *Organisation, initiative, cohesion* (Paris: Temps Nouveaux, 1902) pp 1ff.
59. See *Quarante ans*, pp 440-41. Also, *Les Temps Nouveaux*, Feb. 4-10 and 11-17, 1905.

7

BETWEEN SYNDICALISM AND INDIVIDUALISM, 1905-1913

THE 1895-1905 PERIOD ENDED WITH GRAVE'S increasing recognition of two intra-anarchist currents which threatened anarcho-communism. The first, anarcho-syndicalism, involved with revolutionary activity among unions, envisioned a socialist world of participatory democracy under the aegis of unions. The second, anarcho-individualism, representing alienated and rebellious individuals who lived in the world of bohemia (some even engaged in criminal activity), rejected all social ties outside of its small-group associations. Grave, during this period, saw that his principal task was to protect doctrinal purity: The "Pope of Mouffetard Street" had to steer a course that would avoid, on the one hand, anarcho-syndicalist organisation and, on the other, anarcho-individualist rejection of even the informal bond of mutual aid for general society.[1]

Anarchism and syndicalism were closely intertwined as early as the 1860s when Proudhonian Mutualism was well ensconced in the French union movement and Bakunin advocated syndicalist activity to spearhead the general revolutionary strike.[2] This tradition was vitiated by the fall of the 1871 Paris Commune, which led to the propaganda-by-deed period. But with its failure, anarchism once again focused more on union activity.[3] Although unions accepted capitalism for a brief period of time after the Paris Commune's defeat, in the Marseilles Labour Congress of 1879, they embraced socialism and tied themselves to its various parties.[4] In 1884 unions became fully legal, and soon afterward saw themselves as not mere adjuncts of socialist parties, but as independent entities.[5] (Socialist parties had a marked tendency to subordinate union activity to the winning of elections.) There were two main unions by the mid-nineties, the Fédération des

THE ANARCHISM OF JEAN GRAVE

Bourses du Travail founded in 1892[6] and the Confédération Générale du Travail (CGT) founded in 1895. In 1902, the two combined to form the new CGT.[7]

By the late nineties, anarchist influence in unions again reached the significant dimensions of the earlier mutualist period through workers' anarchism or anarcho-syndicalism which had a general anarcho-communist background and outlook.[8] Many of its militants were intimately associated with Grave and *Les Temps Nouveaux*, including Pelloutier, Delesalle, Amédée Dunois and Pierre Monatte.

The leading spirit of the Bourses du Travail, one of their founders and outstanding general secretary from 1895 to 1901, and father of anarcho-syndicalism, was Pelloutier (1867-1901). Of significance, once an anarchist, he would always regard himself as an adherent of anarcho-communism, refusing to see any basic differences between it and anarcho-syndicalism. Pelloutier, born into a bourgeois family, was first an editor for a decade of a left-wing republican newspaper, then joined Guesde's Parti Ouvrier Français in 1892, but soon left, when it rejected the general strike and union independence, to become an anarcho-communist. His mature understanding of the social struggle may be readily observed in his various articles from 1895 to 1901 in *Les Temps Nouveaux*.[9]

The theory of revolutionary syndicalism, conceived by Pelloutier in the nineties, was essentially a mixture of various Proudhonian and Bakuninist views with the additional anarcho-communist insistence to abolish wage labour and freely distribute goods. From Proudhon there was the basic idea of forming distinct proletarian institutions to act as educators and points of resistance to the bourgeoisie. Instead of only forming working-class productive associations, Pelloutier also envisaged the union as the primary proletarian institution to lead the class struggle against capitalism through Bakuninist direct action in the form of industrial strikes culminating in the always-imminent general one. (Incidentally, both Grave and Pelloutier approved the use of sabotage during a strike, but Grave never endorsed the syndicalist slogan of "Bad Pay, Bad Work," fearing that performing unsatisfactory work would injure one's basic personality.)[10] Pelloutier rejected parliamentary or representative democracy for a participatory one in a decentralised setting, within the confines of unions, which would emerge as the key cells of the new society. For him a union is "a free association of free producers"[11] with "no laws, no statutes, and no rules which would force an individual to submit to any punishment not previously determined." (This quotation is taken by Pelloutier from Grave's *La Société future*.)[12] He agreed with Grave that authoritarian tendencies might indeed arise within union structures, especially in the federal bureaucracy (unions federated nationally), but insisted that recall provisions for elected officials could effectively control this problem.[13] Although differences existed between Grave and Pelloutier, it is important to remember that there was basic agreement in most areas, like the nature of the state, private property, and religion.[14]

In connection with revolutionary syndicalism, Georges Sorel (1847-1922), the leading ideologue of the movement popularised it among intellectual circles. Although a civil engineer who never had formal ties with the CGT, he was a close friend of Delesalle, visiting his bookstore weekly for many years to engage in lively discussion with a group of friends on the labour movement and maintaining a long-standing correspondence with him.[15] The whole range of Sorel's thought cannot be covered here except for its essential elements. In a key work, *Réflexions sur la violence* (1910), he stressed the importance of the general strike as a "myth" (similar to Christian millenarianism) to inspire the proletariat to do battle with and defeat the bourgeoisie, in the course of which the workers would become the new aristocracy of the future.[16]

Some anarchists like Pouget basically agreed with Pelloutier and saw few, if any, differences between anarcho-communism and revolutionary syndicalism. A typical representative of the more action minded/less intellectual anarchists, Pouget emphasised the class struggle with unions as the main proletarian weapon. This was reflected in his editorship of many newspapers, including the well-known *Le Père Peinard*. When *La Voix du Peuple*, the CGT's official newspaper, was founded in 1902, he became its general editor and was largely responsible for giving it an anarchist coloration.[17] Even Faure's *Le Libertaire*, which at first was unfriendly to syndicalism, became more receptive with a "Mouvement Ouvrier" column written by Dunois and Georges Yvetot, anarchist closely tied to syndicalism.[18]

THE ANARCHISM OF JEAN GRAVE

The rise of revolutionary syndicalism was related not only to anarchist influence, but also to economic difficulties faced by the French working class during the fifteen-year period before World War I when wages could not keep up with inflation. Even in the first decade of the twentieth century, an average working-class family's budget, according to one respected authority, was largely devoted to food (about seventy percent), the remainder going for rent (about ten percent) and other necessities of life. Worker response to economic misery came in the form of increased strike activity, especially in the 1906-1907 and 1910-1912 periods.[19]

After Pelloutier's death, union activity in *Les Temps Nouveaux* was covered by Delesalle, a contributor from 1895. Born into a proletarian family (his father a skilled mechanic), union work led to an assistant secretaryship of the Bourses du Travail in the nineties, in which capacity he served the CGT after the 1902 merger. In addition to writing the "Mouvement Ouvrier" column, he reported on other social problems.[20] Delesalle's association with the newspaper came to an abrupt end in May 1906 when he wrote an anti-Semitic letter,[21] to which Doctor Pierrot objected.[22] He wished to reply, but resigned when Grave overruled him.[23] Despite this quarrel, Delesalle and Grave remained fast friends; the depth of their friendship was measured by Grave's aiding Delesalle during periods of severe psychological depression in which he contemplated suicide.[24] Delesalle is best known for presenting the basic ideology of revolutionary syndicalism at the Amiens Labour Congress of the CGT in 1906. (Anarcho-syndicalism became revolutionary syndicalism at this congress, finally freeing itself from close dependence on anarcho-communist intellectuals.) In 1908, he left the union movement to devote his time to a lifelong dream, a bookstore concerned with the working class.

After Delesalle's departure, the "Mouvement Ouvrier" column was written by Dunois, whom Grave had known for many years. Even as a middle-class youth, he had a deep social concern, coming to the newspaper to help in any manner. An excellent writer, he contributed many articles outside his regular column. His friendship with Grave ended when, after leaving the newspaper, he wrote that it was only good to be read by sentimental old ladies.[25] He was replaced by Georges Dumoulin, an assistant treasurer of the CGT, and by Doctor Pierrot.

BETWEEN SYNDICALISM AND INDIVIDUALISM

Especially did Grave and revolutionary syndicalists have similar views in opposing reformist unionism: (1) that workers under capitalism were doomed to live at subsistence level, which although rising, only did so slowly; (2) that deep socioeconomic cleavage between workers and bourgeoisie would thus always remain and encourage revolution;[26] (3) that strikes for higher wages were illusory, but would be supported to intensify the class struggle; (thus, if workers would successfully strike for a wage increase in an industry, its entrepreneurs would simply accelerate the introduction of labour-saving machinery or raise prices, either causing more unemployment and lowering general wage levels or forcing workers in other areas to strike in order to stay abreast of price increases);[27] (4) that many unionised and skilled workers considered themselves "labour aristocrats," superior to semiskilled and unskilled workers.[28] The last point indicated that as bourgeois society became more complex through technological development, a counterrevolutionary tendency was developing in the proletariat because increasing wage differentials among skilled workers, on the one hand, and semi-skilled and unskilled workers, on the other, lessened their social solidarity. On the whole, Grave's respect for revolutionary syndicalist theory was shown by the fact that he thought revolution was possible through a series of strikes leading to the general one.[29]

Although Grave agreed with revolutionary syndicalists in many key areas, he had serious theoretical differences with them. He was fearful that hierarchical organisation even in revolutionary unions might tend to make them authoritarian and thus prone to compromise with the status quo.[30] And, if there were a successful socialist revolution through unions, he could not accept Pelloutier's view that they should be the basic productive and educational cells of anarchism itself;[31] they might develop bureaucratic and authoritarian tendencies precisely because their members were engaged in production. To obviate this danger, Grave envisaged society from the standpoint of individuals engaged in many areas of work and thus not identified with any particular occupation or union,[32] this not easily achieved, but possible.

These differences never prevented Grave from sympathising with and, indeed, often supporting revolutionary syndicalism. One such instance occurred in the spring of 1906 when the CGT was preparing to launch a general strike on May Day for an eight-hour day. Proletarian militancy was reinforced by a tragic mine disaster in the Nord Department, triggering a series of strikes reaching Paris.[33] After Prime Minister Clémenceau had failed to agree with the striking miners, he used force against them.[34] *Les Temps Nouveaux*, of course, depicted the confrontation in the most revolutionary manner possible. Delesalle, sent to the strike-torn area, wrote many timely articles on the atrocious working conditions of the miners and their uncompromising mood.[35] Grave himself penned articles against parliamentary democracy which intimated that change could come only through revolution.[36] By late April, tension throughout France, but especially in the Paris area, was extremely high.[37]

Clémenceau, taking no chances, arrested prominent syndicalists and anarchists and closed down *Les Temps Nouveaux* and other newspapers on May Day.[38] Grave was involved in these events through correspondence with Monatte, a CGT organiser who had gone to the strike-torn Nord. When the police arrested Monatte in late April, they found a letter from Grave among his belongings. This and other bits of information led to unproductive police raids on the newspaper and lodgings of Grave and Delesalle, among others, that tried to connect them to strike activity.[39] In Grave's case the police were so infuriated at their failure to find incriminating evidence that they confiscated some pamphlets which Grave later recovered after a formal protest.[40] Striking back courageously at these harassments, Grave and Delesalle wrote articles in the newspaper which contrasted the Clémenceau of the Dreyfus Affair with the strikebreaker.[41] May Day itself was very tense, but social explosion did not occur.[42]

The importance of revolutionary syndicalism within anarchism was underscored in the Amsterdam International Anarchist Congress of August 1907 (the first such congress since 1881).[43] Grave, like most French anarchists, opposed it as a form of organisation and did not attend.[44] This congress witnessed one of the great debates of anarchism between Monatte and Malatesta. (Monatte, a CGT leader; Malatesta, the greatest Italian revolutionary after Garibaldi, already known for his revolutionary daring in Italy during the seventies, was to be a spark of "Red Week" in June 1914,

BETWEEN SYNDICALISM AND INDIVIDUALISM

when the Italian left almost toppled the government, and was to have a significant role in the 1920 Italian general strike.) For Monatte, revolutionary syndicalism was workers' anarchism: The unions were the proper institutions to lead the class struggle and to construct the future anarchist society. For Malatesta, however, these conceptions inevitably narrowed the base of anarchism to the industrial proletariat alone, and in agreement with Grave, he regarded sydicalism as only one of many possible means for change.[45] The debate itself did not resolve anything, but significantly, the congress voted for an International Correspondence Bureau to facilitate communication between various anarchist groups. This organ, however, was short-lived, expiring in 1911.[46]

Tragically for French anarchism, the loss of a mass working-class base inevitably led to its decline as a viable revolutionary movement, this is the opinion of no less than two well-known anarchists: Daniel Guérin, a French activist, and Sir Herbert Read, a distinguished English literary critic and essayist.[47]

The syndicalists, for an anarcho-communist like Grave, emphasised the dangers of organisation, but in the other direction lay the risks of an anti-social individualism, which eschewed large-scale solidarity and mutual aid represented by the individualists, a small group quite prominent in anarchist circles in the decade-and-a-half before World War I. Indeed, Grave's memoirs devoted much attention to them.[48]

But first, the following events: In June 1909, after a courtship of many years through correspondence, Grave married Miss Thomas in a civil ceremony at Folkestone, England. The new Mrs. Grave was obviously not a run-of-the-mill bourgeois because she contributed to anarchism by writing short stories for *Les Temps Nouveaux* and by indefatigably aiding her husband in his work. She was a bourgeois, however, on lodgings, successfully persuading Grave to leave his scanty ones in Paris for a spacious house in the Paris suburb of Robinson.[49] In his new surroundings Grave may have been influenced to see the world somewhat differently. Madame Paul Delesalle told me that as Grave became increasingly attuned to a bourgeois existence, he was more apt to emphasise doctrinal purity than direct action.

THE ANARCHISM OF JEAN GRAVE

The leading figure of the individualists was Albert Libertad whose actual name and background are wrapped in mystery. Of unknown parentage, brought up in an orphanage, he, nevertheless, claimed that he was the son of a high government official. Libertad, who would not have been out of place in the American counterculture of the 1960s and 70s, was an emaciated cripple who wore sandals and had long hair; he supposedly resembled Christ. An excellent orator, unafraid of physical danger, often involved in brawls, he drew to himself a group of followers, soiled, unkempt, and in a perpetual state of rebellion.[50]

Two of Libertad's better known followers were Victor Kilbatchiche and Ernest Armand. The first, Le Rétif from 1909 to 1919, later became well known as Victor Serge, a follower of Leon Trotsky, serving in the Soviet government before fleeing with him from the Soviet Union.[51] The second had earlier been a Christian anarchist and and succeeded Libertad after his death as editor of *L'Anarchie*, the journal of the individualists.[52]

The individualists were greatly influenced by the following thinkers: (1) Johann Kaspar Schmidt, a German teacher better known by his pen name of Max Stirner, who praised the free individual realizing herself/himself through conflict with others (the individual was part of a union of egoists against the general society), even committing crime, including murder. The individual/small group, however, would not have any power over others. Obviously, these contradictory views have a powerful antisocial element.[53] (2) Friedrich Nietzsche, who glorified the egoistic individual in constant revolt—who despised the many, forged his/her own morality and lived dangerously. Against socialism, he wished for a superman group, an intellectual and military elite to rule the masses.[54] (3) Félix Le Dantec, a teacher of the biological sciences at the University of Paris and author of numerous scientific-philosophical works, who extolled the virtues of a stridently anti-social individual. In a typical work, *La Lutte universelle*, living organisms are in constant struggle to survive.[55]

Grave recognised that his ideas in certain critical areas were similar to those of the individualists: both were for individual sovereignty as against the primacy of the group; both had a deep fear of and antipathy to any social organisation based on hierarchy; and both regarded the state as the very negation of freedom. Also, despite the fact that the individualists were against anarcho-communist collective property, many approved the individual-ownership part of Proudhonian Mutualism, allowing for some ideological affinity with Grave.[56]

Despite some doctrinal similarities, Grave not only disliked many individualists, but also had deep reservations with their general views. Differences especially revolved around the axis of individualism. For Grave, although the individual and the community were distinct entities, they were not antagonistic but complementary. For the individualists, however, the individual (which may include the small in-group) and society were forever in deadly conflict.[57]

These differences reflected antithetical mind sets on revolution and the class struggle. Contrary to Grave's general optimism for the revolutionary potential of the people, individualists, viewing the future as bleakly as the present, regarded them as apathetic to change. In addition, they rejected Gravian class struggle and sympathy for proletarian unions for individual or small in-group action. Thus, for example, whether one was a worker or a bourgeois had no consequence for revolution.[58] For instance, they regarded unions as authoritarian and capitalist organisations that promoted a narrow craft mentality tied to parochial economic interests, in which majority rule impinged on individual autonomy.[59] Revolution, therefore, would have to be undertaken by the individual and like-minded comrades. Kilbatchiche has Libertad saying in this respect:

> Do not wait for revolution. Those who promise revolution are practical jokers. Make your own revolution. Be free and live in camaraderie.[60]

These views reflected a general antisocial tendency which permitted individualists to engage in what Grave believed was gross sexual immorality and to participate in or be sympathetic to criminal activity. Grave could neither tolerate such sexual license as Libertad's having concurrent relations with two sisters,[61] nor condone theft.[62] For him, means and ends were intertwined; antisocial means could not bring about a good end, a non-exploitative and non-authoritarian society.[63] Ultimately for Grave, individualist practices and views could only reinforce bourgeois society, which underneath its rhetoric of freedom viewed the world in stark Darwinian terms.

To say the least, the individualists were not enamoured of Grave. Le Rétif voiced a typical view of him: "We are becoming disgusted by the type of academic anarchism of which Jean Grave at *Les Temps Nouveaux* is the pontiff."[64] Grave, in turn, specifically accused Armand and Le Rétif of being used by the police to discredit anarchism through the sensationalism of the general press equating anarchism with crime.[65] Not relishing Grave's accusation, the two threatened Grave who kept a revolver nearby.[66] Although Grave was unjust in calling the two police spies, *L'Anarchie* was indeed a focal point for criminals and their apologists.[67]

The 1900-1914 period ended with anarchism still wrestling with the problem of how much organisation it would tolerate. This was seen in the last important French anarchist congress held in Paris from August 15 to 17, 1913. Grave, actively involved in the preparations, wrote a paper and attended. *Ce que nous voulons* repeated his usual fears of organisation, but along with the overwhelming majority, he agreed to form a Federation of French Anarchists (a significant departure from his past position), with the reservation that official party organs not be formed.[68]

There were strong underlying pressures for federation, as many anarchists felt that more coordination—and organisation—was needed to wage a more effective campaign against a threatening world war, especially through the medium of a general strike. Anarchist federation would undoubtedly have strengthened ties with revolutionary syndicalists, thus propelling anarchism toward the mainstream of socialism. The federation did not materialise because World War I intervened.

Notes
1. See *Mouvement libertaire*, pp 79-80 and p 166.
2. Maximoff, *The Political Philosophy of Bakunin*, pp 382ff. Pierre Kropotkine, "Le 1er mai 1891," *La Révolte*, October 18-24, 1891, pp1-2, demanded mass union action. *HMA*, p 252, indicated that such well-known anarchists as Michel and Malatesta urged anarchists to join unions.
3. *HMA*, p 249.
4. Blum, *Les Congrès ouvriers*, as cited in Blum I, pp 404ff.

BETWEEN SYNDICALISM AND INDIVIDUALISM

5. On the 1884 law, see Sylvain Humbert, *Le Mouvement syndical*, Vol. IX of *Histoires des partis socialistes en France*, ed. A. Zévaès (Paris: Marcel Rivière, 1912), pp 3-12.

6. Blum, *Les Congrès ouvriers*, as cited in Blum I, pp 454-55. The various Labor Exchanges (the first was founded 1887 in Paris) federated at the 1892 Saint-Etienne Labor Congress.

7. Louis Levine, *Syndicalism in France*, (New York: Columbia University Press, 1914), pp 162ff.

8. On revolutionary syndicalism, see also Edouard Dolléans, *Histoire du mouvement ouvrier, 1871-1920*, II (Paris: Armand Colin, 1957), pp 13-56, 89-116, 117-48, and 151-205; Peter N. Stearns, *Revolutionary Syndicalism and French Labor; A Cause without Rebels* (New Brunswick, N. J.: Rutgers University Press, 1971); F. F. Ridley, *Revolutionary Syndicalism in France; The Direct Action of Its Time* (Cambridge: At the University Press, 1970). On anarchism and syndicalism in France, see HMA, pp 249-322. Paul Delesalle, *L'Action syndicale et les anarchistes* (Paris: Les Temps Nouveaux, 1901), pp 4-16; and Fernand Pelloutier, *Histoire des Bourses, origine, institutions, avenir*, preface by Georges Sorel (Paris: Schleicher Frères, 1902) pp 171ff.

9. On Pelloutier's life and ideas, see Jacques Juillard, *Fernand Pelloutier et les origines du syndicalisme d'action directe* (Paris: Seuil, 1971).

10. Jean Grave, "L'Anarchisme et la cooperation," *Les Temps Nouveaux*, Feb. 9-15, 1901, p 2. *Quarante ans*, pp 116-17.

11. Fernand Pelloutier, "L'Anarchisme et les syndicats ouvriers," *Les Temps Nouveaux*, Nov. 2, 1895, pp 2-4.

12. *Ibid.*

13. *Ibid.*

14. See Juillard, *Pelloutier*; the second section contains much of Pelloutier's writings.

15. Interview with Madame Paul Delesalle by me in Paris, Aug. 9, 1964. Georges Sorel, *Lettres à Paul Delesalle, 1914-1921*, introduction by Robert Louzon (Paris: Bernard Grasset, 1947).

16. On Sorel, see James H. Meisel, *The Genesis of Georges Sorel* (Ann Arbor, Mich.: Wahr Publishing Co., 1951); George Humphrey, *Georges Sorel; Prophet Without Honor, A Study in Anti-Intellectualism* (Cambridge, Mass.: Harvard University Press, 1951). See his *Reflections on Violence* (New York: Collier Books, 1961).

17. On Pouget, see Christien Demay de Goustine, *Pouget; Les Matins Noirs du syndicalisme* (Paris: Editions de la Tête de feuilles, 1972).

18. On Faure, see Jeanne Humbert, *Sébastien Faure: l'homme, l'apôtre, une époque* (Paris: Editions du Libertaire, 1949).

19. On an average worker's family budget, see Stearnes, *Revolutionary Syndicalism and French Labor*, p 114. On inflation and strike activity, see *ibid.*, p 120. On the number of strikes and strikers per year from 1899 to 1913, see *ibid.*, p 121. On living standards, see *ibid.*, pp 111-12ff.

20. On Delesalle's life, see Jean Maitron, *Le Syndicalisme révolutionnaire*; *Paul Delesalle* (Paris: Les Editions Ouvrières, 1952). See, for example, Paul Delesalle, "Mouvement Ouvrier," *Les Temps Nouveaux*, May 5, 1906, pp 6-7.
21. Paul Delesalle, *ibid.*, May 5, 1906, p 2.
22. Marc Pierrot, *ibid.*, May 12, 1906, p 3.
23. *Mouvement libertaire*, p 159.
24. Interview with Madame Paul Delesalle, August 9, 1964.
25. On Dunois, see *Mouvement libertaire*, pp 159-60. Interview with Madame Paul Delesalle, who knew Dunois well, August 9, 1964. A good article by Amedée Dunois: "L'Action directe contre la guerre," *Les Temps Nouveaux*, July 22, 1905, pp 1-2. On Dumoulin, see Dolléans, II, p 198.
26. Grave and the revolutionary syndicalists were on solid ground in their pessimism concerning higher wages under capitalism in France. Charles P. Kindleberger, *Economic Growth in France and Britain, 1851-1914* (Cambridge, Mass: Harvard University Press, 1964), pp 232ff informs us that wages in France during the 1880-1914 period increased only slightly.
27. On the various problems discussed in the paragraph: minimum subsistence for workers, etc., see Karl Marx, *Capital: A Critique of Political Economy* (New York: The Modern Library, n.d.), pp 466ff.; Jean Grave, *L'Anarchie; son but, ses moyens*, pp 263-264; Jean Grave, *Ce que nous voulons* (Paris: Les Temps Nouveaux, n.d.), pp 1-6. Grave mentioned that shorter hours of work all too often lead to work intensification. This brochure was to be read by him before the 1913 French Anarchist Congress. Jean Grave, *Le Machinisme* (Paris: Les Temps Nouveaux, 1898), p 14. (From *La Société future*.)
28. Sorel, *Reflections on Violence*, pp 123-24. Grave, *L'Anarchie; son but, ses moyens*, pp 239ff.
29. Grave, *L'Anarchie; son but, ses moyens*, pp 262ff.
30. Jean Grave, *Réformes, révolution* (Paris, P. V. Stock, 1910), pp 222-223; and Grave, *La Société mourante et l'anarchie*, p 82.
31. Fernand Pelloutier, "L'Anarchisme et les syndicats ouvriers," *Les Temps Nouveaux*, November 2-8, 1895, pp 2-4. Pelloutier, *Histoire des Bourses du Travail*, pp 163-64. Cole, II, p 335-36, stated that the basic differences between the anarcho-communists and the anarcho-syndicalists stemmed over the role of unions in future society.
32. Jean Grave, *Terre Libre (Les Pionniers)*, illustrations by Mabel Holland Thomas (Paris: Les Temps Nouveaux, 1908) p 19; Grave, *Réformes, révolution*, p 225; and Jean Grave, *La Conquête des pouvoirs publics* (Paris: Les Temps Nouveaux, 1911) p 3.
33. For background, see Levine, *Syndicalism in France*, pp 175-77. On the mine disaster in the Nord Department, see Paul Delesalle, "Chez les mineurs," *Les Temps Nouveaux*, April 7, 1906, pp 2-3.
34. Levine, *Syndicalism in France*, pp 175ff.

35. Paul Delesalle, "Chez les mineurs," *Les Temps Nouveaux*, April 14, p 3 and April 28, p 4, 1906.
36. Jean Grave, "Le Mensonge électoral," *ibid.*, April 14, pp 1-2 and April 28, p 4, 1906.
37. Levine, *Syndicalism in France*, pp 174ff.
38. Dolléans, II pp 134-35, for general information.
39. *Mouvement libertaire*, pp 178-80. Jackson, *Clemenceau*, p 142, took a dim view of Clemenceau's suspension of civil liberties. Pierre Monatte, "Le Complot," *Les Temps Nouveaux*, June 16, 1906, pp 2-3, ridiculed the government's charge that the unions were working with reactionary Bonapartist elements.
40. *Mouvement libertaire*, pp 178-80.
41. Jean Grave, "La Gangrène du pouvoir," *Les Temps Nouveaux*, May 5, 1906, pp 1-2; and Paul Delesalle, "Le Complot," *ibid.*, p 3.
42. On the great social tension in Paris on May Day, see John L. Charpentier, "Glanes; le premier mai," *ibid.*, May 12, 1906, pp 1-2.
43. On this congress, see Le Bureau International, *Résolutions approuvées par le congrès anarchiste tenu à Amsterdam, Août 24-31, 1907* (London: Workers' Friend Printing, n.d.), pp 4-12; and *HMA*, pp 308-09.
44. *Les Temps Nouveaux* gave scant coverage to the congress. The only important article on it was by Errico Malatesta, "le Congrès d'Amsterdam," September 21, 1907, pp 1-2, and September 28, 1907, p 2.
45. The arguments and various tensions within the congress are discussed by *HMA*, pp 303-09.
46. *Ibid.*, pp 416ff.
47. Daniel Guérin, *L'Anarchisme; de la doctrine à l'action* (Paris: Gallimard, 1965), pp 85ff., saw anarchism's decline in France when it refused to enter syndicalism. For Herbert Read, a distinguished British literary critic and outstanding anarchist thinker, the only viable anarchism to meet "modern conditions" is anarcho-syndicalism—Herbert Read, "The Necessity of Anarchism," in *Anarchy and Order; Essays in Politics*, intro. Howard Zinn (Boston: Beacon Press, 1971), p 99.
48. On the individualists (and the criminals), see *Quarante ans*, pp 384-437; *HMA*, pp 394ff. and pp 484-92. Also, see Jean Maitron, *le Mouvement anarchiste en France* (2 vols.; Paris: Maspero, 1975) Vol. I: *des origines à 1914*, pp 409-39; Vol. II: *de 1914 à nos jours*, pp 174-83. To be cited as *Mouvement anarchiste*.
49. On the second Madame Grave, I am indebted to an interview with Madame Paul Delesalle in Paris, August 9, 1964. *Quarante ans*, p 571.
50. On Libertad, see *HMA*, pp 394-96; *Quarante ans*, pp 387ff.
51. Jean Maitron, "De Kilbatchiche à Victor Serge; Le Rétif (1909-1919)," *Le Mouvement Social*, XXXXVII (April-June, 1964), 45-78.
52. On Armand, see *Quarante ans*, p 397, pp 408-10. On *L'Anarchie*, see *Mouvement anarchiste*, I, 472-73.

53. On Stirner's life and ideas, see Victor Basch, *L'Individualisme anarchiste: Max Stirner* (Paris: Félix Alcan, 1928); pp 228-50, especially, for an excellent summary of individualist anarchism. Compare, for example, Max Stirner [Johann Kaspar Schmidt], *The Ego and His Own*, trans. from German by Steven T. Byington (New York: Boni and Liveright, n.d.), pp 378-81 with Grave's views.

54. On Nietzche, see Walter Kauffman, *The Portable Nietzche* (New York: Viking Press, 1965).

55. Félix Le Dantec, *La Lutte universelle* (Paris: Ernest Flammarion, 1917); pp 1-25 for a general view of his thought which is clearly of the conservative Social Darwininan variety so prevalent in the intellectual circles of the period.

56. On general individualist ideas, see *Mouvement anarchiste*, II, 174-83.

57. Stirner, *The Ego and His Own*, p 209, for example.

58. A. Lorulot, "Syndicalism et organisation," *L'Anarchie*, Oct. 12, 1905.

59. A. Libertad, "Le Premier Mai," *L'Anarchie*, May 4, 1905. A. Lorulot, "La Faillite du syndicalisme," *L'Anarchie*, July 20, 1905.

60. Victor Serge, *Memoires d'un révolutionnaire de 1901 à 1941* (Paris: Editions du Seuil, 1951), p 25. For eternal rule by a minority no matter what the social system, see Max Nomad, *Apostles of Revolution* (New York: Collier Books, 1961), pp 9-19. Contempt for the masses and hatred for their rulers was expressed by Zo d'Axa, an individualist anarchist and literary figure whose surname was Galland. He was editor of *L'En Dehors*, an anarchist literary magazine. On his life and ideas, see Victor Meric, *A travers la jungle politique et littéraire; coulisses et trétaux* (Paris: Librairie Valois, 1921), II, 5-7. Also, see *Quarante ans*, p 247 and pp 529-30.

61. *Mouvement libertaire*, p 184; *HMA*, p 397.

62. *Mouvement libertaire*, pp 186-87. On a defense of criminal activity, see E. Armand, "Les Illégaux," *L'Anarchie*, Nov. 22, 1906.

63. *Mouvement libertaire*, pp 186-87, for example.

64. Serge, *Mémoires d'un révolutionnaire*, p 25.

65. *Mouvement libertaire*, pp 198-200.

66. *Quarante ans*, p 410.

67. The best example of criminal activity in the *L'Anarchie* crowd is the Bonnot gang, which flourished in the 1908-1912 period: see Victor Meric, *Les Bandits tragiques* (Paris: S. Kra, 1926). No proof has ever been found to substantiate Grave's charge that leading individualists were police spies.

68. *Les Temps Nouveaux*, August 9, 23, and 30, 1913, has much information on the 1913 congress. Jean Grave, "Ce que nous voulons," *ibid.*, September 13, 1913, pp 1-3. This article was later published as a *Temps Nouveaux* pamphlet. Grave's pamphlet was passed up for that of Sébastien Faure's "Manifesto," Nos. 257-58 in *Le Mouvement Socialiste* (Nov.-Dec., 1913), pp 402-04. For Grave's favorable views concerning federation, see *Les Temps Nouveaux*, August 23, 1913, pp 4-5.

8

IN THE WORLD OF ART

GRAVE WAS INTIMATELY INVOLVED WITH the world of art. Not only did he create art from his own wellspring of experience as seen, for example, in the largely autobiographical *La Grande famille*, but he also appreciated its importance for the realisation of socialism. Indeed, he was an outstanding pioneer of early socialism in combining art with the social struggle.[1] Undoubtedly, Grave's membership in 1889 in the Club de l'Art Social in Paris, where various anarchist and other socialist militants met with their sympathetic counterparts in the art world, stimulated his interest in art. Representative of the former in the club was Michel, while Camille Pissarro, Luce and Descaves were typical of the latter.[2]

These artists just indicated were not of an unusual bent of mind since a sizeable segment of the prestigious French artistic community had deep sympathy, if not open alliance with anarchism in the 1890s.[3] The artist was alienated by and in revolt against a society whose individualism was largely directed to making money and obeying a rigid social conformity.[4]

Important literary journals reflected the close ties between art and anarchism. *Les Entretiens Politiques et Littéraires*, a Symbolist monthly of the nineties, was permeated by anarchism. Its staff, headed by Lazare and Vielé-Griffin (both sympathetic to anarchism), invited as contributors such anarchists and sympathisers as Elie and Elisée Reclus and Paul Adam. *La Revue Blanche*, the leading literary monthly of the period, enlisted Lucien Pissarro, Félix Fénéon, Kropotkin, Lazare and Stuart Merrill.[5] One of its reviewers, Léon Blum, a distinguished literary critic who later became the first socialist premier of France in 1936-1937, summed up the importance of anarchism at the time by stating that everyone in his artistic and intellectual circles was either an anarchist or interested in anarchism.[6]

The strong ties between anarchism and the artistic community did not, however, preclude differences between anarchist theoreticians and artists who relegated good art only to those who had the requisite education to understand it - "art for art's sake." For Grave, this attitude could easily lead artists to identify their interests with those of the bourgeoisie at the expense of the proletariat, for the former had more education than the latter; indeed, vital art avoided the shoals of an artificially contrived and recondite snobbery for a universal understanding,[7] his example being Zola's proletarian novel, *Germinal*.[8] From a historical perspective, Grave's art criticism reflected the Enlightenment's clarity and balance, the French Revolution's egalitarian élan, and Romanticism's individuality in the commonplace.

The ideas of Kropotkin will throw more light on the anarchist position on art. For him, significant art was more likely to be created in a social milieu of artist and society in intimate and constant interaction, as in the brilliant Renaissance period in Italy, in a city-state milieu which, despite capitalist development, provided the requisite human solidarity to nourish it. But in the last few centuries, with the continued advance of capitalism and rise of the nation state, social solidarity atrophied, leading art to reflect this malaise.[9] But artists, the quintessence of creativity and conscience of humanity, should transcend limitations imposed by capitalist society and opt for an art to change it. Art, yes, for revolution.[10]

The foundation of anarchism's view of art had been principally constructed by Proudhon whose preoccupation with it was of long duration. In *Du Principe de l'art et de sa destination sociale*, he suggested that art should present the interaction between individual and environment in a clear and precise way to effect a more complete understanding of the various values of human existence.[11] Grave and Kropotkin, following in Proudhon's footsteps, concurred and saw that most of human activity under anarchism would be devoted to art for the workday would be brief. Indeed, all would engage in art since it was an integral part of life. Anarchism itself represented art.[12] Grave summed up the nexus between art and anarchism by

IN THE WORLD OF ART

noting that art could best flourish in a society free from authority, where the unencumbered artistic imagination was unrestrained in its search for truth and beauty. "Art, that supreme manifestation of individualism."[13]

Grave's view of art was also similar in many respects to that of the German composer Wagner who, as already stated, participated with Bakunin in the 1849 revolution in Dresden. In fact, Grave was so captivated by Wagner's *Die Kunst und die Revolution* (1849) that it was published by *Les Temps Nouveaux* in 1898 as *L'Art et la révolution*. Wagner combined art with social revolution as the critical ingredients for a genuine fraternity, which in turn would reinvigorate art, liberating it from the shackles of economic domination and a parochial nationalism.[14]

With the overriding importance of art in Grave's outlook, it was not surprising that he actively engaged in its creation, in literature. We shall examine the novels not already covered, his only play, a children's tale, and a short story, his major literary contributions. Grave's approach to literature, greatly influenced by his anarchist perspective, was in the grand tradition of Balzac, Stendhal and Tolstoy who wrote in the stream of realism, of interaction between individual and social totality to capture the complexity of human existence.[15]

In addition to *La Grande famille*, Grave wrote two other novels, *Malfaiteurs!* And *Terre Libre*. In *Malfaiteurs!* the protagonist, Pierre Armel was a Parisian worker, an idealist and anarchist in his late twenties. An orphan, he had been raised by friends of his parents, the Mouniers, who regarded him as a son and prospective husband to the younger of their two daughters, Solange. Complications began when Pierre embraced anarchism because Mounier was concerned that as an anarchist, Pierre would not be a good provider as he would probably be imprisoned. In contrast to Pierre was his best friend Albert Jouffray courting Louise, the older daughters. He too was a worker and revolutionary (a Marxist-Guesdist), but Mounier liked him since he was clever and had a good possibility of being elected to high public office, with a salary more than sufficient for marriage.

It developed that the daughters—Solange despite her parents' bitter opposition—married the two friends. Solange and Pierre had a happy marriage; although he was imprisoned for writing in an anarchist newspaper, their love and idealism sustained them. Albert and Louise, however, were unhappy despite material success: Albert had the usual mistress and was preoccupied with knowing the right people. In the meantime, Pierre and his father-in-law became reconciled since it became apparent that he might have a promising literary career. At the end of the tale, the parents were domestics in the spacious country house of Albert who, elected to the Chamber of Deputies, achieved fame by delivering fiery revolutionary speeches in defence of the workers. Albert and Pierre themselves had broken their friendship when Albert became an opportunist, marrying in church and becoming a deputy. This novel is in the tradition of the "angry young man" in revolt against a corrupt and class-ridden society; Stendhal's *The Red and the Black* with its well-known hero, Julien Sorel, is undoubtedly its prototype.

Although not a great novel, *Malfaiteurs!* deftly delineated a key drama of the human condition, the struggle to retain a revolutionary integrity in a bourgeois society dominated by social climbing and moral compromise. It's main weakness was in a deficient character development; for instance, the various economic, social, and other pressures which made Albert into an opportunist were not sufficiently explored, thus stripping him of his essential humanity.[16]

Terre Libre (1908) is Grave's utopian novel, set in the late nineteenth century. After crushing a general strike, the French government deported three hundred insurgents along with their wives and children to a penal colony in New Caledonia. The ship taking them to exile was lost in a storm, struck a reef, and half-sank. Fortunately, supplies from the ship were plentiful and the nearby island could support humans. Once the survivors settled down, the prisoners overthrew the old order represented by the guards to form an anarchist society. Always tolerant, the anarchists allowed the guards their separate existence, but wisely, in event of future conflict, brought the ship's cannons to their encampment. The quiet hero in the revolutionary camp was Berthaut whose life was dedicated to the destruction of authority. When an attempt was made to set up a system of representative government, he intervened to prevent this syndicalist-inspired aberration to introduce hierarchy and ultimately destroy liberty. With respect to decision-making, this anarchist society featured majority vote under the aegis of participatory democracy.[17]

The new society would endure, but not without the usual crises. The guards not unexpectedly launched a surprise attack, fortuitously discovered in time by an indolent member (although most worked, no one was forced to), which was repulsed. The final conflict came when a French warship arrived to impose the old order. It was sunk by the artillery fire of the anarchists after an extended engagement; all aboard were lost, including the guards on the island who had boarded the ship, anarchists now assured that their island utopia was safe.

This was an ideal place permeated by the guiding principle of mutual aid. In its stimulating and free environment, curiosity and ingenuity were so enhanced that within a brief period of time, for example, electric automobiles were produced. Grave's interest in technology was evident as he took great relish in describing the work involved in the various processes of production.[18]

The sole play of Grave, *Responsabilités!*, was modeled on Greek tragedy, in which two values, seemingly of equal merit, vie for supremacy within one's conscience. Robert Renaud, a married worker with two children, had lost many jobs and even imprisoned for his anarchist ideas. In desperation, his wife murdered the children and committed suicide. A friend, Durier, who had influenced Renaud to become an anarchist, asked himself if he were not responsible for the three deaths: if Renaud had not met him, the tragedy might not have occurred. A friend (fate) consoled Durier, pointing out the many victims of the present society. The moral is that despite the fact that innocent people lose their lives, the fight for anarchism is just and must continue.[19]

Les Aventures de Nono was Grave's contribution to the realm of make-believe, showing his love for children. Nono, the principal character, was a nine-year old boy from the Parisian proletariat. One night, in a dream, he went on a trip to the fairyland of Autonomy, a haven where all worked and played together in harmony, to encounter such good and wise people as Labour and Liberty. But evil lurked nearby in the guise of

Monnaius (money), a bloated and ugly ogre (he claimed that his gold ring gave him all that he wished) who enticed Nono to go to his land of Monnaia by promising everything he ever wanted. But Nono noticed that having what one desired was confined only to the wealthy few who lived at the expense of the many, the poor. In Monnaia's rigid class structure, Nono observed that the master class had faces of predatory or scavenger birds and animals, like the vulture and tiger (Monnaius himself looked like a vampire), while the poor had faces resembling those of sheep. Transformation occurred at an early age when Monnaius chose each person's occupation. Fortunately, Nono was rescued from this frightful place by two of his friends from Autonomy, Hans and Mah (a girl), and awakened in his mother's arms, safe from Monnaius chasing him.[20]

Nono involved Grave in a controversy with a contemporary writer, Camille de Sainte-Croix, who accused him of plagiarism: he had earlier written a children's work which he claimed Grave copied. This baseless charge was not pursued legally. In a *Les Temps Nouveaux* article, Grave convincingly claimed that he had begun the book during his Mazas incarceration in 1894, then worked on it intermittently, finishing in the Midi while convalescing from a serious attack of pneumonia from February to April 1901.[21]

There was even a Kafkaesque piece in Grave's work, a short story—"Comment on s'enrichit"—in which two men became partners with a third to market a toy. The mistake made by the two, one of whom was the inventor, was to become entangled with the third, an established capitalist who, true to form, insatiable for money, contrived to wrest control of the enterprise from them. Slick lawyers and the majesty of the law intervened on behalf of the unscrupulous capitalist, who after a lengthy court trial captured control of the company and had the two innocents thrown into jail.[22]

Grave's commitment to the world of art and social theory persisted in the *Supplément Littéraire* of *Les Temps Nouveaux*, in which he continued the legacy of *La Révolte* by providing his readers with timely literature and incisive social commentary from well-known thinkers, novelists, dramatists and poets. (The importance of the two supplements was duly noted by

IN THE WORLD OF ART

Kropotkin in a brilliant article titled "anarchism" for the eleventh edition of the *Encyclopaedia Brittanica* in 1910, which regarded them as rich repositories of anarchism gleaned "from the works of hundreds of modern authors expressing anarchist ideas," including Emerson, Thoreau, Tolstoy, Wagner, Mill, Ibsen and Whitman.)[23] Concerning literature, such first-rate novelists as Tolstoy,[24] Zola,[25] and Mirbeau,[26] continued to be featured, while for social theory and comment, such stalwarts of anarchism as Kropotkin,[27] Bakunin,[28] and Proudhon[29] retained their usual importance.

Another group of writers sympathetic to anarchism, not well known today but widely read during the period, furnished much of the material in the literature category. They included Descaves, Ajalbert, Richepin and Emile Verhaeren. Descaves, perhaps the most-remembered of the group, was a prolific writer of proletarian life.[30] A contributing editor of the newspaper and a good friend of Grave, he said that Grave exerted a great influence on his life.[31] Ajalbert, Grave's lawyer, wrote in a realistic vein about the life of the people.[32] Richepin, a poet of considerable talent, was always cooperative in contributing the social-problem segment of his work.[33] Verhaeren, who greatly impressed Grave, was an outstanding Belgian poet particularly sensitive to social misery.[34]

Not only did *Les Temps Nouveaux* excel as a literary vehicle, but it also displayed the visual arts through lithographs donated by such leading contemporary painters as Alexandre Steinlen, Camille Pissarro, Signac and Luce - all good friends of Grave.[35] The lithographs portrayed the intense social suffering of the workers yet saw them as the harbingers of revolution to create a new society. Steinlen, a world-renowned lithographer, was especially interested in disseminating popular art depicting the various dimensions of working-class life.[36] Signac, a well-known neo-impressionist, was most sympathetic to anarchism. His friendship with Grave may be measured by the fact that he considered him as most responsible for developing his sensitivity to the social problem.[37] Luce, another talented neo-impressionist, was very close to Grave and instrumental in introducing him to many artists.[38] Camille Pissarro, yet another outstanding neo-impressionist, was also a good friend. This gentle and idealistic French Jew also contributed more than two thousand francs to the weekly.[39] Other friends and neo-impressionists who contributed lithographs included Charles Angrand,[40] Henri-Edmond Cross,[41] Theo van Rysselberghe,[42] Félix Valloton,[43] Lucien Pissarro (Camille's son),[44] and Hermann-Paul.[45]

Grave's correspondence with his artist friends well revealed the ordinary and significant concerns of life. Only letters from the more prominent will be examined, from Signac, Camille Pissarro, Steinlen and Luce. The correspondence with Signac, twenty letters, 1893-1929, indicated a warm and long-lasting friendship which covered many areas: various illnesses, sorrow concerning the deaths of their beloved friends, Camille Pissarro and Cross, regret that Grave did not visit him at Saint-Tropez or that he was unable to see the Graves at Robinson before leaving Paris, and condolences on the death of Grave's wife. Pissarro's correspondence, twenty letters, 1892-1902, involved collaboration on drawings for a book, hoping for a visit from Grave, contributing money to Les Temps Nouveaux, and lithographs for the newspaper. Steinlen's correspondence, twenty letters, 1903-1912, encompassed personal concerns (grief over the death of his wife), art exhibitions, lithographs for Les Temps Nouveaux, and thanking Grave for an autographed copy of Réformes révolution. Luce's correspondence, nine letters, 1908-1916, included news about such mutual friends as Signac, Cross, and Delasalle, and lithographs.[46]

Notes

1. Eugenia W. Herbert, *The Artist and Social Reform: France and Belgium, 1885-1898* (New Haven: Yale University Press), pp 14ff, asserted that Grave was the leading figure in socialism to use art to propagate its ideals in the pre-World-War I period.

2. *Ibid.*, pp 23ff.

3. Grave, *La Société mourante et l'anarchie*, p 6, saw anarchism's penetration of painting and literature by the very truth and force of its ideas.

4. The great Radical Romanticist was Shelley, who fused anarchism with Romanticism. See, for example, Howard Mumford Jones, *Revolution and Romanticism* (Cambridge, Mass.: Belknap Press of Harvard University Press, 1974.); and Gerald McNiece, *Shelley and the Revolutionary Idea* (Cambridge, Mass.: Harvard University Press, 1969).

5. Herbert, *The Artist and Social Reform*, pp 96ff and Blum, I, xxi and following pages. Also A. B. Jackson, *La Revue Blanche, 1889-1903* (Paris: Minard, 1960).

6. Blum, I, xii and following pages.

7. Grave, *La Société future*, pp 35-58. Also, see Charles Albert, *L'Art et la société* (Paris: Bibliothèque du Groupe L'Art Sociale, n.d.), pp 13-14, who saw that economic gain killed the desire for beauty.
8. Grave, *La Société future*, pp 359-60.
9. Peter Kropotkin, *The Conquest of Bread* (New York: G. P. Putnam's, 1907), pp 138-42.
10. Pierre Kropotkine, *Paroles d'un révolté*, preface by Elisée Reclus (Paris: Flammarion, 1885), pp 65ff.
11. Pierre-Joseph Proudhon, *Du Principe de l'art et de sa destination sociale*, as cited in *Oeuvres complètes* (Paris:Marcel Rivière, 1939), XV, 278ff.
12. Grave, *La Société future*, p 362; and Peter Kropotkin, *The Conquest of Bread*, pp 142-43.
13. Grave, *La Société future*, p 368.
14. Richard Wagner, *L'Art et la révolution*, trans. by Jacques Mesnil (Brussels, 1898).
15. On realism in literature, see appropriate section in Arnold Hauser, *The Social History of Art*, trans. Stanley Godman (New York: Alfred A. Knopf, 1952), ii; and Georg Lukacs, *Studies in European Realism* (New York: The Universal Library, 1964).
16. Jean Grave, *Malfaiteurs!* (Paris: P. V. Stock, 1903), pp 13ff, for a description of Armel.
17. Grave, *Terre libre*, p 221, wherein general community decisions were made by all.
18. *Ibid.*, pp 134ff.
19. Jean Grave, *Responsabilités!* (Paris, P. V. Stock, 1904).
20. Jean Grave, *Les Aventures de Nono*, illustrations by Alexandre Charpentier, Heidbrinck, Herman-Paul, Camille Lefevre, M. Luce, Lucien Pissaro, and Rysselberghe (Paris: P. V. Stock, 1901).
21. Jean Grave, "Froissements de la vanité," *Les Temps Nouveaux*, May 4-10, 1901, pp 1-2.
22. Jean Grave, "Comment on s'enrichit," *Ni Dieu, Ni Maître: 1903 Almanach de la Révolution*, Paul Delesalle (ed.) (Paris: Charles Blot Imprimerie, 1902), pp 22-25.
23. Emile Capouya and Keith Tomkins (eds.), *The Essential Kropotkin* (New York: Liveright, 1975), p 119, and from "Anarchism" pp 108-20.
24. *Les Temps Nouveaux, Supplément Littéraire*, Vol. VI (1908-11), pp 23, 77, and 87. To be cited as *TNSL*.
25. *Ibid.*, p 53 and p 102.
26. *Ibid.*, p 16, p 41, and p 52.
27. *Ibid.*, p 773, for example.
28. *Ibid.*, I (1895-97), p 496, among others.
29. *Ibid.*, p 37, p 215, and p 219. Other writers included Wilde, France and Flaubert.
30. *Ibid.*, I, p 104, p 321, p 369, p 388, and p 417.

31. *Mouvement libertaire*, p 152; and Lucien Descaves, *Souvenirs d'un ours* (Paris: Les Editions de Paris, 1946), p 122.
32. *TNSL*, VI, p 457 and p 556. His memoirs: Jean Ajalbert, *Mémoires en vrac* (Paris: Albin Michel, 1938).
33. *TNSL*, I, p 124, p 332, and p 393. On Richepin: Howard Sutton, *The Life and Works of Jean Richepin* (Genève: E. Droz, 1961).
34. *TNSL*, I, p 335, p 383, p 420, and p 642.
35. On the painters discussed, see John Rewald, *Post Impressionism: From Van Gogh to Gauguin* (New York: Simon Schuster, n.d.); and Herbert, *The Artist and Social Reform*. On Grave and the various artists, see R. L. Herbert, "Les Artistes et l'anarchisme d'après les lettres inédits de Pissarro, Signac et autres," *Le Mouvement Social*, XXVI (July-September, 1961), 1-19. Also, see on Kropotkin, Grave, and many neo-impressionists vis-à-vis anarchism and art, the excellent work by Donald D. Egbert, *Social Radicalism and the Arts: Western Europe: A Cultural History From the French Revolution to 1968* (New York: Alfred A. Knopf, 1970); pp 220-66.
36. On Steinlen, see Francis Jourdain, *Un Grand imagier: Alexandre Steinlen* (Paris: Editions Cercle d'art, 1954). Steinlen was born in Lausanne in 1859 and came to Paris in 1881. He was always in the streets drawing people there. This work is well-illustrated.
37. On Signac, see *Quarante ans*, p 305, p 439, and p 453.
38. On Luce, see *ibid.*, p 305, pp 348-49, and pp 453-54.
39. On Camille Pissaro, see Adolphe Tabarant, *Pissaro* (Paris: Reider, 1924). Also, see *Quarante ans*, p 255, p 305, p 392, p 540, p 549, and p 551. For Grave's eulogy on Pissaro, see *Les Temps Nouveaux*, November 21-27, 1903, p 2.
40. GA, thirteen letters from Angrand to Grave, 1899-1925, concerning principally lithographs. *Quarante ans*, pp 439-460 and p 551.
41. GA, nine letters from Cross to Grave, 1896-1909. *Quarante ans*, p 551.
42. GA, about twenty letters from Rysselberghe to Grave, 1897-1912, concerning topics related to the newspaper. *Quarante ans*, p 551.
43. GA, six letters from Valloton to Grave, 1896-1909, concerning artwork. *Quarante ans*, p 551. On his life, see Francis Jourdain, *Félix Valloton* (Genève: Editions Pierre Callier, 1953).
44. GA, two letters from Lucien Pissaro to Grave. *Quarante ans*, p 551. *Les Temps Nouveaux*, April 15-21, 1899, p 4, where one of his paintings was offered for a raffle.
45. GA, Herman-Paul, three letters during 1914-1918. On his life, see *DB*, XIII, 43.
46. The letters of Signac, C. Pissaro, Steinlein, and Luce are in GA.

9
WAR AND SOCIAL REVOLUTION, 1914-1920

ANARCHO-COMMUNISTS DURING THE 1914-1920 period were confronted with the great opportunities and pitfalls that occurred with World War I and accompanying social upheaval. Grave's critique of the various forces that brought about the holocaust of global war, his activities, along with those of other anarchists, during the conflict, and the significance of the Communist November 1917 Revolution in Russia for French anarchism will be delved into.

Grave and other anarchists were acutely aware of the inner dynamism of imperialism leading to war.[1] For instance, Grave related it to commercial factors, such as finding new markets,[2] which themselves were part of a larger mosaic that not only included the civil and military bureaucracies in imperialism's service,[3] but also a largely predatory bourgeois *Weltanschauung* tied to nationalism that expropriated the lands of conquered peoples[4]—colonialism, a curious "hybrid of patriotism and mercantilism."[5] Thus an unprofitable imperialistic venture, for example, could be justified by appealing to a jingoistic patriotism.[6] Furthermore, he was aware of the intimate links between imperialism and racism, of people in the economically advanced nations so alienated and dehumanised that they were immune to colonialist savageries and even accepted the racism of most bourgeois ideologues.[7]

In contrast to Grave's uncompromising opposition to colonialism, there were many socialists who had illusions about it. One such was Jean Jaurès, not only the outstanding French socialist leader in the generation before 1914, but also a brilliant scholar and humanitarian. He thought French presence in Morocco, for instance, no matter what its faults, could aid in transforming a feudalistic society into a more modern one. His formula in achieving this called for civilising the area by building schools, hospitals and other social facilities.[8] What Jaurès did not take into sufficient account, however, was that the colonialist administration would inevitably reinforce the traditional power structure, thus making it more difficult for progressive social change.

Grave was also aware of the inherent war danger of an ever-increasing armaments race between the great powers that strengthened such powerful interest groups as war suppliers and military establishments whose bellicose views exacerbated war hysteria. He strenuously opposed the extension of the military draft from two to three years in 1913, appealed to humanity's higher social instincts to curb the bloated military budget for the sake of aiding the needy,[9] and warned that war would inevitably further atrophy mutual aid.[10]

Although *Les Temps Nouveaux* expected war and made the usual customary references to its possibility, it did not view with alarm, until almost the end, the immediate events leading to World War I. The assassination of Francis Ferdinand and his wife at Sarajevo on June 28, 1914 was justified in the July 4 issue by Grave on the basis that Austria-Hungary had earlier annexed Bosnia against the wishes of its inhabitants. This article was inconspicuous, only of two paragraphs.[11] In the July 11, 18 and 25 issues, again, there was no apparent awareness of imminent war: The problems discussed were the usual ones of social affairs and anarchist theory. But the August 1 issue sensed danger. Page one had a drawing by Paul Iribe: a Russian functionary asking the Czar what good was an alliance with France if Premier Poincaré did not arrest a few French republicans. On page two, there were three brief paragraphs asserting the possibility of retribution against a world of authority through the medium of war. The rest of the issue was devoted to conventional affairs.[12]

The last issue, August 8, contained only two pages. The leading article, which covered the first page, was titled "Aux Camarades." Printed in larger than usual type, it blamed the people's docility to authority and submission to politicians and military, all in the name of nationalism. It praised worker demonstrations against the war on its eve, but regretted their inability to prevent it. Then it went on to condemn all governments for the war whose immediate cause was blamed on the militarism of Germany and Austria-Hungary, France pictured as trying to avoid war to the very end. The last paragraph held out one last flicker of hope, that the German people would overthrow their government. A brief tribute to Jaurès was also inserted; he was assassinated on July 31, while trying to marshal international socialist support to abort the conflict.[13]

Not many weeks after the war's beginning, Grave, in a quixotic act, wrote letters to pacifist intellectuals and artists like Anatole France, Mirbeau, Severine and Hermann-Paul, to form a group opposing anti-German feeling, as he made a clear distinction between the innocent, the German people, and the guilty, their political masters. This rather fraternal project failed to arouse sufficient interest and was consequently shelved.[14]

By early September, the Graves left their rented home in the Paris suburb of Robinson for Clifton, England, the wealthy suburb of Bristol, to live with close relatives. Two considerations were responsible for this move: Grave's journalistic work was momentarily suspended because war gave the government an excuse to close down much of the socialist press, including *Les Temps Nouveaux*. And, near the end of August, when Paris was in a state of alarm over the swift and menacing German advances, many of the wealthier people fled the city. Once in Clifton, Grave had many occasions to socially encounter the local bourgeois elite, learning of their views toward various problems.[15]

World War I engendered splits within socialism including its anarchist segment. Although the vast majority in most socialist parties supported their respective governments during the conflict, most anarchists were pacifists. An influential minority which included Grave, however, supported the war, justifying it as defending France and freedom.[16] An excellent example of this was Kropotkin's position that favoured French victory on the basis of superior revolutionary tradition; a French defeat would inevitably strengthen reactionary forces throughout the world.[17]

That Grave would be a member of any prowar group was, to say the least, unexpected since he had always been a staunch antimilitarist. In fact, as a militant pacifist, he had always opposed bourgeois nationalism for working-class internationalism.[18] There is strong evidence that in this painful change, the influence of Kropotkin was decisive. A letter of September 2, 1914 from Kropotkin to Grave clearly indicated this:

> In what world of illusion do you live in to speak of peace? We must think of destroying the German army, to reconquer bleeding Belgium which is in a state of turmoil, and then to defend Paris.[19]

Once in the prowar group, Grave indefatigably propagated its program. When in early 1916, he and his wife visited the Kropotkins at the seaside resort of Brighton, he persuaded Kropotkin of the need for a manifesto to warn of possible dangers inherent in a German victory. After Grave returned to Clifton, he wrote the tract and sent it to Kropotkin for suggestions.[20] Among those signing it, in addition to Grave and Kropotkin, were Malato and Paul Reclus.[21] (There were sixteen names in all, fifteen of individuals and one of a geographical location.)[22] This *Déclaration* (also called the *Manifeste des Seize*), dated February 28, 1916, appeared first in general circulation on March 14, 1916 in the CGT's prowar newspaper *La Bataille*. It began by stating that its wish for peace was impossible at present since the German workers were incapable of preventing the imperialism of their government. Then, it claimed that the German proletariat was not represented at the antiwar Zimmerwald Conference in Switzerland in 1915,[23] the obvious implication being that the various antiwar groups, those which Grave himself was against, were weaker in Germany than in other nations. The key statement, indeed, accused the German people of backing their government's imperialism:

> The German Empire, knowing that its armies are only ninety kilometres from Paris for eighteen months, and *backed in its dreams for new conquests by the German people*, does not see why it should not keep the conquests already made.[24]

The response to this manifesto from the antiwar anarchists was not long in coming. It was led by Malatesta's stinging attack entitled *Anarchistes de Gouvernements*. It saw all Europe as imitating Prussian militarism, including the prowar anarchists who had joined the reactionary chorus in supporting the war effort of their respective governments. The defeat of one side in the war would not solve any long-range problems; instead, it would only perpetuate the ideas of revenge to only foster more war. Therefore, all anarchists should return to their original views: "Down with capitalists and governments, all capitalists and all governments." The pamphlet concluded with the cry of "Long live the people, all the people!"[25]

Malatesta was supported by a group of Grave's former collaborators at *Les Temps Nouveaux*, principally Girard and Benoît, who conducted antiwar propaganda as Groupe des *Temps Nouveaux* (hereinafter *Groupe*), that along with others, notably Signac and Faure, issued another rejoinder to the prowar manifesto entitled *La Paix par les Peuples*. It charged that the war was caused by imperialistic rivalry that had already enslaved the people of Asia and Africa. Then it condemned all governments equally for the war, defended the Zimmerwald Conference, and restated the traditional aims of anarchism, pacifism and total disarmament.[26]

Grave's decision to support the war caused consternation among some friends. The painter Signac, particularly troubled, wrote Grave:

> Nourished by your principles, by those of [Elisée] Reclus, by those of Kropotkin—because it is you who have formed me—I cannot understand why you support the war, and why you do not protest against the execution of this horror?[27]

Inexorably, the arguments between those for and against the war provoked personal animosity. This was well illustrated by former militants of *Les Temps Nouveaux*. When the *Groupe* criticised Grave's prowar position, Grave retaliated by informing them to stop using the name and offices of the weekly at Broca Street in Paris because he had no wish for its name to be associated with their position. When the *Groupe* persisted in its course, Grave peremptorily locked them out.[28] The *Groupe* then decided to publish another brochure in February 1917, *Projets d'Avenir*, which recalled the argument with Grave and reaffirmed their antiwar stance. Of greater importance, it announced a new monthly, *L'Avenir International*,[29] which did not appear until January 1918, with Girard and Benoît as chief contributors.[30] (A featured writer was Romain Rolland of *Jean Christophe* fame, a noted antiwar figure and later a member of the French Communist Party.)[31] The position of this organ was consistently antiwar and internationalist.

After this fracas, Grave and other prowar anarchists published a monthly bulletin (irregularly issued from May 1916 to June 1919) called *Publication des Temps Nouveaux* with offices at Broca Street.[32] If anyone were identified with this organ, the honour belonged to Grave its editor; entire issues were of little else than his articles. Other important contributors included Kropotkin, Malato and Jacques Guérin, the last performing much of the daily irksome work associated with publishing. The central thrust of the articles was to support the French war effort. Toward the end of the war, Grave wrote a notable article on the League of Nations which pictured it as a form of supergovernment under bourgeois control that inevitably would lead to more organisation and hierarchy.[33]

While the war progressed, Grave, safely sheltered in Clifton, accepted at face value the assertions of wealthy friends that capital was against war because it disrupted commerce.[34] Now, for him, the real culprits were the various governments, which, unfortunately, had been unduly influenced by their respective armies,[35] negating his earlier analysis which intertwined authority with capital and state.

The always-active Grave found time to help a close friend, Doctor Jean Wintsch who published a prowar anarchist newspaper, *La Libre Fédération*, in Lausanne, Switzerland.[36] Not only did Grave send the addresses of former subscribers of *Les Temps Nouveaux* to increase circulation, but he contributed many articles. A significant one urged the resurrection of the Jacobin tradition, the arming of the entire people to repel German aggression.[37]

A few of Grave's articles also appeared in *Freedom*, the noted British anarchist journal. Although this monthly was antiwar, it allowed prowar anarchists to state their views.[38] Grave's main tack here was that the basic issue was not war, but foreign domination, which only reinforced the power of authority and reaction.[39] This argument recognised that a conquered people falls under the double authority of its indigenous power structure and that of the imperialists, making the task of liberation all the more difficult.

The principal journalistic work of Grave during the war was in collaboration with the revolutionary syndicalists. In October 1914, he and other prowar anarchists, like Paul Reclus and Luce, were invited by officials of the CGT, principally Léon Jouhaux and Monatte, to write for its newspaper, La *Bataille Syndicaliste,* close ideological and personal ties prompted this. Just prior to the war, this newspaper called for a "War on War"[40] through the unity of the international working class in a general strike,[41] but with the war's advent, it soon endorsed national defence against Germany.[42] On October 3, 1915, the newspaper's name was changed to *La Bataille.*[43]

From October 30, 1914 to February 11, 1919, Grave wrote approximately 180 articles for these newspapers, many featured on page one, often partly blank, a few entirely so, since the censors thought them detrimental to the war effort.[44] Their basic tack revolved around problems caused by or related to war and peace. Ideally he had hoped for revolution to greet war, but since anarchism was weak, this was impossible.[45] Under existing conditions France should protect itself against German aggression and fight until victorious.[46] Germany, of course, was severely castigated with respect to war guilt: at times, a distinction was made between its masses and ruling groups;[47] at other times, the entire nation would be blamed, the rulers, however, more so than the people.[48] Toward the end of the war, articles were increasingly concerned with a peace settlement, urging restraint and moderation with respect to Germany. Payment for war damage in northern France was supported, but any idea for revenge was rejected.[49] Practical suggestions to ensure the coming peace included the abolition of tariffs, the freeing of subject nationalities, the ending of secret treaties, and the nationalisation of the armaments industry.[50]

The last important event in the Grave/Kropotkin collaboration occurred when Kropotkin, just before departing for Russia in the summer of 1917, sent Grave his well-known "Open Letter to the Western Working Class," published in *La Bataille,* thanking the workers for their personal warmth and generosity during forty years of work and struggle and also urging them to continue their support of the war.

Kropotkin had wished to see Grave before leaving England, but failed to do so because his ship left a few days earlier than originally planned.[51] Thus, it was by letter that Kropotkin said farewell to his friend.

THE ANARCHISM OF JEAN GRAVE

I do not know how to tell you how difficult and sad it is to leave without embracing you and dear Mable. Sophie is also sorry. After so many years of working together, almost forty, not to be able to embrace and to talk about a thousand things together. It is more than sad.[52]

The demands and accompanying tensions of World War I erupted into revolution in the most autocratic and backward of the great European powers, Russia. The March 1917 Revolution, which overthrew the reactionary Romanov dynasty, lifted the hopes of Kropotkin and Grave (this was true for all democrats and socialists) who saw it as a harbinger of the better world to come after the war.[53] In November 1917, the Bolsheviks led by V.I. Lenin and Leon Trotsky, representing the majority of the Russian proletariat, overthrew the inept coalition of moderate socialist and bourgeois parties led by Alexander Kerensky that had persisted in continuing the war and postponing the sweeping socio-economic changes proposed by the masses.[54]

Bolshevik success in Russia and German defeat in November exposed much of Europe to the possibility of socialist revolution during the 1918-1920 period: in Germany in November-December 1918, the moderate Majority Socialists and left-wing Independent Socialists held the reins of government, with the latter and the Spartacists demanding sweeping changes to inaugurate socialism. In Italy, during the summer of 1920, hundreds of thousands of workers seized six hundred factories. In France, in 1919-1920 the CGT, led by Monatte and others, launched a series of strikes involving over two hundred thousand workers, and, in December 1920, the overwhelming majority of the French Socialist Party at the Tours Congress formed the French Communist Party. But revolution was contained outside of Russia; the traditional power structures survived.

French anarchism could not but be influenced by this revolutionary ferment. There was a marked tendency for the antiwar group to be friendly to the Bolsheviks, while the prowar element, including Grave, was unsympathetic. In *L'Avenir International*, for example, the young anarchist nobleman, Jean de Saint-Prix, wrote in favour of both anarchism and Communism,[55] while Girard called for the defence of Communist Russia from foreign encroachment.[56] But Grave from the very beginning, was most critical of the Bolsheviks, opposing their wishes to end the war and to extend revolution to the advanced Western European nations, primarily on the basis that Germany would be greatly strengthened.[57] Furthermore, he averred that since Communism was supported by only a minority of the Russian people, a period of chaos would inevitably follow as it tried to consolidate its position.[58]

Grave's criticism of Communism was especially rejected by revolutionary syndicalism, the popular base of anarchism despite the 1906 break, now strongly attracted to Communist revolution.[59] In fact, the erosion of anarchist strength and influence in France may be dated to the successful Bolshevik revolution in Russia which generated a great revolutionary élan among the French proletariat. Revolutionary syndicalist leaders—Monatte, the outstanding example—in the CGT now called for support and extension of Bolshevism.[60] (One must remember that Lenin's *State and Revolution* had marked anarchist overtones, particularly of the revolutionary syndicalist variety.)[61]

When Grave returned to Paris in July 1919, he became editor of a new journalistic venture.[62] Along with Doctor Pierrot and Guérin, former prowar collaborators, he resurrected *Les Temps Nouveaux* as a monthly whose chief aim was to foster the formation of anarchist groups; he had earlier wished for a daily, but monies were insufficient.[63] From the beginning, Grave was not satisfied with a review top-heavy with theoretical discussion because it could not adequately cover the social scene for lack of space. The monthly itself had two to three hundred subscribers.[64] His contribution to the review, not particularly distinguished, consisted of five articles: Three, on the advantages of free trade, stressed the importance of economic interdependence to lessen future threats of war; the remaining two were of an earlier brochure on syndicalism and an enthusiastic endorsement of the Versailles Treaty with its vindictive war reparations.[65]

Grave did not have a pleasant time on the review; there was interminable squabbling with other staff members, especially Guérin, the administrative head, over insertion of articles. In early 1920, after Guérin died, when the staff's eulogy called him its leading spirit, Grave left in a fit of anger.[66]

THE ANARCHISM OF JEAN GRAVE

Notes

1. For representative anarchist criticism of war, colonialism, and the arms race, see Charles Albert, *Patrie, guerre et caserne* (Paris: Les Temps Nouveaux, c. 1905); André Girard, "La guerre imminente et les financiers," *Les Temps Nouveaux*, August 26, 191 1, p 1; Pierre Kropotkine, "La Guerre," *Ibid.*, March 2, 1912, pp 1-2; March 9, 1912, pp 1-2; March 16, 1912, pp 2-3; March 30, 1912, pp 1-2.

2. Grave, *La Société mourante et l'anarchie*, pp 177-78. Grave neglected the role of overseas capital movements in search of higher investment returns which was popularized by J. A. Hobson, *Imperialism: A Study* (London: A. Constable, 1905). Also, see V. I. Lenin, *Imperialism: The Highest Stage of Capitalism* (New York: International Publishers, 1939), pp 62ff., on capital exportation.

3. Grave, *La Société mourante et l'anarchie*, p 174. Grave's connection of imperialism not just to purely economic factors, but to the dynamics of a capitalist class structure, was akin to Hobson's position in *Imperialism*; see, for example, p 88ff.

4. Grave, *La Société mourante et l'anarchie*, p 174. The chapter entitled "La Colonisation," pp 171-82 of *Ibid.* was published in pamphlet form: Jean Grave, *La Colonisation* (Paris: Les Temps Nouveaux, 1900).

5. Grave, *La Société mourante et l'anarchie*, p 171. In connection with imperialism, Grave envisaged its demise by national liberation; only then would "economic emancipation" arrive—AM, letter Grave to Nettlau, June 20, 1923.

6. Grave, *La Société mourante et l'anarchie*, p 1 7 7.

7. *Ibid*, pp 77-79 and 171ff.

8. *Oeuvres de Jean Jaurès*, comp. Max Bonnafous (9 vols.; Paris: Rieder, 1931-34), II, 33 and VII, 426. On Jaurès' life and ideas, see Goldberg, *Jean Jaurès*.

9. Jean Grave, *Contré la folie des armaments* (Paris: Les Temps Nouveaux, 1913), pp 4ff. (24pp).

10. The criminality and pettiness of the military mind is amply shown by Henri Chapoutot, *Livre d'or des officers français de 1789 à 1815; d'après leurs mémoires et souvenirs*, preface by Jean Grave (Paris: Editions des *Temps Nouveaux*, 1904), a French anarchist who, in examining the memoirs of various generals of the period, found their accusing one another of cowardice, theft, and other such chivalric virtues.

11. Jean Grave, "Qui frappe par l'épée périra par le révolver," *Les Temps Nouveaux*, July 4, 1914, p 1.

12. Jean Grave, "Où nous sommes," *Ibid.*, August 1, 1914, p 2.

13. Editorial Staff, "Aux Camarades," *Ibid.*, August 8, 1914, pp 1-2.

14. *Quarante ans*, pp 476-78. Appropriate letters are in GA.

15. *Quarante ans*, pp 478-92; Alfred Rosmer, *Le Mouvement ouvrier pendant la premiere guerre mondiale de Zimmerzvald à la Révolution Russe* (Paris: Mouton, 1959), p 137; Jean Grave, "En Angleterre," *La Bataille Syndicaliste*, October 30, 1914, p 1.

16. On anarchism and World War 1, see Woodcock, *Anarchism*, pp 324-25; Woodcock and Avakumovic, *The Anarchist Prince*, p 380, saw that most anarchists were in the antiwar group.

WAR AND SOCIAL REVOLUTION

17. For Kropotkin's remarks, see *Le Temps*, October 31, 1915.
18. See, for example, Grave, *La Société mourante et l'anarchie*, pp 151-71.
19. GA, letter, Kropotkin to Grave, September 2, 1914; *Ibid.*, letter, Kropotkin to Grave, April 4, 1916, in which he stated that the allies must fight "like ferocious beasts." Jean Grave, "Ce qui est à faire," *La Libre Fédération*, October 2, 1915, called for victory over Prussian militarism.
20. *Mouvement libertaire*, pp 261-62; Woodcock and Avakumovic, *The Anarchist Prince*, p 384, stated that the author of the *Manifesto of the Sixteen* (the *Déclaration*) could have either been Grave or Kropotkin.
21. GA, letters Malato to Grave, March 7 and 28, 1918, which contain a prowar position.
22. Jean Grave and others, "Déclaration," *La Bataille*, March 14, 1916; Rosmer, *Le Mouvement ouvrier*, p. 111.
23. The Zimmerwald Conference was held in September 1915, in Switzerland. Although both German and French labor movements were represented, neither the German nor French Socialist parties were officially there. The miniscule group of Russian, Italian, French and German delegates, among whom was Lenin, stated that the war was not a workers' war and called for the immediate cessation of hostilities. On this conference, see Dolleans, II, 234-38.
24. Grave and others, *La Bataille*, March 14, 1916.
25. Errico Malatesta, *Anarchistes de Gouvernement (Résponse de Malatesta au Manifeste des Seize)*—a brochure of seven pages in my possession, a gift of Mlle Colette Chambelland of Le Musée Social. It was issued by the *Groupe des Temps Nouveaux* in 1916. Errico Malatesta, "Pro-Government Anarchists," *Freedom* (April, 1916), p 28, was the English version of the above. Also, see GA, letter Malatesta to Grave, November 5, 1916, in which he informed Grave that the prowar anarchists have "committed a great fault." For a very early anarchist manifesto against the war, see Errico Malatesta, F. Domela Nieuwenhuis, and others, "International Manifesto on the War," *Freedom* (March, 1915), p 21.
26. Groupe des *Temps Nouveaux*, "La Paix par les peuples," *Deuxième lettre: un désaccord, nos explications* (Paris: Imprimeric Spéciale du Groupe des *Temps Nouveaux*, 1916), pp 54-62.
27. GA, letter Signac to Grave, August 1, 1916. However, Grave's friend Luce supported the prowar position: *Ibid.*, letter, Luce to Grave (1916).
28. Groupe des *Temps Nouveaux, Deuxième lettre*, pp 3-42, contained a series of letters between the Groupe and Grave. See Grave's open letter to the Groupe in *La Bataille*, March 8, 1916, reaffirming the break between him and the Groupe on pp 14-16.
29. Groupe des *Temps Nouveaux, Troisième lettre: Projets d'Avenir* (Paris: Imprimerie Spéciale des *Temps Nouveaux*, February, 1917), pp 3-18.
30. *L'Avenir International*, January, 1918, p 23.

31. Romain Rolland, "Biologie de la guerre (Dr Nicolai)," *Ibid.*, March, April, May, and July, 1917.
32. *Publications des Temps Nouveaux, Bulletins* were irregularly issued from May 1916, to June 1919. Sixteen issues were printed.
33. *Ibid.*, No. I (May, 1916). Jean Grave, "La Société des Nations," *Ibid.*, No. 9 (January 1918), pp 4-23.
34. Jean Grave, "Les Causes profondes de la guerre actuelle (Pas de raisons économiques)," *La Bataille*, April 30, 1916, p 4.
35. *La Bataille Syndicaliste*, March 2, 1915, where Grave argued that all governments were responsible for the war, but the German more so.
36. *La Libre Fédération* was published irregularly (thirty-four issues) from October 2, 1915, to October 31, 1918.
37. *Mouvement libertaire*, p 258. See, for example, Jean Grave, "Ce qui est à faire," *La Libre Fédération*, October 2, 1913, p 1. Other articles by Grave appeared on October 14 and 27, November 23, December 9 and 23, 1915. Other articles appeared in 1916.
38. *Freedom: A Journal of Anarchist Communism* was begun in 1886 and lasted to 1927. A new series that began in 1929 lasted to 1939.
39. Jean Grave, "Ought Anarchists to Take Part in the War," *Ibid.*, (November, 1915), pp 84-85. Jean Grave, "What Can We Do?," *Ibid.*, (December, 1914), pp 94-95. A letter from Grave on the war in *Ibid.*, (February 1915), p 15.
40. *La Bataille Syndicaliste*, July 29, 1914, p 1.
41. *Ibid.*, July 26, 30, 31, 1914.
42. *Ibid.*, August 3, 6, 1914.
43. *La Bataille Syndicaliste* changed its name to *La Bataille* on October 3, 1915. From January 4, 1921 to 1939, it remained the official daily of the CGT as *Le Peuple*. The circulation in the World War I period was about fifteen thousand.
44. *La Bataille*, for example, April 16 and 23, 1916.
45. Jean Grave, "Les Anarchistes et la guerre," *La Bataille Syndicaliste*, February 27, 1915; also, Jean Grave, *Ibid.*, December 21, 1915.
46. *Ibid.*, October 30, 1914 and December 5, 1915, *La Bataille*, July 22 and 24, 1918.
47. *La Bataille Syndicaliste*, December 17 and 23, 1914; January 13, March 7, April II, 1915. *La Bataille*, May 7, 1916 and April 19, 1917.
48. *La Bataille*, December 13 and 24, 1915; April 9 and September 10, 1916.
49. *La Bataille Syndicaliste*, November 29 and December 11, 1914. *La Bataille*, June 11, 1917; December 11, 1918.
50. *La Bataille Syndicaliste*, January 16, 1915. *La Bataille*, July 23, 1916; January 25 and 27, May 8 and June 23, 1917.
51. *La Bataille*, July 2, 1917, p 1 and *Mouvement libertaire*, p 20 concerning the letter. On vacationing together, *Quarante ans*, p 172.
52. GA, letter Kropotkin to Grave, June 3, 1917.

WAR AND SOCIAL REVOLUTION

53. See, for example, Jean Grave, "Une éclaircie dans l'horizon," *La Bataille*, June 7, 1917, p1.
54. On the Russian revolutionary period of 1917 and after, see E. H. Carr, *The Bolshevik Revolution, 1917-1923* (3 vols.; Baltimore, Maryland: Penguin Books, 1966) and William Henry Chamberlin, *The Russian Revolution, 1918-1921* (2 vols.; New York: Grosset and Dunlap, 1965). In I of Chamberlin, 365ff, we note that in the Constituent Assembly vote of November, 1917, the Bolsheviks received about twenty-five percent and the Socialist Revolutionaries about sixty percent. The Bolsheviks received the majority of votes in key areas: Petrograd, Moscow, and of the military in the northern regions.
55. Jean de Saint-Prix, "Sur le mouvement anarchists russe," *l'Avenir International* (August 1919), pp 9-14. De Saint-Prix died in February 1919. The entire issue of May 1919 was devoted to him. See especially the eulogy of Romain Rolland, "A notre jeune frère," pp 5-6.
56. André Girard, "Oserons-nous sauver la Russie," *Ibid.* (November, 1919), pp 3-4.
57. Jean Grave, "Au coeur des événements de Russie: à coté d'Icieux," *La Bataille*, August 13, 1917, p1.
58. Jean Grave, "La Faillite de la Révolution Russe," *Ibid.*, November 1, 1918, p 2.
59. On the various differences between anarcho-communists and Bolsheviks and on the drift of revolutionary syndicalism to communism, see the brilliant work by Annie Kriegel, *Aux Origines du communisme français, 1914-1920* (2 vols.; Paris: Mouton, 1964), I, 270-347, and II, 713-54. Also, see Val R. Lorwin, *The French Labor Movement* (Cambridge: Harvard University Press, 1954), p 51; Dolléans, II, 310ff.
60. Dolléans, II, 287ff.
61. V.I. Lenin, *State and Revolution* (New York: International Publishers, 1932), p 98: "Under Socialism, all will take a turn in management, and will soon become accustomed to the idea of no managers at all."
62. *Mouvement libertaire*, pp 269-72.
63. The second *Les Temps Nouveaux* was issued twenty-two times, from July 15, 1919 to April-May, 1921. Its subtitle of *Revue Internationale des idées communistes* was changed on July 15, 1920 to *Revue Internationale des idées communistes et libertaires*. Hereafter cited as *TN2*.
64. *Mouvement libertaire*, p 274, concerning the subscribers.
65. Jean Grave, "Le Mensonge du protectionnisme," *TN2*, No. 5 (November 15, 1919), pp 6-9; *Ibid.*, No. 6 (December 15, 1919), pp 8-10. Jean Grave, "Comment le protectionnisme favorise le travail national!," *Ibid.*, No. 8 (February 15, 1920) , pp 5-8. Jean Grave, "Association, Organisation," *Ibid.*, No.II (May 15, 1920), pp 8-12. Jean Grave, "Sur le traité de paix," *Ibid.*, No. 3 (September 15, 1919), pp 5-10.
66. *Mouvement libertaire*, pp 272ff. Interview with Madame Paul Delesalle, July 26 and August 9, 1964. As Grave grew older, he became more suspicious and cantankerous.

10

TWILIGHT AND DEATH, 1921-1939

EVEN IN THE TWILIGHT OF HIS LIFE, GRAVE continued to propagate his anarchist vision. Shortly after Grave resigned from *Les Temps Nouveaux*, he inaugurated in 1921 a new publication that he edited until its demise in 1936, *Les Publications de "La Révolte" et "Temps Nouveaux"*—hereinafter *Publications*.[1] Grave's hope was to attract a new readership, to find correspondents from other nations, and to serve as a centre for the founding of anarchist groups. As before, Grave continued to be the indefatigable searcher of truth, reading widely and commenting on the human condition. In his regular column, *A Travers nos Lectures*, he reviewed hundreds of books (including Marx's *Capital*) in such fields as history, economics, sociology, and literature.[2] As always, Grave's prose was lucid and cogent as he valiantly tried to revivify the dying spirit of anarchism which had been weakened by Communism.[3]

The *Publications* tried as much as possible on limited publication (approximately a hundred issues from 1921 to 1936) to cover the anarchist scene. Examples: a letter from China seeking funds to continue a labor university; a hunger strike by Malatesta in Italy; the agony and triumph of Nicola Sacco and Bartolomeo Vanzetti, two intrepid Italian anarchist immigrants in the United States, who, after being convicted of robbery and murder, were electrocuted in 1927 (the American Left saw them as innocent martyrs of fear and prejudice); a lengthy letter from Alexander Berkman, a daring anarchist, commenting on famous labour trials in the United States.[4]

One of the major themes of the *Publications* was its antipathy to the Soviet Union, usually pictured as economically foundering,[5] but the focus

TWILIGHT AND DEATH

of attention was on its distorted form of socialism: the inordinate power of the bureaucracy over the people, the terrorism exercised by the secret police, and the denial of speech and press freedoms.[6] In particular, Grave asserted that the bitter civil war, in which the struggle was not only between Left and Right but between various groups within the Left itself, such as Communists and anarchists, unquestionably proved that the Communists did not have a majority. That revolution was sparked by a conscious minority was admitted, but the broad masses themselves must actively accept and participate in the change. The Bolshevik crime was to impose their will on a majority which did not want their form of socialism.[7]

The League of Nations again received attention with two articles in 1925 that essentially restated Grave's earlier opinions: It would lead to a world government under bourgeois domination, which in turn would increase the difficulty for the proletariat to win its ultimate freedom. For peace, the people had to force their respective war-prone governments to bring about the destruction of permanent armies, to remove all tariff barriers, and to settle disputes by mutual agreement.[8]

Concerning the fusion of art and politics, in which Grave was forever involved, the *Publications* was in the grand tradition of *La Révolte* and *Les Temps Nouveaux*: Front covers from No. 28 (August 10, 1924) to No. 70 (April 25, 1931) were lithographs for *Les Temps Nouveaux* by Luce, Signac and Steinlen.

Ultimately, Grave lost the battle to continue the *Publications*. With less than a hundred subscribers, printing ceased in September 1936.[9] That he was understandably disappointed was obvious:

> As one can see on the last page, in two months' time... I have received one subscription! Before such indifference, what is the use of trying to talk to those who are not interested. This is the last bulletin. Publication has ceased.[10]

Grave's old age was not unpleasant. There was ample housing which was provided by his wealthy wife's purchase of the villa at Robinson where they lived before the war. Then too the Graves were not lonely; their good friends, the Delesalles often visited and only death terminated their close friendship.

THE ANARCHISM OF JEAN GRAVE

The hallmark of Grave in his old age is his indefatigable intellectual activity. In addition to his journalism and wide reading, he was engaged in writing his memoirs, *Quarante ans de propagande anarchiste*, and in conducting an extensive correspondence with many well-known figures, much of it with Max Nettlau, a prominent Austrian anarchist who worked untiringly as an historian and bibliographer of anarchism. In response to an ever curious Nettlau, Grave not only described his activities in Paris, such as the founding of the Social Study Group, but imparted his well-formulated opinions on anarchism.[11] Grave also had a brief correspondence with such well-known writers as Barbusse,[12] Paul Eltzbacher, author of *Anarchism*,[13] and H.G. Wells whose best known utopias are *A Modern Utopia* and *Men Like Gods*.[14]

As for Kropotkin, Grave received his last letter, dated July 20, 1920, from a friend of Kropotkin's daughter in early 1922: he wrote about his life at the small village of Dimitrov (about thirty miles from Moscow) where he spent his last years. Although complaining of ailments associated with old age, he was enthusiastic about his significant work, *Ethics*.[15] (Kropotkin's great humanity was amply revealed in the correspondence with Grave through his optimism, revolutionary energy, and great warmth.)[16]

With advancing age, Grave's social perspective rejected the class stereotypes of his earlier years: a somewhat virtuous working class as opposed to a wicked bourgeoisie. Instead, he opined that most individuals, irrespective of class, were engrossed in self-interest, related to the accumulated authoritarian patterns and prejudices of the past.[17] He retained, however, the vision that mutual aid would overcome the destructiveness of individual, social, and national antagonisms. Anarchist ideas could even remain dormant for long periods of time only to return again to play their proper role in human destiny.[18] Thus, despite despair, hope in Grave ultimately prevailed; he had not lost the idealism of youth. (An example in literature in which Grave represented this, but which atrophied to futility, was Rebecci in André Malraux's *Les Conquérants*. An anarchist in his youth, one nurtured by Grave's struggles and ideals, he lived out his later life by running a pinball parlour in Canton, China. Lamenting the past, he stated: "Jean Grave was not just a good man for me; he was my youth.")[19]

TWILIGHT AND DEATH

With old age Grave faced the inevitable tragedy of the deaths of loved ones and self. The first great shock was the death of Kropotkin on February 8, 1921. A magnificent memorial issue in the *Publications* was devoted to him in which many tributes were offered by friends. Particularly appropriate was a drawing by Luce entitled "Kropotkin on His Death Bed," showing the venerable octogenarian dying peacefully.[20] On January 17, 1929, Grave suffered the heaviest blow of all, the death of his wife, but managed to carry on despite a heart condition from the early 1920s that severely restricted physical activity. Money from his wife's estate provided more than enough for physical needs. Her will stipulated that he only receive the interest lest he give away the fortune. In the early thirties, Grave was operated on for prostate gland problems, but recovered rapidly and enjoyed fairly good health. During the last years of his life, he lived with a housekeeper, Madame Barotte. Grave died on December 8, 1939, after being in pain for about two weeks at Vienne-en-Val in the Loiret Department. He had earlier left Paris, fearing its fall to Nazism. He was buried in the municipal cemetery of Robinson.[21]

Jean Grave was a rare individual; one who had the courage of his convictions. While years of prison and failure to see anarchist success may have dampened his spirit, they never broke it. He was a critic and visionary. His aim was a world of equality interwoven with liberty and fraternity. Its achievement would be his proper epitaph and triumph.

Notes

1. *Publications de "La Révolte" et "Temps Nouveaux"* was published in Robinson (Seine) from 1921 to 1936, and was a continuation of *Publications du Groupe de Propagande par l'Ecrit* which began in early 1921, and comprised the first nine numbers. All told, there are ninety-nine numbers of which approximately twenty are missing. To be referred to as *Publications*. On aims, see Ibid., No. 12 (April 1, 1922), pp 16-18.

2. At times Grave's column was entitled *Bibliographie*. Infrequently others contributed to the column.

3. For the fascination of Communism on French writers and intellectuals, see David Caute, *Le Communisme et les intellectuels français, 1914-66* (Paris: Gallimard, 1967); Sartre and Gide are conspicuous examples.

4. *Publications* No. 51 (December 25, 1927), p 11. Ibid., No. 7 (1921), pp 12-13. Ibid., No. 46 (March 15, 1927), p 4. Ibid., No. 57 (November 20, 1928), p 16. Bartolomeo Vanzetti and Nicola Sacco were two Italian anarchists tried for murdering a guard in

a robbery in Massachusetts in the early 1920s. They were executed in 1927 despite the fact the many leading intellectuals thought that they were victims of a hysterical witch hunt against radical immigrants. An informative work concerning them is by Robert P. Weeks (ed.), *Commonwealth vs. Sacco and Vanzetti* (Englewood Cliffs, NJ: Prentice-Hall, 1958).

5. Jean Grave, "La Faillite Bolchevik," *Publications*, No. 29 (September 1924), pp 14-15.

6. Jean Grave, "La Décomposition de l'anarchisme," *Ibid.*, No. 28 (August 10, 1924), pp 14-15.

7. Jean Grave, "Association, organisation," *Ibid.*, No. 7 (1921). Jean Grave, "La Révolution peut-elle se faire par étapes?" *Ibid.*, No. 30 (November 15, 1924), pp 3-9. A good article by one of Grave's collaborators, J. Erboville saw the Soviet system as state capitalism; "Les Moscovites," *Ibid.*, No. 16 (October 15, 1922), pp 11-15.

8. Jean Grave, "La Société des Nations," *Ibid.*, No. 31 (January 19, 1925), pp 3-6. Jean Grave, "Ce que doit être la vraie Société des Nations," *Ibid.*, No. 32 (February 28, 1925), pp 3-18. Jean Grave, "Projet de fédération," *Ibid.*, pp 18-23. Jean Grave, "Pour la paix," *Ibid.*, No. 58 (January 30, 1929), pp 3-4.

9. *Ibid.*, No. 50 (October 15, 1927), p 19. Over one-half of money received was donated by friends. The monetary deficit in running the bulletin was very high; by issue No. 50 (October 15, 1927), p 19, it was almost 8,250 francs.

10. *Publications*, No. 99 (September 1936), p 2.

11. AM, letters Grave to Nettlau, November 4, 1925; July 7, 1934, for example.

12. GA, letter Barbusse to Grave, May 26, 1931.

13. *Ibid.*, letter Eltzbacher to Grave, June 26, 1925.

14. *Ibid.*, two letters in January 1926; one from Herbert Wells, one from Catherine Wells (Wells' wife), concerning articles Wells had written in the *Daily News*. They undoubtedly had something to do with future war because Grave was referred to see Wells' soon-to-be published work, *War and the Future*.

15. GA, letter Kropotkin to Grave, July 20, 1920.

16. *Ibid.*, see the many letters from Kropotkin to Grave.

17. AM, letter Grave to Nettlau, July 7, 1934. Grave, *Publications*, No. 30 (November 15, 1924), pp 8-9.

18. *Mouvement libertaire*, pp 298-99.

19. André Malraux, *Les Conquérants* (Paris: Bernard Grasset, 1928), p 33.

20. *Publications*, No. 6 (1921).

21. On Grave's last years: personal interview with Madame Paul Delesalle in Paris July 26 and August 9, 1964; AM, letter Grave to Nettlau, December 22, 1933; and Jean Maitron, "Jean Grave, 1834-1939," *Revue d'Histoire Economique et Sociale*, XXVI I 1, No. I (I 950), 110.

PORTRAIT DE JEAN GRAVE
A L'ÈPOQUE DU PROCÈS DES TRENTE

GRAVE'S HISTORICAL IMPORTANCE

Georges Weill, *Histoire du mouvement social en France, 1852-1902* (Paris: Félix Alcan, 1904), devoted pp 266-72 to anarchism, much of the material consisting of notes form Grave's works. George Plekhanov, *Anarchism and Socialism* (Chicago: Charles H. Kerr Co., 1918), pp 107ff, launched numerous attacks on Grave's "unscientific" work. Max Nomad, *Rebels and Renegades* (New York: Macmillan Co., 1932), p 24, observed that Grave, the chief theoretician of French anarchism, was the "favourite disciple of Kropotkin." Alfred Rosmer, *Le Mouvement ouvrier pendant la guerre; de l'Union Sacrée à Zimmerwald* (Paris: Librairie du Travail, 1939), often cited Grave. Grave is a prominent figure in the two key works concerning French anarchism by Jean Maitron: *Histoire du mouvement anarchiste en France, 1880-1914* (1st ed.; Paris: Société Universitaire, 1951); and *Le Mouvement anarchiste en France*; Vol. I: *des origines à 1914*; Vol. II: *de 1914 à nos jours* (Paris: Maspero, 1975). Eugenia W. Herbert, *The Artist and Social Reform; France and Belgium, 1885-1898* (New Haven: Yale University Press, 1961), assigned a significant role to Grave as one of the pioneers of socialism in using art to further it. Two widely known general histories of anarchism noted the importance of Grave: George Woodcock, Anarchism; *A History of Libertarian Ideas and Movements* (Cleveland: Meridian Books, 1962) and James Joll, *The Anarchists* (New York: Universal Library, 1966). A popular work which gave proper attention to Grave and French anarchism is by Barbara W. Tuchman, *The Proud Tower; A Portrait of the World before the War: 1890-1914* (New York: Macmillan Co. 1966). Two fairly recent works on French anarchists related Grave's importance: Reg Carr, *Anarchism in France: The Case of Octave Mirbeau* (Montreal: McGill-Queen's University Press, 1977), gave more attention to Grave than anyone other than Mirbeau. Marie Fleming, *The Anarchist Way to Socialism; Elisée Reclus and Nineteenth-Century European Anarchism* (London: Croom Helm, 1979), cited him often.

11

REVOLUTION AND UTOPIA, BACKGROUND

THE ETHOS OF MODERN SOCIALISM IS BASED on equality. In *Homage to Catalonia*, George Orwell expressed this central notion cogently and succinctly:

> The thing that attracts ordinary men to Socialism and makes them willing to risk their skins for it, the 'mystique' of socialism, is the idea of equality; to the vast majority of people, Socialism means a classless society, or it means nothing at all.[1]

The idea of a general equality is not of recent vintage. Indeed, modern socialism is the inheritor and outcome of a complex tradition of past class struggles that left their indelible mark on the religious and philosophical systems developed by humanity whose central axis again progressively revolves around the idea of equality.

In the evolutionary development of humanity, equality has been the norm. Paleolithic humanity, whose existence goes back hundreds of thousands of years, lived in societies characterised by mutual aid with its corollaries of socio-economic equality and participatory democracy. Indeed, without this close co-operation and equality, it is doubtful if humanity could have survived.

The discovery of agriculture in the Neolithic about ten thousand years ago inexorably led to civilisation first in Sumeria and Egypt, characterized by class and caste societies of great inequalities in wealth and power. Many observers posited this change to larger economic surpluses made possible by the agricultural revolution that resulted in the proliferation of labour division and rise of private property, necessitating the appearance of the state with accompanying bureaucratic structures in the various production and control organisations. Exploitation of labour became general after this time. The economic surplus permitted the slaves, serfs and modern workers to support themselves and to provide simultaneously an additional amount to their respective socio-economic superiors, masters, noblemen and capitalists. The scourge of war now became a regular feature of the historical drama; its roots, however, lay in the late Neolithic Age.

Even with the advent of civilisation that brought forth oppressive and exploitative class and caste societies, the ideals of the earlier egalitarianism linked with continuing class struggles were instrumental in perpetuating a powerful egalitarian consciousness in the aspirations of humanity. There is ample evidence of this in the Old Testament. The Hebrew prophetic revolution of the eighth and seventh centuries B.C.E., of Amos, Micah, and Isaiah, denounced the wealthy for oppressing the poor and urged a return to the earlier equality. The seventh century B.C.E. Code of Deuteronomy, an outgrowth of the prophetic revolution, promulgated laws to ensure a society of democracy and general equality with election of officials by the people, cancellation of debts every seven years, and prohibition of interest to fellow Hebrews.

Equality, no less than for the Hebrews, was also important in the religio-philosophical thought of a Greek world characterised by deep socio-economic divisions and intense class struggles in its city-states. The founder of "Greek Communism", Pythagoras of Samos, who lived in the sixth century B.C.E., founded brotherhoods and sisterhoods that eschewed private property, stressed economic equality, and condemned economic exploitation. He first coined the term: "From each according to his ability, to each according to his need."

Plato—along with Aristotle the most influential of the Greek philosophers—in *The Republic* presented a society in which a partial communism is the central idea. In following Pythagoras and Spartan society, Plato envisaged the ruling group of his ideal state (the philosophers and military of the guardians) living communistically with no private property and community of wives and husbands as the norm to eliminate selfishness. But the average people (mostly farmers and workers), were expected to be perfectly selfish, to accumulate private property and have traditional marriage. But even with a virtuous ruling group, Plato, ever fearful of revolution, conditioned the populace to accept the "noble falsehood" that God made the guardians to rule and defend the state, the others (those representing human appetite) to work and trade. Plato equated goodness with communism, which only the enlightened elite who exploited the multitude could attain; the many or selfish, involved with the reality of production, lacked virtue. There may be a profound economic truth here: That the goodness of communism is predicated on a lifestyle which then was only possible for the few. Or to put it another way, the forces of production had not yet matured to allow communism for all.

Aristotle, in *The Politics*, opposed Plato's limited communism and rejected the audacious proposal of Phaleas of Chalcedon for a society of economic and intellectual equals to avoid the perils of civil strife. Importantly, he examined the class struggle related to economic inequality, contrasting the oligarchic view (since men are unequal, only those who have wealth, the most virtuous, should rule) with the democratic (men without wealth wish all citizens to enjoy freedom and equality). Moreover, like Marx, he formulated a technological aspect of the class struggle from a ruling-class perspective:

> So any piece of property can be regarded as a tool enabling a man to live; and his property is an assemblage of such tools, including his slaves; and a slave, being a living creature like any other servant, is a tool worth many tools. For suppose that every tool we had could perform its function, either at our bidding or itself perceiving the need, like the statues made by Daedalus or the wheeled tripods of Hephaestus, of which the poet says that 'self-moved they enter the assembly of the gods'—and suppose that shuttles in a loom could fly to and fro and a plucker play on a lyre all self-moved, then manufacturers would have no need of workers nor masters of slaves.[2]

The various religio-philosophical ideas and class struggles of the Eastern Mediterranean merged into the formation of Christianity. Its founder, Jesus of Nazareth, greatly influenced by the Essenes, propounded a millenarian message in which the wealthy and powerful would be punished, while the poor and humble exalted. He also stressed brotherhood within the framework of socio-economic equality. Unable by historical circumstances to effect a secular revolution for equality, the most alienated of the masses would achieve it through the supernatural. While waiting for God's imminent utopia, the early Christian community at Jerusalem lived a life of communism by sharing all goods.

In the Middle Ages, a powerful Christian monastic tradition, based on poverty, chastity and obedience, partially preserved the early ideals of Christian sharing in this manner: The poverty aspect of monasticism permitted a certain social solidarity with the masses, and the notion of collective property to eliminate individual selfishness had an obvious connection to socialist views. That these patterns were potentially revolutionary in a world of sharp social distinctions was evident in the ideas of St.Francis of Assisi who was against all forms of property, private as well as collective, and urged members of his order to work with their hands as he did.

The Renaissance witnessed increased economic activity and the rise of such cities as Florence and Venice in which class warfare was common. In Florence, the *ciompi* or wool workers gained power for a brief period of time. In addition, the intellectual richness of the period is shown by Sir Thomas More's *Utopia*. A synthesis of Greek philosophy and the Judeo-Christian religious tradition, it depicted a communist society without wage labour and a general equality between men and women. More's vision reflected a progressive Renaissance spirit allowing for simple material comforts, religious toleration, and even democratic government. Even the sin of work was made pleasant since a six-hour day and variety of work were the norm.

The Protestant Reformation in the sixteenth century displaced Catholicism in much of Northern Europe: Although mainly led by the nobility and rising bourgeoisie, its millenarian/social protest side was not insignificant. The German Peasants' Revolt of 1524-25 (tied to Anabaptism) brought forth such a spokesperson as Thomas Müntzer, who called for a communist theocracy, a republic of virtue to replace the hateful rule of the wealthy. The Anabaptist tradition has had a great influence on later radical Protestant sects.

In the early seventeenth century, two well-known utopias appeared: *City of the Sun* by Tommaso Campanella and *Christianapolis* by Johann Andrea (the first author was an Italian monk, the second a German Lutheran and teacher). Both societies, like More's *Utopia*, had neither private property nor wage labour, but Andrea's retained the traditional nuclear family, while Campanella's discarded it. New innovations in these utopias stressed the importance of science and scientific education, but Andrea's also added integrated labour or the combination of manual and intellectual labour to reinforce equality. Politically, these utopias had various forms of democracy. Also, there was, as in More, a general equality among men and women.

It was in the seventeenth century that utopias introduced the absence of formal government in a communist setting. The English revolutionary period of the 1640s produced its fair share of socio-religious radicalism, primarily the Levellers, the Diggers, the Fifth Monarchy Men, and the Quakers. A visionary utopia of this period by the Digger, Gerrard Winstanley, *Law of Freedom*, combined communism with a minimal State. He was followed in the later part of the seventeenth century, by Gabriel de Foigny, a French cleric who wrote *A New Discovery of Terra Incognita Australis* where communism existed within no formal government; the populace met three times a year in local assemblies to discuss common problems.

The near roots of contemporary socialism are located in eighteenth century Enlightenment thought, then in the outbreak of the American and French Revolutions and the Industrial Revolution in England.

In the Enlightenment, equality was central to the social speculations of such proto-socialist luminaries as Morelly, Baron d'Holbach and William Godwin, and such egalitarian revolutionary democrats as Rousseau, Diderot, Thomas Paine and Thomas Jefferson. The most important social theorist of the period Jean-Jacques Rousseau is considered by many as the father of modern democracy and by extension a progenitor of modern socialism. Rousseau criticised the inequality of estate society and regarded private property as the root cause of social oppression. For him, not only was equality interwoven with liberty, but it was also the pre-condition for the general will of economically equal citizens democratically legislating. (Equality and democracy were also used interchangeably, for example, in Alexis de Tocqueville's *Democracy in America* (1835), which described a young and vibrant America.)

A cardinal event in the rise of modern socialism was the French Revolution of 1789. Although primarily a bourgeois one, it released such powerful democratic and egalitarian forces into the historical stream as democratic and quasi-egalitarian Jacobinism, championing the lower-middle class, and the precursors of libertarian and state socialism represented respectively by Jacques Roux and the Enragés, and Gracchus Babeuf and the Conspiracy of the Equals.[3]

The Industrial Revolution, which began in the middle of the eighteenth century in England, and its further development in the nineteenth century in other nations, solidified the rise of the bourgeoisie and marked the appearance of a large proletariat. The resulting class struggle brought forth such anarchists as Proudhon and Bakunin and the founders of Marxism, Marx and Engels.

Why the persistence of socialist utopia in history? For Grave, "anarchism is nothing more than the continuation of the eternal protest of the exploited and oppressed against the exploiters and oppressors."[4] For the German sociologist Karl Mannheim in *Ideology and Utopia*, utopia expresses the inner longings of the exploited masses for equality.[5] Despite a powerful "religion" of inequality so very fashionable among bourgeois ideologues, the utopian egalitarian spirit has persisted. As Herbert Marcuse stated in *Eros and Civilisation*, in the chapter "Phantasy and Utopia":

> Imagination envisions the reconciliation of the individual with the whole, of desire with realisation, of happiness with reason. While this harmony has been removed into utopia by the established reality principle, phantasy insists that it must and can become real, that behind the illusion lies *knowledge*.[6]

REVOLUTION AND UTOPIA

Notes

1. George Orwell, *Homage to Catalonia* (Boston: Beacon Press, 1962), p 104.
2. Aristotle, *The Politics*, translated and introduced by T. A. Sinclair (Baltimore MD: Penguin Books, 1962), p 31.
3. See the following works on the overview of utopia and the good society and other problems discussed: Martin A. Larson, *The Religion of the Occident* (Patterson, NJ: Littlefield, Adams, and Co., 1959). Erich Fromm, *The Dogma of Christ and Other Essays on Religion, Psychology and Culture* (Greenwich, CT: A Fawcett Premier Book, 1955). Erich Fromm, *Psychoanalysis and Religion* (New Haven: Yale Unversity Press, 1963). Norman Cohn, *The Pursuit of the Millennium: Revolutionary Messianism in Medieval and Reformation Europe and Its Bearing on Modern Totalitarian Movements* (New York: Harper Torchbooks, 1961). Christopher Hill, *The Century of Revolution, 1603-1714* (New York: W.W. Norton, 1961). Lewis Mumford, *The Story of Utopias* (Gloucester, MA: Peter Smith, 1959). Joyce Oramel Hertzier, *The History of Utopian Thought* (New York: Macmillen Co., 1923). Marie Louise Berneri, *Journey Through Utopia* (Boston: Beacon Press, 1950). Martin Buber, *Paths in Utopia* (Boston: Beacon Press, 1960). Glenn Negley and J. Max Patrick, *The Quest for Utopia: An Anthology of Imaginary Societies* (Garden City, NY: Doubleday Anchor Book, 1962). That socialist ideas were widespread in the Enlightenment is amply indicated by André Lichtenberger, *Le Socialisme au XVIII siécle* (Paris: Félix Alcan, 1895).
4. Grave, *L'Anarchie, son but, ses moyens*, p 70 recognized Morelly, Campanella, Babeuf, Fourier, and Buonarotti as precursors of socialism. The quotation is from Grave, *L'Anarchie, son but, ses moyens*, p 77.
5. For the persistence of utopia, see Karl Mannheim, *Ideology and Utopia: An Introduction to the Sociology of Knowledge*, trans. Louis Wirth and Edward Shils (New York: A Harvest Book, 1963), p 257: Utopia results from the longings of the exploited masses in a world where they are the "outsiders." Woodcock, *Anarchism*, pp 23-24, stated that most utopias (obviously those embodying authority) are repellent to anarchists.
6. Herbert Marcuse, *Eros and Civilization: A Philosophical Inquiry into Freud* (New York: Vintage Books, n.d. [copyrighted by Beacon Press, 1955]), p 130.

12

ROAD TO REVOLUTION

THE THEORETICAL VIEWS OF GRAVE AND anarchism in certain key areas—criticism of bourgeois society, revolution, and other related topics—are expanded upon here.

Grave's thought was greatly indebted to Proudhon, Bakunin, contemporary anarcho-communism (Kropotkin's and Elisée Reclus' influence is obvious), and to Marx(ism), especially in its view of the capitalist economic structure and primacy attached to class struggle. In fact, there were many similarities between anarcho-communism and Marxism and from a general theoretical perspective, the two were closely related. Grave himself was also familiar with past utopian and socialist thinkers, the Enlightenment *philosophes* (Diderot was his favourite), the English classical economists, history, sociology, economics, and literature. His erudition is reflected in such major works as *La Société au lendemain de la révolution* (1893); *La Société mourante et l'anarchie* (1893); *La Société future* (1895), *L'Individu et la société*; (1897), and *Réformes révolution* (1910).

In *La Société mourante et l'anarchie*, Grave postulated that anarchism's major struggle was against authority:

> Anarchy is the negation of authority. Authority, however, pretends to justify its existence by its necessary defence of existing social institutions, the family, religion, property, and so forth, and has created a complex of machinery to buttress its power and legitimacy. It has founded the law, the courts, legislative power, the executive, and so forth. In confronting this situation, anarchism should attack all social prejudice, examine in depth all human understanding, and finally demonstrate that its conceptions conform to the physiological

and psychological nature of man, while showing that the present social organisation, established contrary to all logic and good sense, has brought about unstable and revolutionary-prone societies from the accumulated hatred of those oppressed by its arbitrary institutions.[1]

This multifaceted concept not only encompassed oppressive economic, social, political and religious structures associated with class society, but also such concomitant cultural attitudes as patriotism and racism. Before examining authority in detail, we shall observe its relationship to scarcity and mutual aid.

Grave interlaced authority with the concept of scarcity, arguing that a parsimonious nature was an element in promoting social disharmony in certain constructs. (Scarcity was a factor in the social thought of many other thinkers, including Marx/Engels and Jean-Paul Sartre, noted libertarian Marxist and Existentialist.) This problem for Grave and Marxism was not as critical as class struggle in social development, although related.[2]

The underlying factor for the destruction of authority was mutual aid, a sociobiological concept developed by Kropotkin, embodying a force stronger than love, the need to cooperate for survival. In the evolution of animal life, he postulated that within species cooperation was more important than competition in the struggle for existence. As applied to the human condition, he saw mutual aid as its key element, but unfortunately weakened by the advent of civilisation and concomitant rise of class society and social oppression. In the present period the basic depository of mutual aid (although in vitiated form) resided in the working masses, while their rulers embodied authority through domination and exploitation. His hope was that the mutual-aid component in the life of workers and peasants would so succeed in strengthening itself that the class struggle would intensify to the point where it would lead to their victory over the ruling groups. For Grave, this too was the expectation.[3]

According to Grave, the present general historical tendency was propitious for achieving anarchism through mutual aid. The masses had ameliorated their position from slavery to serfdom to civil freedom with extensive political rights under capitalism which should aid mutual aid for anarchism. In fact, the progressive advance of mutual aid has now so weakened authority that it only continues with the consent of the people themselves.[4] From a practical perspective, mutual aid mandated that individuals worked together to liberate humanity from the chains of oppression. Grave's suggestions to combat state authority included evasion of military draft, refusal to pay taxes, joining unions and utopian colonies, and doing propaganda work, which also involved criticism of bourgeois ideologues.[5] An example of the last was his rejection of Malthus' thesis in *Essay on Population*, that the poor were responsible for their own misery; Grave saw this view as a shallow attempt to justify the status quo.[6]

For Grave, the strengthening of mutual aid would necessarily propel the revolution forward, In fact, this was necessary because the human personality needed freedom and equality; lacking them, it would not be at peace with itself, but engage in destructive individual and collective acts. Indeed, without the strengthening of mutual aid at the expense of authority, greater disasters would engulf humanity. This line of thought is reminiscent of Christian millenarianism in which a small minority (for the anarchists, a revolutionary elect; for the Christians, the pure remnant) knows the truth leading to the promised land.[7]

Grave's anthropological views should shed further light on the basic underlying assumptions of his thought. He postulated that humanity through evolution was progressing to a higher plane, in which as an active and creative agent it changed itself by altering its "conditions of life." At first, however, humanity was "more animal than human," signifying that its moral sense as yet was not fully developed. Early humans lived in associative groups of general equality, but competitive elements were stronger than those of solidarity. In time, as groups became larger, inequality arose from differences in strength and intelligence. Yet he mentioned that some tribes did not develop "authority," indicating that before the advent of civilisation there was equality and fraternity; this at a later stage of human development than the earlier one when humanity was "more like an animal."[8] In viewing early humanity as cooperative and competitive (the former element was dominant), he was aware of contradiction. In this schema, Grave synthesised the anthropological views of Bakunin and

Kropotkin: from the former, the competitive element, linking it to a deficient moral sense; from the latter, the importance of mutual aid.[9]

The rise of organised authority, presumably with civilisation, was related by Grave to the development of private property, the greatest bulwark of bourgeois society and the root cause of social inequality and misery. Like Proudhon, he regarded it as theft whose roots originated in early history when, as competition developed, the more ruthless were able to appropriate the labour of others.[10] To counter this crime, Grave advanced the following arguments. First, humans were basically equal in essential qualities and if differences existed in the matter of strength or intelligence, they were minimal.[11] Second, since it took eons to form the world's natural resources, they should be the equal birthright of all.[12] Third, because humanity was the recipient of the accumulated knowledge and achievements of past generations (present day technology and what has been built are thus a common heritage) and because there is more extensive labour division since the advent of large industry, making for ever greater interdependence in the processes of production, no one should profit from these realities; this despite the fact that some individuals are more intelligent than others.[13] These arguments of Grave (and Kropotkin) have both ethical and rational components.

The institution of private property itself spawned the state and its different arms (bureaucracies, court systems, police and armies, among others). The state itself was in the hands of elites, especially those controlling the larger segments of property (the bourgeoisie in the contemporary period) thus not an impartial umpire in class struggle. (This interpretation is also that of Marxism.) Indeed, the fall of the bourgeoisie would necessarily lead to the demise of the state.[14]

For Grave, religion completed the triad of authority: Anarchism, representing atheism, opposed religion's defending the master classes, rationalizing social oppression by admonishing the poor to accept their difficult lot in life for future reward, thus reinforcing their feelings of passivity. Following general anthropological views, Grave situated the origins of religion in human dependence on and fear of an incomprehensible nature and asserted that with increasing mastery of science, religion would disappear.

THE ANARCHISM OF JEAN GRAVE

In rejecting traditional religion, Grave replaced it with a humanistic anarchist philosophy, which accepted the finality of individual death, but which did not succumb to the despair of the life-is-absurd orientation. Life had its own validity without being tied to the supernatural. Indeed, every generation was of critical importance in the chain of life, both culturally and biologically.[15] (Grave is not entirely correct in viewing religion as a reactionary force. In the United States, for example, the Protestant Social Gospel was highly influenced by Walter Rauschenbusch, a fundamentalist and socialist).[16]

Grave's criticism of bourgeois society reached a fairly large audience. For instance, his most widely known work, *La Société mourante et l'anarchie* was translated into many languages, including English, as *The Dying Society and Anarchy*. In this and other works, he mentioned such obvious failings of present society as chronic unemployment, armaments races, war, colonialism and its corollary of racism, the parasitical military, civil and other bureaucracies, the deadening effects of extensive labour division reducing workers to be "machines of machines," the barbarous behaviour of governments toward the labour movement, and the general social misery of the people as contrasted to the opulence and privileges of the rulers. A fuller statement of the last: for the governors there are "joys and abundance," for the masses, "misery, privation and anomie."[17] In this cruel and pitiless world, irony and paradox dominated. Every advance in mechanical invention enriched the bourgeoisie at the expense of the proletariat whose insecurity and misery would increase by further unemployment. Labour itself was reduced to a mere commodity in the market place, the new arbiter of value.[18]

Before proceeding further, let us for the moment focus again on one of the most important malignancies of bourgeois society which Grave commented on, racism. Is it not of interest to note that in Grave's *La Société mourante et l'anarchie* there is a chapter entitled "There Are No Inferior Races." Perceptively, Grave linked Western racism to colonialist exploitation of subject people and added that those who talk of "inferior races" wish to justify the crimes of the "superior races."[19]

In a world of deep socio-economic division characterised by authority, a key concept to describe a basically limited and unfree human condition is "alienation," one that has been widely used in the last two centuries to explain humanity's tragic fate. Although many commentators use "alienation" to portray human awareness of finite existence, or the impossibility to approach the perfection and power of God, others use it to signify that one's full human potential is thwarted by an oppressive society. Certainly, when Rousseau in *Discourse on the Origins of Inequality* isolated the rise of private property as the cause of social oppression and general unhappiness, he was aware of the latter use of alienation. The brilliant German philosopher, Georg F.W. Hegel in various works (*The Phenomenology of the Mind*, for example) commented on the alienated human condition by contrasting the lord and slave. It was Marx, however, who in *Economic and Philosophical Manuscripts*, *Capital*, and other works, systematically related alienation to class oppression that inexorably pitted the proletariat against the bourgeoisie. He condemned capitalism for its alienating socioeconomic structures, dooming the worker to be a mere "machine" in the capitalist mechanism, while "the more value the worker creates the more worthless he becomes." Also, he added that work is often so mechanical and repetitive, so difficult and arduous that one "feels himself to be freely active only in his animal functions, eating, drinking, and procreating."[20]

Grave, no less than Marx, was aware of the many facets of alienation in describing workers as "machines of machines,"[21] who laboured on an increasingly sophisticated technology under capitalist control, which was at once characterised by the twin tendencies of greater labour division and more unemployment.[22] That this alienation is an inherent part of bourgeois ideology is apparent as bourgeois political economists from Smith in the eighteenth century to Keynes in the twentieth have regarded the worker as largely a mere factor in the cost of production, like a commodity. Grave was not opposed to modern technology, but insisted that it not be used by one segment of the community to exploit the other.[23] In Grave's literary work, alienation is the norm, the example of Caragut in *La Grande famille* the most obvious. To summarise: Both Grave and Marx advocated that to end alienation, the present bourgeois society should be replaced by a socialist one of free, equal and creative individuals.[24]

Before exploring in greater detail Grave's views of the class struggle and revolution, in which he rejected voting and reform, a brief historical background is needed. Grave was in the vanguard of a Parisian working class whose revolutionary experiences in 1789-94, 1830, 1848 and 1871 led it increasingly to prefer class struggle and revolution to fickle and uncertain social reform as portrayed by the representative parliamentarism of the Third Republic. Grave's antipathy to this republic was based on its domination by conservative bourgeois and aristocratic elites, which not only played the leading role in destroying the Paris Commune of 1871, but which opposed basic social reform—the farmers and workers, comprising more than eighty percent of the people, carried the heavy burden of sustaining the privileged groups. Because of these circumstances, social compromise was impossible. For him, therefore, only by waging an incessant class struggle could the working class, including independent artisans, with the aid of the peasantry, be able to overthrow the bourgeois and aristocratic oligarchy.

For Grave, following Bakunin and Marx, the class struggle was the principal historical engine to overcome the power of the ruling classes, in the Middle Ages between the serfs and nobility, while after the industrial revolution, between the bourgeoisie and workers: it occurred at once in the economic, social, political and cultural spheres, but the economic one dominated the others because any dislocation in this area would exacerbate tensions in the others.[25]

The importance that Grave attached to the economic aspect resided in the fact that capitalism made for a state of economic interdependence in which any breakdown adversely affected its entire mechanism. Class antagonism was sharpened by economic crises thus: Ever motivated by profit, capitalism had an inherent tendency to increase the use of labour-saving machinery to relatively depress wages and increase unemployment; even the use of colonies as outlets for goods could not for long delay this progression. Succeeding depressions would eliminate small enterprise, until finally the few wealthy capitalists would be overthrown by the proletarianised majority to inaugurate socialism.[26]

In Grave's revolutionary model, the spearhead of the industrial workers would be aided by the majority of the peasantry. For Grave and other anarchists, the revolutionary potential of most of the peasantry resided in their being part of the exploited masses. Indeed, the anarchist program for the peasantry allowed for ownership of land directly used, although the ideal was to have voluntary collectivisation.[27]

Grave also held that in the relationship between masses and leadership to effect revolution, the first element was more important, but the second was also essential in providing necessary direction.[28] In disdaining formal organisation, Grave envisaged leadership in his Bakuninist phase in the form of small, clandestine groups committing propaganda by deed, while in his reformist-revolutionary phase, he counselled militants to concentrate on education and propaganda. For Marx, however, the leaders of the workers' party would direct the revolution.[29]

In the actual revolutionary change, some fighting would occur between the revolutionaries and the bourgeoisie because Grave generally did not believe that any ruling class would voluntarily relinquish its privileges. Once in motion, the revolution would rapidly destroy state authority and its various appendages (the military, civil administration, and exploitative private property) within months.[30]

Grave, well aware of the international implications of a proletarian-led revolution in France, replayed the model of the French Revolution, expecting foreign-government intervention, but hoping it would spark revolution throughout the world.[31]

The Gravian model of imminent revolution regarded reform as inefficacious, as a dampening influence on the revolutionary temper of the people,[32] but at about 1900, it cautiously superimposed a layer of reformism on it, which over the years became significant. In agreement with many other socialists, including Marxists, Grave finally realised that capitalism would endure for a lengthy period of time since the expected revolution did not materialise, based on the basic apathy of the people themselves, who in large measure still supported the aspirations and assumptions of capitalism, and their habits of subservience imposed by economic insecurity. It was, however, still possible to effect piecemeal reform by the majority for pressing socio-economic needs. He postulated that although most people were literally ignorant as to the basic causes of social oppression, they could well understand the need for urgent and specific reform.[33]

With the postponement of revolution, what were Grave's views on the possible peaceful transition from capitalism to anarchism? He was acquainted with, but largely rejected, the Proudhonian mutualist vision which theorised a long period of evolutionary change from capitalism to anarchism through cooperatives, a basic difference between mutualists and anarcho-communists. Although Grave admitted that producer cooperatives might bring about economic amelioration, he was fearful that capitalist influences within them, especially the profit motive, might intensify with economic success. Thus, he was not overly sanguine that sections of the proletariat could resist the temptations of *embourgeoisement*. This view had affinity to Lenin's thesis (later modified) that proletarian consciousness did not go much beyond union activity. As for consumer cooperatives, in a more optimistic vein, he saw their educating workers to defend their purchasing power, but remained cautious, opining that they should always be motivated by ideals of anarchism. In this analysis, he was not dogmatic, and even saw the remote possibility of producer cooperatives becoming important institutions to achieve anarchism.[34]

Even after Grave became a "reformist," he did not see reform as an end in itself, but as a necessary and integral part of the revolutionary spirit that continued to operate even within the confines of democratic political structures. On, for example, the most significant political reform in nineteenth-century Europe, universal male suffrage, he envisioned it, on the one hand, as a delaying tactic of the status quo to deflect popular discontent, but, on the other hand, admitted to its usefulness as a mechanism for further reform, which at a critical juncture might lead to revolution. In fact, in *La Société future*, he argued that it was perfectly possible for social tensions to intensify from greater social equality through reform, a pattern analogous to that in de Toqueville's *Democracy in America*. In general, he still feared that while reform could expand both liberty and the general welfare, it also contained the seeds to further pacify the people by instilling a false consciousness with respect to the authoritarian nature of capitalism. This view is analogous to Marcuse's distinction between the "repressive tolerance" of democratic and class-ridden societies and the genuine tolerance of those based on equality. Ultimately, Grave's ambivalence to reform indicated his unrelenting hope for imminent revolution; in this vein, he was still, for example, against voting.[35]

Although Grave accepted the importance of reform, he partially rejected Proudhon's insistence in De la capacité politique des classes ouvrières for the proletariat to establish both a countersociety through cooperatives and a counterculture through newspapers and other informational organs to do battle with the bourgeoisie. He downplayed Proudhonian countersociety, but actively engaged in the counterculture aspect through his newspaper work, theoretical speculations and in participating to establish an anarchist school for children. Grave's interest in the formation of a proletarian counterculture has its counterpart in the Communist movement: Antonio Gramsci, one of the founders of the Italian Communist Party and principal inspirer of Euro-Communism, advocated the creation of such mass proletarian institutions as workers' councils and the establishment of popularly based Communist parties to engage the bourgeoisie in a protracted war of position by challenging their cultural hegemony.[36]

For Grave, sooner or later, the revolution would still erupt: At a certain critical juncture of events, involving economic and other related crises (similar to the imminent revolutionary model), the workers would overthrow the bourgeoisie for socialism.[37] But since he had allowed for a lengthy period of reform before revolution, which presumably would have mitigated social hatreds, revolutionary violence might be minimal.[38]

From a general perspective on the immediacy of revolution, Grave and anarcho-communism were more hopeful than Marxists and other socialists of the Second International. By the 1880s and 90s, Western European Marxists had basically rejected revolution for reformist politics, while Grave and his comrades maintained their purist revolutionary stance through electoral abstention. When the expected revolution, however, did not occur, Grave became pessimistic and predicted in La Société future that it was generations away.[39]

The question arises why anarcho-communists like Grave were more revolutionary than the Marxists in such parties as the German Social Democratic Party and the French Unified Socialist Party? Individual temperament in a given sociohistorical environment undoubtedly played a role; the anarchists tended to be more idealistic and thus not willing to compromise. Grave, for example, as has been noted, may be regarded, at least during his younger years, as a "true believer." There is usually enough dissatisfaction in most societies that individuals like Grave are not unknown.[40] At any rate this very utopianism and talk of revolution, added to the terrorism and crime of a few anarchists, led an Italian criminologist at the turn of the last century, Cesare Lombroso, to characterise anarchists as belonging to the criminal type, thus their revolutionary bent.[41] How silly!

Although few in number, anarchists were more politically conscious and active than their counterparts in the other socialist groups, allowing for the widespread dissemination of their ideas. They were concentrated in urban areas and were in many occupations, although, as one commentator stated, often in those where one could often talk. A *Le Matin* article in 1894, partly based on a police report, had about five hundred anarchists in Paris in the early 1890s. Leading occupations and numbers included 10 journalists, 25 typographers, 17 tailors, 16 shoemakers, 15 mechanics, 12 hairdressers and barbers, 15 cabinetmakers, 10 bricklayers, 3 grocers, an architect, and an insurance agent. The same article estimated eight thousand anarchists in France of whom twenty-five hundred were in the Paris area, two thousand in Lyons, and a thousand in Marseilles. Jean Maitron, undoubtedly the foremost authority on French anarchism, was much more conservative as to their number during the nineties: He calculated that there were only a thousand active anarchists concentrated in about forty or so groups, supported by an inactive element of between five to ten thousand; and, if there were an anarchist party, it might have received a hundred thousand votes. Grave's *Mouvement Libertaire* was very optimistic in estimating twenty thousand French anarchists in 1914.[42]

A brief postscript on Grave's later thought in which one can find a few aberrations. To begin, he rejected the concept of class:

> Classes no longer exist. There are only people, many of whom are not capitalists, who in trying to survive do so very well in the society of today. Some, who live very poorly, nevertheless defend existing society. Others, who do not know any better, support it. Then, there is a group that wishes to do away with capitalism: it includes some members of the bourgeoisie.[43]

Too, Grave's reformism became more pronounced. Change would come basically in piecemeal fashion in which shifting groups would temporarily merge to support specific reforms. Indeed, because society had made progress, advancing from slavery to serfdom to political freedom, the possibility of continued reform might occur without cataclysm. Thus, Grave emphasized the importance of speech and press freedoms to ensure this.[44] To be sure, anarchists, as conscious minority, would have their usual important role as advocates for the ideals of humanism.[45]

As for organisation, Grave continued to unalterably oppose it: Although association was normal for humans, as they were social animals, once they admitted any formal organisation, like Sisyphus, they would be doomed to climb forever the mountain of authority. Therefore, he still condemned the syndicalist position that society be organised through unions.[46] As for anarchism's future, he hoped that it would remain receptive to the exigencies and demands of a changing world.[47]

Notes
1. Grave, *La Société mourante* pp 1-2. Octave Mirbeau's Preface hailed the work as a "masterpiece of logic full of enlightenment."
2. Cf *ibid*, pp 39-48, concerning scarcity, technology, and class oppression with the generally similar views of Jean Paul Sartre, *Critique de la raison dialectique* (Paris: Gallimard,1960), I, 200ff, and Marx, *Capital*, 1, 91-92.
3. On mutual aid, see Jehan Le Vagre [Jean Grave], *La Révolution et l'autonomie selon la science* (Paris: A. Bataille, 1885), pp 5-11. The key work on mutual aid is by Peter Kropotkin, *Mutual Aid: A Factor in Evolution* (New York: Alfred A. Knopf, 1919), pp 1-10 are especially interesting.
4. Grave, *L'Anarchie: son but, ses moyens*, p 11ff. On the historical tendency comments, see Jean Grave, "Il n'y a pas plus de raison de se décourager que de s'illusioner," *Publications*, No. 28 (August 10, 1924), pp 4-14.
5. Grave, *L'Anarchie: son but, ses moyens*, pp 207-08; Grave, *La Société mourante*, pp 45-71; and Karl Marx, *Theses on Feurbach* in Lewis S. Feuer, ed., *Marx and Engels: Basic Writings in Politics and Philosophy* (Garden City, NY: Anchor Books, 1959), pp 243-45.
6. Grave, *La Société future*, pp 19-20 and 46-49. Jean Grave, *Les Scientifiques* (Paris: Les Temps Nouveaux, 1913), pp 2ff.
7. Cf Grave, *L'Anarchie: son but, ses moyens*, pp 11-12, 17-'8 and Grave, *L'Individu et la société*, pp 145-71 with Norman Cohen, *The Pursuit of the Millennium: Revolutionary Messianism in Medieval and Reformation Europe and Its Bearing on Modern Totalitarian Movements*, pp 272-306.
8. Grave, *L'Individu et la société*, pp 23-25.

9. Grave, *La Société mourante*, pp 44-47; Grave, *L'Individu et la société*, pp 23-25; Maximoff, *Bakunin*, p 94.
10. Grave, *La Société mourante*, pp 49ff. Other who regarded private property as the root cause of social misery, for example, are Rousseau and Winstanley.
11. *Ibid.*, p 51 and 58.
12. *Ibid.*, pp 50-51.
13. Grave, *L'Anarchie: son but, ses moyens*, p 7 and p11.
14. Cf Grave, *La Société mourante*, pp 83ff and his *Réformes, révolution*, p 44 with Frederick Engels, *Socialism: Utopian and Scientific* (New York: International Publishers, 1935), pp 69ff. Both saw the state under bourgeois control.
15. On Grave and religion, see his *La Société mourante*, pp 43-44, 51; *L'Individu et la société*, pp 50-53, 260-74; *L'Anarchie: son but, ses moyens*, p 19. Erich Fromm, *Psychoanalysis and Religion*, pp 21ff stated that Christianity developed authoritarian attitudes when it became a state religion; obedience and submission are the hallmarks of this authoritarianism. Also, the teachings and life of Christ are seen as essentially humanistic, wherein "joy" not "sorrow" or "guilt" is stressed. Erich Fromm, *Escape from Freedom* (New York: Farrar and Rinehart, 1941), pp 10ff posits that Calvinistic predestination, which emphasizes man's wickedness, is basically authoritarian.
16. See, for example, Walter Rauschenbusch, *Christianity and the Social Crisis* (New York: Macmillan, 1914), pp 44-142.
17. Cf Grave, *L'Anarchie: son but, ses moyens*, pp 11-12 with Thorstein Veblen, *The Theory of the Leisure Class: An Economic Study of Institutions*, intro. C. Wright Mills (New York: A Mentor Book, 1957), pp 21ff—both see that power and wealth are exalted at the expense of poverty, weakness, and virtue.
18. Grave, *La Société mourante*, pp 56-59 and 126ff.
19. *Ibid.*, pp 183-97. On Gobineau, Chamberlain and the linkage of racism with slavery and imperialism, see Georg Lukacs, *La Destruction de la raison* (2 volumes, Paris: L'Arche, 1958), II, 233-74. Elisée Reclus was another pioneer in attacking racism—Fleming, *The Anarchist Way*, pp 48-50.
20. Erich Fromm, *Marx's Concept of Man: With a Translation from Marx's Economic and Philosophical Manuscripts*, by T. B. Bottomore (New York: Frederick Ungar, 1961), pp 93ff. The first manuscript titled *Alienated Labor*, pp 93-109 states that the worker, considered as a commodity of production under capitalism, despised his work for that very reason. The quotations are on page 97. On Hegel's progressive thought, see Jacques d'Hondt, *Hegel et son temps* (Paris: Editions Sociales, 1968). Also, see Erich Fromm (ed.), *Socialist Humanism: An International Symposium* (Garden City, NY: Anchor Books, 1966), Part III: "On Alienation."
21. Cf Marx, *Alienated Labor* in Fromm's *Marx's Concept of Man* with Grave's *La Société au lendemain de la révolution*, p 113 in which the worker is seen as essentially being a robot.
22. See Grave, *La Société au lendemain de la révolution*, pp 108ff, and Grave, *L'Anarchie: son but ses moyens*, pp 11ff and p 70.
23. Grave, *La Société au lendemain de la révolution*, p 113.

24. On Marx's basic egalitarianism, see Karl Marx, *Critique of the Gotha Programme: With Appendices by Marx, Engels, and Lenin*, ed. by C. P. Dutt (New York: International Publishers, 1938), pp 8ff and V.I. Lenin, *State and Revolution* (New York: International Publishers, 1932), pp 35ff.

25. On Gravian determinism (there are certain social "laws"), see Grave, *L'Anarchie: son but, ses moyens*, p 116. Grave's use of the term "people" indicated its broad nature, *ibid.*, p 139. On the general historical pattern discussed, see Grave, *La Société future*, pp 21-24.

26. Cf the revolutionary pattern of Karl Marx and Friedrich Engels, *Manifesto of the Communist Party* (New York: International Publishers, 1948), pp 9-21, with Grave, *La Société mourante*, pp 269ff and Grave, *L'Individu et la société*, pp 226-27 and pp 295-96. For a similar anarchist view, see Pierre Kropotkine, *L'Action anarchists dans la révolution* (Paris: Les Temps Nouveaux, 1914), pp 2ff. Fleming, *The Anarchist Way*, pp 187-93 saw the Marxian connection in Elisée Reclus' revolutionary pattern.

27. On Grave and the peasantry, see Grave *L'Anarchie: son but, ses moyens*, pp 307-24. Also, see Elisée Reclus, *A Mon frère le paysan* (Amiens: Editions de Germinal, 1905), pp 1-8; and Errico Malatesta, *Entre paysans* (Paris: Les Temps Nouveaux, 1901), pp 1-32. All three authors have similar views.

28. Grave, *L'Anarchie: son but, ses moyens*, p 37 and pp 193ff. Peter Kropotkin, *The Great French Revolution, 1789-1793* (New York: G. P. Putnam's Sons, 1909), pp 11-15 insisted that mass movements make revolution. On Marx and revolution by the masses, see Michael Harrington, *Socialism* (New York: Saturday Review Press, 1972), pp 36ff.

29. On the role of a conscious revolutionary elite, see Jean Grave, *L'Entente pour l'action* (Paris: Les Temps Nouveaux, 1911), pp 11ff; Grave, *Réformes, révolution*, p 86; Grave, *L'Individu et la société*, pp 250ff; and Marx and Engels, *Manifesto of the Communist Party*, p 19.

30. Grave, *La Société future*, p 207; Grave, *La Société au lendemain de la révolution*, pp 14ff. On p 35, Grave even envisaged a transitory period (he does not specify the time frame) after the revolution in which anarchists do not hold power—probably other socialists hold it.

31. Grave, *L'Anarchie: son but, ses moyens*, p 14, pp 202-03. Grave, *La Société au lendemain de la révolution*, pp 14ff.

32. On Grave's advocacy of immediate revolution, see Grave, *L'Anarchie: son but, ses moyens* (1899), pp 107ff. For a Gravian blast against reformism, see Jean Grave, *Si J'avais à parler aux électeurs* (Paris: Les Temps Nouveaux, 1911), p 3.

33. Cf the Grave for immediate revolution in *L'Anarchie: son but, ses moyens* (1899), pp 107ff with the more patient one in *Réformes, révolution* (1910), p 40. There was not any exact year with reference to this change; for example, in *La Société future* (1895), pp 1-5, revolution would take generations. Generally, after 1900, Grave was more patient with respect to revolution. On the ignorance of the people as to the cause of their social misery, see Jean Grave, *La Panacée-Révolution* (Paris: Les Temps Nouveaux, 1898), p 14.

34. On Grave and cooperatives, see *Réformes, révolution*, pp 145-62; and A. D. Bancel, *Le Coopératisme devant les écoles sociales*, Préface Jean Grave (Paris: Bibliothèque Artistique et Littéraire, 1897), pp i-iii. On Lenin's ideas concerning the tendency of workers to stay at the stage of mere union activity, see Thomas H. Hammond, *Lenin on Trade Unions and Revolution, 1893-1917* (New York: Columbia University Press, 1957), pp 17ff.

35. On pacification of the masses, see Grave, *L'Anarchie: son but; ses moyens*, p 136. Grave's view that social tensions increase with the approach of equality in *La Société future*, pp 1-5 is similar to that of Alexis de Tocqueville, *Republic of the United States of America and Its Political Institutions*, trans. Henry Reeves (2 vols. in 1; New York: A. S. Barnes, 1867), I, 9. This work is more well known as *Democracy in America*. Herbert Marcuse, "Repressive Tolerance" in Robert Paul Wolff, Barrington Moore Jr., and Herbert Marcuse, *A Critique of Pure Tolerance* (Boston: Beacon Press, 1965), pp 81-123.

36. Pierre-Joseph Proudhon, *De la Capacité politique des classes ouvrières* (Paris: Marcel Rivière, 1924). On Gramsci's life and ideas, see Guiseppe Fiori, *Antonio Gramsci: Life of a Revolutionary* (New York: Dutton, 1971). Also, see Quinton Hoare and Geoffrey Nowell Smith (editors and translators), *Selections from the Prison Notebooks of Antonio Gramsci* (New York: International Publishers, 1971), pp 228-45 on the great resiliency of Western capitalism which necessitated that revolutionaries adopt a more patient stance.

37. For an example of revolutionary violence, see Grave, *La Société au lendemain de la révolution*, p 18. On peaceful transition to socialism in Marx and Engels, see George Lichtheim, *Europe in the Twentieth Century*, (New York: Praeger, 1972), p 139.

38. This is implied in Grave's work during the last twenty years of his life. More on this later.

39. Grave, *La Société future*, pp 1-5.

40. On the mind set of the revolutionary believer and the socioeconomic background, see Eric Hofer, *The True Believer: Thoughts on the Nature of Mass Movements* (New York: A Mentor Book, 1958), pp 51ff. Cohn, *The Pursuit of the Millennium*, pp 307-19. André Malraux's *La Condition humaine* (Paris: Gallimard, 1946) has an excellent example of the revolutionary fanatic, Tchen.

41. Cesare Lombroso, *Les Anarchistes* (Paris: Flammarion, 1896), pp 59ff saw anarchists as belonging to the criminal type.

42. *Le Matin*, "Contré l'anarchie," March 5, and 9, 1894; *HMA*, pp 115-24 and 432, *Mouvement libertaire*, p 287.

43. On Grave's attack, on *Capital*, see his "Le Capital de Karl Marx," *Publications*, No. 24 (Dec. 25, 1923), pp 8-15; and, "A Travers nos lectures," *ibid.*, No. 28 (Aug. 10, 1924), pp 15-16 on Marx. The quotation in the text is from p 15 of the first citation.

44. That peaceful reform may replace revolution to achieve anarchism, see Grave, *Publications*, No. 7 (1921); pp 4-11.

45. *Ibid.*

46. AM, letter, Grave to Nettlau, July 24, 1934. Jean Grave, "Un monde qui ne différerait guère de l'autre," *Publications*, No. 90 (Dec., 1934), pp 3-6.

47. Jean Grave, "A propos d'une ânerie," *ibid.*, No. 54 (June 20, 1928), pp 3-6.

13

UTOPIA

THIS SECTION IS ON GRAVE'S UTOPIAN VIEWS. The first part explores differences between Grave and Marxists after a socialist revolution has been achieved; the second details Grave's specific plan for utopia; and the third involves critical views with respect to anarchist utopian conceptions.

It was only after a socialist revolution that Marxists (and Marxist-Leninists) developed theoretical differences with Grave and other anarchists concerning the state and related problems. Their respective outlooks, however, were not too dissimilar. The Marxists, while ultimately calling for the destruction of the state, insisted that it would still be necessary for a rather lengthy period of time in the first phase of communism or "socialism" under the "dictatorship of the proletariat." First, in order to meet the threat of possible bourgeois counterrevolution, the workers had to control the state apparatus with its centralised power of coercion. Second, the state itself was an expression that not all economic and social contradictions could be immediately resolved. A significant contradiction in this respect involved manual as opposed to mental labour, the former less valued than the latter. For Marxists this reflected the fact that the present technology was of such nature that a division of labour and consequent economic inequality were necessary.[1] Thus, large industry and resulting hierarchy would continue. The state itself would wither away only under "communism," the second and final stage, in which technological and social development (including the advent of integrated labour) would allow for the necessary elevated productive levels to resolve vexing contradictions.[2]

THE ANARCHISM OF JEAN GRAVE

However, even in the first phase ("socialism") there was a strong Marxian affinity to anarchist outlook. Marx's *The Civil War in France* (1871) favoured such "anarchist" views as the armed people, the importance of the local commune with respect to the national government of only limited functions, basic equality between the people and their representatives (delegates would be elected by universal suffrage, earn average workers' wages, and be subject to immediate recall), and rejection of parliamentary democracy (the delegates to the various assemblies were limited in their actions by the specific instructions of their constituents).[3] It must be emphasised that for Marx, even in the first phase of communism or "socialism," economic inequality, even if existent, would not be of major proportions. Lenin, in *State and Revolution*, written just before the Bolshevik Revolution of November 1917, accurately reflecting the egalitarian mood of the masses,[4] followed these principles of Marx, endorsing basic wage equality and popular participation in managing society.[5] Specifically, he saw that the functions of officials and managers could be performed by anyone with an average education,[6] thus indicating optimism in resolving the inequality inherent in the dichotomy between manual and mental labour. In War Communism's exultant earliest period, the participatory democracy sketched by Lenin was pervasive. It reflected the Bolshevik slogan of "All power to the Soviets", to the local spontaneously created committees of workers, farmers and military. Workers, for example, ran the factories through local democratically elected committees. It is obvious that Bolshevik stress on participatory democracy well fitted their egalitarianism. Not surprisingly, George Lichtheim, a brilliant mid-twentieth-century observer of socialism, commented on Lenin's "quasi-anarchist pronouncements in 1917."[7] Soon afterward Communism became authoritarian.

Grave and the anarchists, in contradistinction to the views of Marx and Lenin, would destroy all governmental authority in the revolutionary overturn. This included the disbanding of any centralised revolutionary elite that might conceivably transform itself into a new government. But Grave did not posit the end to all authority. Thus, from a broad socialist perspective the state in some form remained. For example, the possibility of a bourgeois counterrevolution was not discounted, but local communes would confront it.⁸ As for the gap between manual and mental labour, it would be quickly eliminated through the expansion of mutual aid. Thus, on equality, Grave was certainly more sanguine than Marx for its rapid achievement.⁹

This is not to imply that Grave was pollyanish on the human condition once the revolution was achieved. He admitted that it would certainly take time to eradicate all of the antisocial tendencies engendered by a class society that existed for millenia. In this respect he recognised the preoccupation of the people for a "better" life, fearing that once anarchism assumed power, without a rise in living standards, a popular backlash might develop against it.¹⁰

Grave's views on anarcho-communist utopia are scattered throughout his writings, but we shall delve into the works especially concerned with this problem: *La Société future*, *La Société au lendemain de la révolution*, and *Terre Libre* (his utopian novel). In addition, works of Kropotkin especially will be examined.

For Grave, anarchism embodied free and co-operative individuals living in an egalitarian environment devoid of any authority associated with hierarchy in such institutions as government, private capital and religion,¹¹ the antithesis of the Liberal view of legally free but economically and socially stratified individuals locked in competition. There was a social contract, so to speak, that united the individual to the general community, the universality of mutual aid, which anarchists would defend by arms if necessary.¹² In the event of civil war, would not anarchism, however, inevitably need organisation and consequent hierarchy in order to defend itself? Perhaps, but one must not discount the various anarchist safeguards that would make hierarchy difficult in the long run, like absence of wage labour, general equality and participatory democracy.

Individual initiative in the form of "free agreement" and free association characterised the contractual nature of Grave's utopia: industrial, agricultural and other associations would be engaged in multifarious activities devoid of all normal authoritarian patterns. The various economic units would be under worker control, Proudhonian self- management being one of the cornerstones of Grave's thought.

THE ANARCHISM OF JEAN GRAVE

There were, of course, certain standards in the associations that, if not met, could provoke conflict between the individual and the group. This was considered as possible in rare instances, with the group having the right to dissociate itself from the individual. Grave did not consider this authoritarian, but simply as inherent in the human condition. The only prohibition involved in economic activity was that of exploiting another's labour lest capitalism and concomitant inequality return.[13] Exploitation under the rubric of "freedom" is inherent in the capitalist, not socialist, conception of liberty. The industrial and other economic associations would be subject to political control. Against anarcho-syndicalism, Grave approached the social construct from a broadly politico-cultural outlook by having anarchism's "political" units dominate economic activity.

The basic "political" units for Grave's anarcho-communism are the communes of a generally limited number of people within a confined geographical area, that federate nationally and internationally. Grave saw ties between the various political levels as informal, cemented by fraternity. Meetings between the different levels would coordinate economic and other activities. General community problems would be handled by local initiative, all having responsibility, including various committees occupied with particular suggestions, and general periodic commune meetings.

An example given by Grave of decision-making was a projected railroad line. To be sure, it would be discussed in various committees and meetings. If differences occurred as to its feasibility or which route was the most suitable, the problem was decided by majority vote. In intertwining the economic and political (reconciling the particular economic needs of the various production associations) spheres in the communes and in the federation of communes, anarcho-communism blunts and diffuses economic conflict. (This may be exacerbated under the anarcho-syndicalist political structure whose economic associations are the nuclei of the political structure.)

Grave's utopianism, as may be readily observed, envisaged a certain degree of conflict as he accepted the fact that not all social contradictions would be immediately resolved, and he tolerated voting! Indeed, he envisioned a lengthy transitional period before the complete attainment of human solidarity. There is, however, no organised state to force a Procrustean uniformity or conformity. That Grave's decision-making process, for example, involves disagreement is axiomatic, but it is of a different proportion from that of a society based on deep inequalities. Thus, the majority vote of an anarchist society is qualitatively different from that of a bourgeois one. Indeed, the general tendency of anarchism is toward a society in which social interaction rests on communication, devoid of authority and conflict, based on social harmony.[14]

Any modern society demands some regulation between production and consumption. Grave did not neglect this problem for he would have statisticians gather information which would then be used to make adjustments. Although he did not give any details about the various levels of the statistical centres, it is reasonable to assume that they were operative in the associations themselves and in the various "political" units. He basically conceived of economic need from the perspective of consumption in which personal needs and desires determined production. This demanded that society respect individual autonomy regarding needs and not try to manipulate it, that central planning for consumption with its authoritarian aspects be avoided.[15]

Industrial organisation was a major concern for Grave. The technology which they would use for the good society was that of their time since they were not usually science-fiction writers. In stressing small and decentralised industry, both would employ integrated labour as much as possible, and consciously utilise the newer scientific technologies like electricity. Indeed, for Grave, this new pattern would replace dull and repetitive work with one that was "recreational," based "on justice and equality." In his *Terre Libre*, a cornucopia of goods was produced by a technology featuring miniaturisation and decentralisation based on integrated labour.[16]

In proposing the general end of labour division, anarchists would not penalise gifted individuals. Indeed, in a society having a much higher cultural level than the present, in which the variety of work inevitably stimulated mental and artistic impulses, there would necessarily be much more rapport between genius and society. Intelligence, however, would not have superior consideration in exploiting others.[17]

THE ANARCHISM OF JEAN GRAVE

Along with general work equality, Grave and other anarchists would immediately abolish the wage system, a bourgeois remnant that demeaned human dignity, distribution made on the basis of need. Even the practical Bertrand Russell in *Roads to Freedom* envisaged the possibility of anarchist free-sharing of basic goods.[18] Grave, however, permitted more interplay concerning personal consumption as he accepted the fact that in a society (as his contemporary one) in which the forces of production did not satisfy all needs, additional individual effort could provide them.[19]

Although small industry would prevail for Grave and Kropotkin, exceptions were recognised. For example, Grave had large-scale manufacturing in the steel industry. Of course, one may ask, who would be condemned to work there? Grave did not answer this question. A possible solution suggested by Russell is less hours of work. Another was for everyone to share in varying degree the dull, repetitive work, which, in any case, under anarchism would be minimal since production of useless commodities for status would be unthinkable. Another, proposed by Murray Bookchin, a leading contemporary American libertarian, was to use technology to design means to liberate humankind from irksome labour. Once, however, one allows for large-scale industry and trade within and between nations, will not co-ordination and hierarchy become inevitable and thus ultimately bring back inequality? Anarchists reply that the prevalence of integrated labour, participatory democracy, and a four-to-five-hour workday should prevent the rise of a bureaucratic class and consequent inequality.[20] Indeed, from the perspective of today's technology, it is feasible to have large-scale co-ordination, under participatory democracy, as envisaged by traditional anarcho-communism. This distinct possibility is contemplated by Bookchin in *Post-Scarcity Anarchism*, through a "humanistic balance...between autarky, industrial confederation, and a national division of labour."[21]

The final problem of Grave's ideal society involves women. Grave was an ardent advocate of equality between the sexes. He was a traditionalist, however, in the area of marriage, which he viewed as a normal arrangement, but which could be expeditiously terminated for incompatibility. As for the traditional inferior social position of women, he proposed physiological and social reasons: women possessed less strength than men and during childbearing were in a normally dependent state. To these factors, he added the rise of private property and consequent rise of social inequality that deformed relationships within the family. Despite women's inferior position, he opined that wealthy women have already emancipated themselves, thus implying that women in the proletariat, reflecting its economic slavery, were still in chains. Once free, he thought that the female personality would change from one of deviousness and subservience to one of frankness. Indeed, with social equality, crimes of passion would progressively diminish since they were engendered by the hypocrisy and duplicity inherent in the present unequal arrangements.[22]

Grave's views on the good society were similar to those of his friends. Kropotkin, for example, stated that an anarcho-communist society had:

> To establish a certain harmonious compatibility...not by subjecting the individual to authority...not in trying to establish uniformity, but in calling for the free development, free initiative, free action, and free association of all people.[23]

For Malatesta, the essential task of anarchism was to bring about "a society of free and equal individuals based on the harmony of interests and on the voluntary will of all for the satisfaction of social needs."[24] Elisée Reclus agreed by calling for the creation of a society which before was only conceivable in literature, in such works as *The City of the Sun*, where "there are neither masters nor official upholders of public morals...neither rich nor poor, in which all will have equal rights and live in brotherhood."[25]

The utopian views of Grave, Kropotkin, and other anarchists, in conjunction with those of libertarian Marxism, are important in contemporary social philosophy. A prime example of this was the thought of Herbert Marcuse (1898-1979), a leading neo-Marxist philosopher and a guru of the New Left in America, who interpreted Marx in the only authentically possible manner—as a critic of contemporary class society, both Soviet and Western, and by maintaining Marx's vision of a classless and stateless society of free and creative individuals.[26]

Marcuse, like Bookchin, held that in the technologically advanced capitalist nations (the United States is the prime example), it was now possible to have the necessary level of productive forces to ensure a communist/stateless society. He would end an exploitative, hierarchical (one driven by an almost endless labour division), polluting, imperialistic (Vietnam was one of his examples), totalitarian-democratic society whose facade of freedom hides an inherent authoritarianism employed by a parasitical capitalist elite.[27] He saw, however, that, especially in the United States, this change would not soon occur because its proletariat, although in a dependent position, largely favoured the status quo as it was basically integrated into the society. For Marcuse, the new technological society veiled its authoritarian nature thus: (1) It produced material abundance for much of the workforce. (2) It masked capitalist exploitation by virtue of the fact that the acceleration of automation made it more difficult for workers to understand its degree. Thus, the domination of labour by capital appeared to be the subjugation of the worker to an administrative network that largely denied a specific focal point for anger to be directed against.[28]

There were, however, sparks of opposition to the capitalist/technological power structure among section of the intelligentsia and middle-class youth (both had sufficient understanding and affluence to understand its authoritarian nature), and among ghettoised ethnic minorities who experienced the repression socially and economically, not greatly sharing in the cornucopia of the new consumerism.[29] The system itself had an inherent contradiction for Marcuse: "capital versus the mass of the working population as a whole,"[30] either going to communism or neo-fascism.[31] Marcuse opined that if the workers came to power (this more likely in Europe than in the United States because of its long socialist tradition), they could rapidly establish an advanced socialist society.

The possibility of this was based, for Marcuse, on the fact that in the technologically advanced capitalist nations, conditions were already favourable to transcend mere economic values,[32] thus providing the means to put into effect within a brief period Marx's "utopianism." The new society, basically stateless/classless, where the means of production were in the hands of the people, proclaimed the "*self-determination* of men and women who assert their freedom and their humanity in the satisfaction of their vital material needs."[33] He also saw the necessity for direct democracy, where

UTOPIA

in any organisation there would be effective control from below.[34] Finally, he would abolish the present "fragmentation of work," i.e., extensive labour division, which condemned most of the workers to repetitive and dull work, by using cybernetics to make it supervisory and creative. These new conditions would eliminate an alienating competition and production of meaningless goods for the sake of profit, thus ending the present "servitude in the guise of technology." This, moreover, would end "pollution as a way of life," and permit future generations to inherit a relatively clean ecostructure. The focus of the coming socialist society was then not on technology as much as on humanity's basic "moral and aesthetic needs."[35] Marcuse did not deny the possibility of conflict in this new world, but believed that it "can be resolved without oppression and cruelty."[36] The probability for this was "political freedom" in the sense that humanity would transcend politics.[37]

The utopianism of anarchism was attacked by noted adversaries. Three examples: It was rejected by a well-known political theorist, the leading Russian Marxist George Plekhanov, in *Anarchism and Socialism*, which characterised *La Société au lendemain de la révolution* and *La Société mourante et l'anarchie* as utopian and out of touch with reality, while Grave himself was dismissed as a "dabbler in metaphysics." The main point of critique was that anarchists were dreamers because they did not engage in formal political action, as in electoral politics to acquire political power. Anarchism itself was simply dismissed as a "bourgeois outgrowth."[38] George Bernard Shaw, in a critical but sympathetic examination of anarchism, *The Impossibilities of Anarchism*, which first appeared in the early 1890s, revealed his admiration for Kropotkin, and even admitted that in the long run, anarcho-communism might be attainable. But he deemed necessary a transitional stage of socialism because humanity as yet had not reached the moral stage required for anarcho-communism: man "must be considered as an obstinate and selfish devil."[39] A recent observer, Aileen Kelly in "Lessons of Kropotkin", in the *New York Review of Books*, stated that Kropotkin's (and by implication Grave's) work was replete with a simplistic messianic view of life, rooted in a theological vision that pitted the good of mutual aid against the evil of authority.[40] That there is a messianic quality in anarcho-communism is certainly true. As inheritor of earlier revolutionary traditions, how can it be otherwise? Indeed, this revolutionary utopianism is the main impetus for socialist revolution in the twentieth century.

Notes

1. Friedrich Engels. *On Authority* as cited in Feuer, *Marx and Engels*, pp 481-85.
2. Marx, *Critique of the Gotha Programme*, pp 8ff, discussed two stages, proletarian dictatorship to be followed by communism.
3. Karl Marx, *The Civil War in France* as cited in Feuer, *Marx and Engels*, pp 366-70.
4. On the revolutionary mood of the Russian proletariat, farmers and military in 1917, see John Reed, *Ten Days That Shook the World* (New York: The Modern Library, 1934).
5. Lenin, *State and Revolution*, p 44.
6. *Ibid.*, p 38.
7. Lichtheim, *Europe in the Twentieth Century*, p 142, observed Lenin's "quasi-anarchist pronouncements in 1917."
8. On the immediate destruction of the State, see Grave, *Réformes, révolution*, p 126 and Grave, *L'Anarchie: son but, ses moyens*, pp 51ff.
9. Grave, *Terre Libre*, has a utopia of integrated labor. An excellent work on utopias is by Negley and Patrick, *The Quest for Utopia*.
10. AM, letter, Grave to Nettlau, July 14, 1934.
11. Grave, *La Société mourante*, pp 13-26.
12. Grave, *La Société au lendemain de la révolution*, pp 14ff.
13. Grave, *La Société future*, pp 202ff.
14. Kropotkin, *The Conquest of Bread*, pp 256-75. Simone Weil, *Oppression and Liberty* (London: Routledge and Kegan Paul, 1958), pp 83-108, pictures the ideal society in terms very similar to Grave's. On the fact that class antagonisms remain for a period of time after the revolution, see Grave, *La Société au lendemain de la révolution*, pp 14ff.
15. Grave, *La Société au lendemain de la révolution*, p 47. AM, letter, Grave to Nettlau, July 24, 1934, on consumption to determine production.
16. On science as a crucial factor in the development of individual autonomy and anarchism, see Grave, *La Société future*, pp 386ff. On industrial decentralization, integrated labor, and so forth, see the pioneer work of pragmatic anarchism: Peter Kropotkin, *Fields, Factories, and Workshops or Industry Combined with Agriculture and Brain Work with Manual Work* (New York: G.P. Putnam's Sons, 1909) pp 177-83 for general conclusions. On "recreative" labor based on "justice and equality," see

Grave, *La Société au lendemain de la révolution*, p 97. Grave, *Terre Libre*, pp 134ff on electric cars.

17. Grave, *La Société future*, pp 168ff, saw knowledge from a cultural-historical aspect, each generation building on the achievements of its predecessors. The genius of a particular generation should therefore recognize this incalculable debt to the past. See, also, Grave, *L'Individu et la société*, pp 183ff. R.H. Tawney, *Equality*, p 131, stated that happiness is not only dependent on leadership but also on social solidarity. On p178, he affirmed that intelligence was greatly influenced by environment. Plato, *Republic*, intro, and trans. A.D. Lindsay (London: J.M. Dent, 1948), pp 100ff, on the intellectual ruling elite.

18. On the elimination of wage labor, see Kropotkin, *The Conquest of Bread*, pp 200-201 and Grave, *La Société future*, p 362. On common storehouses, see Kropotkin. *The Conquest of Bread*, p 126; Grave, *La Société au lendemain de la révolution*, pp 19ff, and, Bertrand Russell, *Roads to Freedom: Socialism, Anarchism, and Syndicalism* (London: Unwin Books, 1966), pp 74-75.

19. Grave, *La Société future*, pp 94ff and pp 206ff implied that human wants (thus needs) vary.

20. On size and organization with respect to production, see Grave, *L'Anarchie: son but, ses moyens*, pp 218-26. On miniaturization of machinery and machines performing monotonous work, see Murray Bookchin, *Post-Scarcity Anarchism* (Berkeley: Ramparts Press, 1972), pp 94-106. For Russell's suggestion, see his *Roads to Freedom*, p. 81.

21. Bookchin, *Post-Scarcity Anarchism*, p 136.

22. Grave, *La Société future*, pp 139-42 and pp 321-29. Simone de Beauvoir, *The Second Sex*, trans. and ed., H. M. Parshley (New York: Bantam Books, 1961), p 97, agreed with Grave that the women of the privileged classes were generally freer than their poorer sisters, and pp 75ff that it was the advent of private property engendered by the agricultural revolution that enslaved women.

23. Pierre Kropotkine, *L'Anarchie: sa philosophie, son idéal* (Paris: P.V. Stock, 1896), p 17.

24. Errico Malatesta, *L'Anarchie* (Genève: Groupe d'Etudiants révolutionnaires de Genève, 1902), p 8. On his life, see the short biography in Max Nomad, *Rebels and Renegades* (New York: Macmillan Co., 1932), pp 1-47.

25. Elisée Reclus, "L'Anarchie," *Les Temps Nouveaux*, May 1825, 1895), pp 1-2.

26. For an attack on Marcuse's thought, see Alasdair McIntyre, *Herbert Marcuse: An Exposition and a Polemic* (New York: The Viking Press, 1970). For a sympathetic treatment see Robert W. Marks, *The Meaning of Marcuse* (New York: Ballantine Books, 1970). For a critique by Marcuse of Soviet society, see his *Soviet Marxism: A Critical Analysis* (New York: Vintage Books, 1961).

27. Herbert Marcuse, *Counterrevolution and Revolt* (Boston: Beacon Press, 1972) pp 1-16. Herbert Marcuse, *Eros and Civilization*, pp 138ff which denies that a higher standard of life alone makes for a better society.
28. Herbert Marcuse, *One-Dimensional Man: Studies in the Ideology of Advanced Industrial Society* (Boston: Beacon Press 1964), pp 1-48.
29. Marcuse, *Counterrevolution and Revolt*, pp 32ff.
30. *Ibid.*, P 15.
31. *Ibid.*, pp 24ff.
32. Marcuse, *One-Dimensional Man*, pp 3-4.
33. Marcuse, *Counterrevolution and Revolt*, P 18.
34. *Ibid.*, p 45. Herbert Marcuse, *Five Lectures: Psychoanalysis Politics and Utopia* (Boston: Beacon Press, 1970), p 76 talks about a "dictatorship" to insure the new communist society but let's remember that it is based on participatory democracy. Herbert Marcuse, *An Essay on Liberation* (Boston: Beacon Press, 1969), p 69 envisages "direct democracy" in which representatives can be recalled at will, underpinning this is "equal and universal education for autonomy."
35. Marcuse, *Counterrevolution*, p 17 on the four preceding quotations. Marcuse, *Eros* p. vii saw automation leading to "working time becoming marginal and free time becoming full time." Marcuse, *Five Lectures*, pp 63ff does not view the new society as utopian because the technological means for it already exist; p 78, labor exists but it is not alienated since humanity continues to transform nature; p 67 on "cybernetics and computers."
36. Marcuse, *Five Lectures*, p 79.
37. Marcuse, *One-Dimensional Man*, p 4.
38. George Plekhanov, *Anarchism and Socialism*, trans. by Eleanor Marx Aveling (Chicago: Charles H. Kerr Co., 1918), pp 107ff.
39. George Bernard Shaw, *The Impossibilities of Anarchism* (London: Fabian Society, 1893), pp 102-03, for example.
40. Aileen Kelly, "Lessons on Kropotkin," *The New York Review of Books*, October 28, 1976, pp 41-42. For criticism of anarchism, see Krimerman and Perry, *Patterns of Anarchy*, section VII.

14

CERTAIN COMMON VIEWS BETWEEN GRAVE AND PROMINENT BOURGEOIS THINKERS

GRAVE'S THOUGHT WAS SHARED IN varying degrees by leading contemporary bourgeois thinkers hostile to socialism. Parenthetically, socialism was greatly influenced by such progressive thinkers, who stressed the importance of change, as Darwin in biology and Hegel in philosophy and history. Both at times accepted the notion of human solidarity/cooperation: as Hegel's "state" in *The Philosophy of Right and Law* and Darwin's cooperative person in *The Descent of Man*.[1]

On elite control of the state apparatus in a socioeconomic model of deep class division and class struggle, there were broad areas of agreement between Grave and four leading contemporary bourgeois thinkers (an excellent cross section of conservatives): the American sociologist William Graham Sumner (1840-1910), the Italian political scientist Gaetano Mosca (1858-1941), the Italian sociologist Vilfredo Pareto (1848-1923), and the German sociologist Max Weber (1864-1920), undoubtedly the foremost bourgeois social thinker of the first half of the twentieth century. When referred to as a group these thinkers are the "four."[2]

The four believed that a small elite group ruled the dissatisfied and at times turbulent masses.[3] For Sumner, Mosca and Pareto class demarcations were more marked than for Weber, more concerned with differences in status groups. For Sumner, there were three basic classes: the wealthy few (the most fit from a Darwinian perspective), the "masses" or average people ("mediocrities"), and the minority proletariat, at the bottom, made up of the unfit. For Mosca and Pareto (although also aware of social complexity), the elite was generally contrasted to the masses. For Weber, the ruling elite in Germany of Kaiser, army and state bureaucracy (not the wealthy bourgeoisie) governed a society in which status groups took precedence over classes; although allowing for a middle class of professionals and others between masses and rulers.[4]

The four did not deny the reality of the class struggle. Sumner apprehensively envisioned a future America in the grips of a rising socio-economic misery, with increasing class conflict between the proletariat and bourgeoisie. For Pareto and Mosca, the class struggle was an equally valid phenomenon between rulers and ruled. For Pareto, as an example, it did not proceed toward the goal of a classless society, but was interminable because revolutionary elites of more able individuals (frustrated by the older elites in their drive to join them) led and used the dissatisfied but incompetent masses against their masters. In his circulation of elites, velocity of change increased during a successful revolution. For Weber, the process was based more on status groups than on classes.

The four posited this gloomy prognosis for socialism: should it assume power an elite would still manage society and deny universal equality. Weber, for example, emphasised that large-scale industry and labour division bureaucratised life—even under socialism—which could not but negate the principle of equality.[5] They also based class or status inequality on either a quasi- or strictly biological basis, and the normal acquired advantages of inherited wealth and power.[6] Obviously, Grave disagreed with their biological assumptions since he adhered to the notion of a general human equality.[7] Basically, for the four, there was only contempt for the helpless masses and admiration for the rulers. One of them, Mosca, in *The Ruling Class*, mentioned Grave's *La Société mourante et l'anarchie* as a work that would destroy such pillars of elite rule as private property and large-scale organisation in order to ensure equality.[8]

This focus on inequality influenced Robert Michels (1876-1936), a protégé of Weber and a socialist who became an ardent admirer of Mussolini's fascism. In *Political Parties* (1911), he described the oligarchic tendencies in the German Social Democratic Party whose bureaucracy of officeholders had a slow rate of turnover. In a democratic organisation whose stated goal was an egalitarian socialist society, an elite group dominated.[9] Anarchists like Grave agreed with this analysis.

CERTAIN COMMON VIEWS

From a broad perspective (to contrast the respective socialist and bourgeois positions on social progression and its end), for Grave and for Marx, the social struggle progresses toward a cooperative egalitarian society in which the human personality blossomed in a non-coercive milieu, analogous to Marcuse's "pleasure principle"; while for bourgeois ideologues, a competitive and class-repressive society characterised by inner loneliness, one ridden by Marcuse's "performance principle," was the eternal present and future.[10]

Notes

1. Concerning Hegel, see his *The Philosophy of Right and Law in The Philosophy of Hegel*, ed. Carl J. Friedrich (New York: Modern Library, 1954). Concerning Darwin, see his *The Descent of Man* (London: J. Murray, 1871), chaps IV and V.

2. On Sumner, see M.R. Davie, *William Graham Sumner: An Essay of Commentary and Selections* (New York: Crowell, 1963). On Mosca, Pareto, Weber, and Michels, see H. Stuart Hughes, *Consciousness and Society: The Reorientation of European Social Thought, 1890-1930* (New York: Alfred A. Knopf, 1961), chap. VII. On Pareto and Mosca, see James H. Meisel, *Pareto and Mosca* (Englewood Cliffs, NJ: Prentice-Hall, 1965). On Weber, see W. J. Mommsen, The *Age of Bureaucracy: Perspectives on the Political Sociology of Max Weber* (New York: Harper and Row, 1974).

3. On the ruling elites (combinations of warriors, religious leaders, and capitalists), see William Graham Sumner, *Folkways* (Boston: Ginn and Co., 1906), p 64. Gaetano Mosca, *The Ruling Class* (trans. Hannah D. Kahn; New York: McGraw-Hill, 1939), pp 50-69. This work was first published in 1884. Vilfredo Pareto, *Mind and Society* (trans. by Andrew Bongiorno and Arthur Livingstone; edited by the latter (four volumes; New York: Harcourt, Brace, and Co., 1935), III, 1423-31. This work was first published in 1916. Max Weber, *Economy and Society: An Outline of Interpretive Sociology* (edited by Guenther Roth and Claus Wittich (three volumes; New York: Bedminster Press, 1968), II, 941-1003. First published in 1922. For Mosca, Pareto, and Weber, bureaucrats have an ancillary role to governing elites.

4. On class structure: Sumner, *Folkways*, p 47. Mosca, *The Ruling Class*, pp 110-19 on "class distinctions." Pareto, *Mind and Society*, III, 1427: "The least we can do is to divide society into two strata: a higher stratum, which usually contains the rulers, and a lower stratum, which usually contains the ruled." Weber, *Economy and Society*, I, 302-307 on "status groups and classes" indicates a wide range of gradations.

5. On the class struggle: William Graham Sumner, *Earth-Hunger and Other Essays* (New Haven: Yale University Press, 1913), p 289. Mosca, *The Ruling Class*, pp 199-221, on revolution. On p 220, that for revolution to grip the masses, economic discontent and so forth are triggering elements. Pareto, *Mind and Society*, III, 1431 ff. Also, see

THE ANARCHISM OF JEAN GRAVE

Vilfredo Pareto, *Les Systemes socialistes* (2nd ed.; 2 vols.; Paris: M. Giard, 1926), I, 16ff which accepts Marxian class struggle, but which ties it to the rise of outside elites leading the masses. First published in 1902. Weber, *Economy and Society*, II, 930-32 has status struggle characterizing social conflict.

6. On the biological superiority of the wealthy vis-à-vis the masses, see Sumner, *Earth-Hunger*, pp 351-52. On the fact that the elite groups pass on economic, cultural, and other advantages to their offspring (this makes for a general stability of elites), see Mosca, *The Ruling Class*, pp 5-69 section.

7. For Grave, the lack of mutual aid, which results in cunning, force, and violence, is the basic cause for social oppression and rise of inequality. Intelligence itself is not a factor in the preceding progression. Concerning this, see, for example, Grave, *La Société mourante*, pp 39-48.

8. Mosca, *The Ruling Class*, pp 293-96 on Grave.

9. Michels, *Political Parties*, pp 117-28, for example.

10. Marcuse, *Eros and Civilization*, pp 3-7.

15

EXAMPLES OF THE ANARCHIST TEMPERAMENT: WEIL, CAMUS, SARTRE, AND THE 1968 FRENCH MAY EVENTS

ALTHOUGH ANARCHISM IN FRANCE WAS finished as a viable movement after the advent of the Bolshevik Revolution, it continued to influence society, especially in the intellectual arena. Three important individuals in France—indeed, they have world-wide reputations—will be presented as examples of the anarchist temperament: Simone Weil, Albert Camus, and Jean-Paul Sartre, who had their greatest impact in the post-World War II period. Then the 1968 French May Events will be examined because of the strong anarchist strain in its aims and development.

Weil (1909-1943) was a rare person, possessing a first-rate intellect and great humanity. She was born into a progressive French-Jewish upper middle-class family. Her physician father, Bernard, an agnostic (the mother also), was sympathetic to anarchism in his youth. She was educated in Paris, at the well-known lycée Henri IV and at the prestigious Ecole Normale Supérieure, graduating with an agrégation in philosophy.

From her mid teens, Weil had a keen interest in working-class developments, regularly reading the Communist daily, L'Humanité. Indeed, she seriously considered joining the Communist Party only to be dissuaded by reservations with its official line. In 1932, she began to work with the Loire Group of Revolutionary Syndicalists and soon afterward wrote articles for the revolutionary syndicalist monthly, La Révolution Prolétarienne, founded by the indomitable Monatte and other dissident Communists.

Weil's revolutionary activism in the Loire Group occurred while a professor in Roanne. In 1935, she decided to pursue an unusual course of action, to become a worker. From December 4, 1934 to August 22, 1935, she worked in three factories in the Paris area, including the Renault automobile plant, principally as a power-press operator and on a milling machine. When the Spanish Civil War erupted in 1936, Weil volunteered to fight for the Republic. She went to Barcelona, associating herself with anarchists, but after being seriously burned by oil in an accident, returned home.

Weil's restless spirit also encompassed religion. After a few mystical experiences involving Christ, she embraced Catholicism, but never formally became a member of the Catholic Church since she refused baptism. A revolutionary, a mystical lover of humanity, Weil died in England of tuberculosis in the prime of her life.[1]

Weil's analysis of the social problem was basically in the anarchist tradition. In *Oppression et liberté* (a series of essays), she surveyed the tragic human condition of class-exploitative society and presented a prescription of the good one. The governing elite, possessing economic and other advantages, ruled the many oppressed in a state of permanent revolt, covert and overt. She agreed with Marx that oppression was linked to the system of production and exchange, which led to conflict, but disagreed with him that the mere expansion of production, coupled to the class struggle, would bring the ultimate goal of communism. Instead, her good society unalterably posited decentralist patterns of individual autonomy and equality: (1) Elimination of all advantages of co-ordinators in production by having each individual in the co-operative workshop control completely what he/she produces, individual autonomy *à outrance*! (2) Insistence on small-scale collectives as the basic production units to humanise the economic arena to instill the indispensable element of fraternity in all social relations. (3) The absolute abolition of a competitive economic spirit, the hallmark of bourgeois society. (4) A comprehensive liberal-technical education for a simultaneously thorough understanding of the socio-cultural as well as the scientific aspects of life. The new society, in other words, would be one of cultural-technical equals.

In the same work, Weil severely criticised Stalinism as a form of state capitalism, in which the new rulers, comprising the controlling bureaucracies, effectively stifled dissent among the proletariat by denying elementary civil liberties (that Marx should be identified with a society that repudiates

EXAMPLES OF THE ANARCHIST TEMPERAMENT

civil liberties and maintains power through terror is unthinkable). Ultimately, for her, "the individual, and not the collectivity, [is] the supreme value."[2]

In *La Condition ouvrière* (a series of essays), the empathy and consequent sympathy that Weil had for an oppressed French proletariat was strikingly depicted. It was based on her factory experiences which described her descent into the hell and alienation of the factory, where workers, she quickly learned, laboured in a state of constant humiliation, subject, as it were, to the demons of repetition and speed, as machines of flesh who served the machines of steel. That was not all, for workers were constantly forced to obey the directions of bosses, who, if displeased with their performance, could immediately discharge them. Moreover, being generally ignorant of the technical processes involved, ill-educated workers were further confronted by the mystery of the machine. In the tradition of Sorel, Weil advocated difficult and demanding work, but insisted that it be performed in a milieu of equality and fraternity.

Weil's anarchist vision was amply demonstrated in a particular social and political event. When the June 1936 general strike erupted after the Popular Front electoral victory brought to France its first socialist premier, Léon Blum, she enthusiastically supported it on the grounds that it gave a new élan and hope to the proletariat. For the unity of the working class, she insisted that the first requirements to consolidate the gains of the general strike were to decrease salary differentials among the workers and to establish worker committees. These changes would further increase proletarian solidarity to allow for more human dignity, thus intensifying the class struggle between the proletariat and the bourgeoisie to hasten the drive for human liberation.[3]

To be sure, Weil drifted to the right in the late thirties, and with the fall of France, she ultimately joined the Free French in England. Her last work, *L'Enracinement* (*The Need for Roots*), written less than six months before her death, was a curious hybrid of her earlier revolutionary syndicalism and a certain authoritarian stance so prevalent among French conservatives. One could find in it such terms as "obedience" and "hierarchism",[4] but they were more than offset by a severe condemnation of capitalism and a sketch of a future society basically Proudhonian. It included the following: (1) The rejection of a capitalist ethos to dominate economically and militarily through imperialism. (2) The elimination of an economic system based on money: "Money destroys human roots wherever it is able to penetrate, by turning desire for gain into the sole motive."[5]

Weil's alternative to the present capitalist society was based principally on Proudhonian Mutualism. The new society had "private property," which at death reverted to the state, collective property of the various associations of workers and peasantry, and that of the state, the patrimony of all. As much as possible, production was decentralised in small economic units where highly skilled workers used sophisticated machinery to make a variety of products. The new society would encourage the formation of a new type of individual with a high level of technological expertise and great awareness of general culture.[6]

Camus (1913-60), the recipient of the 1957 Nobel Prize in Literature, is a major spokesperson and fighter for human freedom. Born into a proletarian French-Spanish family (his father was killed in the early fighting of World War I), his youth was in the slums of Algiers. He finished the local lycée and attended the University of Algiers where he earned a degree in philosophy, then in 1938 became a journalist. During the occupation of France, he joined the underground Resistance group "Combat" and became the editor of its newspaper, *Combat*. Not only a noted novelist (among his works are *L'Etranger*, *La Peste* and *La Chute*), he was also a well-known playwright and political essayist; his finest example of the last was *L'Homme révolté* (1948) translated into English as *The Rebel*.[7]

Camus, an atheist, existentialist, and humanistic socialist, has characters in his works who particularly personify his tragic vision of life and socialist convictions. In *La Peste*, Dr. Rieux fought against the plague because he was against human misery and suffering, solidarity his guiding value. In *L'Etranger*, the protagonist Meursault, alienated and devoid of feeling, accidentally killed a person and sentenced to death not so much for the actual crime, but for his nonconformity, a victim of a brutal and repressive society. In *La Chute*, Clamence, a lawyer and former jurist, was perpetually doing penance because he believes that his solidarity and compassion for others was inadequate.[8]

EXAMPLES OF THE ANARCHIST TEMPERAMENT

In assessing the political thought of Camus, one must first view it in general terms. Basically, he was against all forms of oppression, be they economic, social, political, religious or cultural. He clearly and emphatically identified himself with the oppressed and humiliated, the proletariat. It was this empathy that convinced him to become briefly a member of the French Communist Party in 1934-35, that involved him with *Combat*, and that led him to join with Sartre, Simone de Beauvoir, and others in forming Le Rassemblement Démocratique Révolutionnaire (RDR), a party of two thousand members active in 1948–49; against both capitalism and Stalinism, it was for a socialist France that respected democratic forms and civil liberties.

In *L'Homme révolté*, Camus presented his basic anarchist philosophical reflections on the good society, and revolutionary ethics.[9] He rejected certain traditional anarchist practices and views: Bakunin, for example, was castigated for advocating terrorism and for being an authoritarian on the basis of his penchant for creating centralised and hierarchical elites for effecting revolution.[10] Camus was also fearful of utopia being worked out in advance by intolerant revolutionaries who would use terrorism to impose future happiness and he accused Godwin, Morelly, and Babeuf of this crime.[11] In this charge, he was especially unfair to Godwin.

Camus' anarchism in this work may be tested on several grounds. To begin, he rejected the authoritarian bourgeois/socialist revolutionary tradition, the French Revolution/Russian Bolshevik Revolution complex that maintained state power by the replacement of one elite for another and by the use of terror against the people.[12] His authentic revolution was waged by the Paris Commune of 1871, which was "the last refuge of rebel revolution." For him, the rebel, in contradistinction to the revolutionary who invariably sets himself up as the new master, wishes to free all people permanently.[13] This condition was embedded in the rebel's feelings of human solidarity: "I rebel—therefore we exist." And: "Man's solidarity is founded upon rebellion, and rebellion, in its turn, can only find its justification in this solidarity."[14]

In invoking human solidarity as the general principle and the 1871 Paris Commune as the concrete historical example, Camus amplified his anarchist-oriented position by applauding the revolutionary syndicalist tradition of Pelloutier and Sorel who wished "to create, by professional and cultural education, new cadres [of workers] for which a world without honour was calling and still calls."[15] Indeed, he admired "revolutionary trade unionism," which "started from a concrete basis, the basis of professional employment (which is to be to the economic order what the commune is to the political order), the living cell on which the organism builds itself."[16] Furthermore: "Trade unionism, like the commune, is the negation, to the benefit of reality, of bureaucratic and abstract centralism."[17] He also quoted the Proudhonian labour leader and Communard, H. L. Tolain, that "human beings emancipate themselves only on the basis of natural groups."[18] Revolution, ultimately, would take hold "from bottom to top," not "from top to bottom,"[19] and be based "on the most concrete realities: on occupation, on the village, where the living heart of things and of men is to be found."[20] To realise its ends, the revolution disdained "terror," but did not necessarily reject "violence."[21] For him, the "syndicalist and libertarian spirit," not the "Caesarian," should represent socialism.[22] Broadly conceived, Camus the anarchist was for a socialist society of pluralism, one eclectic in its methods and outlook, having no grand design in the hands of centralised leaders or planners, based on the participatory democracy of local groups. This generous vision was reminiscent of Proudhon, Grave, and Kropotkin.

There are other concrete examples of Camus' anarchism. In a speech delivered at the Labour Exchange of Saint-Etienne in May 1953, entitled "Bread and Freedom," he condemned both capitalism ("The society of money and exploitation has never been charged, so far as I know, with assuring the triumph of freedom and justice.") and Stalinism ("The progressive retreat of socialism based on freedom before the attacks of Caesarean and military socialism."). He also informed the audience that "freedom is the concern of the oppressed and her natural protectors have always come from among the oppressed." Then, he observed that in the fight for human dignity, both freedom and justice were necessarily required.[23] In the "Wager of Our Generation," an interview given for the journal *Demain* in October 1957, he asserted that because of human solidarity "the aim of art, the aim of life can only be to increase the sum of freedom and responsibility to be found in every man in the world." Like Grave, he thought liberty

EXAMPLES OF THE ANARCHIST TEMPERAMENT

would more likely emerge in the West rather than in the Communist East because in the former, there was at least the "quarter truth" of "liberty."[24]

Sartre (1905-1980) is a world-renowned philosopher and literary figure who personifies the conscience of the world's progressives in the post-World War II period, the leading exemplar of the committed artist/intellectual actively engaged in fighting oppression, *l'homme engagé*. Sartre and his mother lived with her parents after his father, a naval officer, died soon after Sartre was born. Sartre's maternal grandfather, Charles Schweitzer, the uncle of Albert Schweitzer and a language teacher from a prominent Alsatian family, was the great influence on Sartre. It was he who commanded the young Sartre to write, which he did unabatedly until his death.

Sartre had a brilliant academic career, graduating from the lycée Henri IV and then from the Ecole Normale Supérieure in 1929 with an agrégation in philosophy, then continuing his studies in Berlin. In the thirties, when he taught philosophy in various lycées and was busily writing, he saw himself as an anarchist who passively supported the Popular Front.

It was during World War II that Sartre became and remained thereafter the committed fighter for human freedom. He joined the Resistance in Nazi-occupied France and in 1947-48 was a founding member of the RDR.[25] Also, although not formally a member of the French Communist Party, he was sympathetic to the general aims of Communism. Against the right in France, he was appalled by the people's acceptance of the army-backed De Gaulle imperial presidency built on the ashes of the Fourth Republic. He was also a determined opponent of French colonialism in Algeria and American imperialism in Vietnam. The Soviets, however, were not spared either for he supported the 1956 Hungarian Revolution and applauded the Prague Spring of 1968 when the Czechoslovakian Communist Party opted for a liberalisation that would guarantee civil rights, and bring about a "socialism with a human face."[26]

Sartre's corpus of writing (his philosophical works as well as his novels and his plays) dissected the human condition of his times in great detail and profundity.[27] In *L'Etre et le néant* (1943), the spiritual malaise of individual existence in a bourgeois-dominated society was amply sketched, the individual seen as essentially alone, in anguish, regarding the Other (other persons) as a barrier to his freedom, revealing the inner image of the outer socio-economic bourgeois relations based on a predatory Social Darwinism.[28] In *L'Existentialisme est un humanisme* (1946), hope emerged as the radically free and solitary individual escaped the anguish of isolation by uniting with others to fight for and expand human solidarity. The freedom and happiness of all now replaced the inner loneliness of the internecine warfare for power and privilege.[29]

With *Critique de la raison dialectique* in 1960, Sartre fitted his humanistic existentialist philosophy within the broader parameters of Marxism, which he recognised as not only the dominant contemporary philosophy, but the one which also best described the complexity of social reality.[30] This work, whose aim was to inject Marxism with the specificity of existentialism, followed in the broad footsteps of Marx, Proudhon, and Grave in that it envisaged history as moving toward a future realm of freedom. The Sartrean vision was faithful to the libertarian Marxist and anarchist traditions in which the interaction between individual and society through various groups was at centre stage. It utilised the full range of the rich and complex Marxian socio-historical perspective, while at the same time exploring the individual's interior-exterior existence through the existentialist connection.

For Sartre, scarcity underlay the historical progression, forcing individuals into performing various tasks requiring labour division and coordination, that led to domination and hierarchy as principal characteristics of the social construct. From scarcity, violence also sprang into being; it is "interiorised scarcity," which "makes people see each other as the Other and as the principle of Evil." Furthermore, an economy of scarcity engendered "a climate of fear and mutual distrust."[31] It was in this maelstrom that humanity made history dialectically; the dialectic itself being "the totalisation of concrete totalisations effected by a multiplicity of totalising individualities."[32] In this historical analysis, Sartre not only delineated the larger contours of history, progressing dialectically through economic, social, political, and cultural changes, but also viewed the individual in his alienated human relationships stemming from antagonistic social groups.

Specificity will be given to the Sartrean analysis of such topics as tensions within human groups, bureaucracy, the state, class struggle, revolu-

EXAMPLES OF THE ANARCHIST TEMPERAMENT

tion, critique of Communist societies and of colonialism/racism in French-occupied Algeria to indicate that Sartre's views follow in the footsteps of Grave and Marx.

For Sartre, alienation/subjection, tied to the individual's interaction with others, has been an inherent condition of history. At first, human association was in "fused groups" (ad hoc groups devoid of structure embodying equality and fraternity), which evolved into "pledged groups" (individuals organised by a pledge of mutual obligations and rights), which in time became institutions (the state, military, and so forth) in which sovereignty or authority based on coercion was paramount. Once these last structures were in place, spontaneity and democratic forms atrophied into bureaucracy, "the opposite of freedom." Sartre, like Orwell in *1984*, was fearful that the rise of the new bureaucratic state, through its control of the communications media, would condition the masses to act against their interests, as the Nazis were able to do in their frenzied anti-Semitism, thus hindering the attainment of socialism. This attempt by the bureaucracy to influence and control events was called "other-direction."[33]

Sartre was definitely in the anarchist tradition in focusing great attention on the primary or more intimate human associations within the larger collectives of state and class. It was what happened in these small groups and their surrounding networks, where individuals intimately involved themselves in love and work, that was most important in determining the intensity of the class struggle in any particular period, but their very complexity, diversity, and alienation from one another made it very difficult to achieve the unity of the proletariat.[34]

Sartre's view of the state is in the Marxist/anarchist tradition: "In this sense, for example, the nineteenth-century bourgeois state reflected the unity of bourgeois society." "The state is a determination of the dominant class, and this determination is conditioned by class struggle." "The state therefore *exists* for the sake of the dominant class, but as a practical suppression of class conflicts within the national totalisation." "In class conflicts it [the state] intervenes to tilt the balance in favour of the exploiting classes."[35]

The class struggle for Sartre, patterned basically on Marxist and anarchist precedents, was the chief propellant of history; in the present historical epoch, the ascending proletariat (the exploited) was engaged in deadly conflict with the descending bourgeoisie (the exploiters). The proletariat, as the chosen class ("the damned of the earth"), was destined to destroy the bonds of all class oppression. His deep sympathy for the proletariat was revealed thus:

> His [the worker's] free activity in its freedom, will take upon itself everything which crushes him—exhausting work, exploitation, oppression, and rising prices. This means that his liberty is the means chosen by the Thing and by the Other to crush him and to transform him into a worked Thing. Hence the moment of the free contract by which in the nineteenth century, the isolated worker, a prey to hunger and poverty, sold his labour to a powerful employer who imposed his own rates, is both the most shameless mystification and reality.

To be sure, there were divisions within the two general classes: in the bourgeoisie, a range from the petite bourgeoisie to the very wealthy; in the proletariat, the differences and tensions inherent in the various status groups from the unskilled to the skilled, including competition for positions. The proletariat also had a difficult time to unite for it must overcome the alienations and divisions imposed by past generations: "The previous generation already defines their [workers'] institutional future" through various " 'obligations'—military, civic, professional, etc." But in spite of "divisions in the working class," the overriding historical tendency was for the class struggle between the workers and bourgeoisie to intensify as the workers became more unified.[36]

Indeed, Sartre used a technological perspective to postulate the progressively increasing class solidarity of the proletariat. "The machine organises men," defining to a large degree the relations of the workers to themselves as well as to the capitalist owners. Thus, when revolutionary syndicalism was in its heyday in the early twentieth century, the few skilled workers who formed the labour aristocracy could simply paralyse a factory by going out on strike. Since the labour aristocrats were not interested in the unskilled workers, mass unionism did not develop; divisions in the working class were too wide to impose unity. Today, however, with the "interchangeability of skilled workers", mass action is possible.[37] He refers to the fact that the recent technological explosion is related to the educational one, a condition which allows for a highly educated work force, largely erasing former status differences, thus furthering the probability for revolution.

Sartre was convinced that proletarian revolution, as in the past, could occur spontaneously at any time. Despite divisions and fissures within the working class, it alone was revolutionary. The "apocalypse," or the revolution would come from individuals coalescing together in the fused groups which at a certain historical juncture would simply act in the spirit of equality and fraternity.[38] This view was that of the young Marx, who saw imminent revolution in the late 1840s and early fifties, of Bakunin, Kropotkin, Grave, and the Lenin of 1917 who urged the Bolsheviks to follow the masses.

Sartre's critique of socialist societies, which developed in economically backward nations, was most perceptive. Although basically sympathetic to them, he indicated such negative features in the early stages of their development as rise of bureaucracy and terror that culminated in the "cult of personality." These deformities should be progressively resolved by "debureaucratisation, decentralisation, and democratisation," in which "the sovereign must gradually abandon its *monopoly of the group* (the question arises at the level of workers' committees)." Sartre did not go as far as anarchists to describe the new socialist bureaucrats as constituting a new capitalist class because the revolution expropriated capitalist property.[39]

Sartre's analysis of colonialism/racism in the work cogently explored their various elements in Algeria. First was violence, that French armies forcibly entered Algeria through the "atrocious massacres" of the people. The second was the brutal expropriation of land. The third, which inexorably followed, was exploiting the Algerian people, polarizing Algeria between the colonialists (including workers) and the native population, wherein the former, the privileged group, became racists, viewing natives as a sub-proletariat, as "*nothing* except a labour force which can be bought for less and less."

In a comparison of Sartre's critique of colonialism/racism with that of Grave's in *La Société mourante et l'anarchie*, certain similar views prevailed:

THE ANARCHISM OF JEAN GRAVE

(1) that there were no inferior human groups; (2) that racism and capitalist/colonialism were interlocked; (3) that violence characterised the relations between the oppressors (colonialists) and the oppressed (the natives), in which the former employed brute force to reduce the latter to an inert mass of inexpensive labour; (4) that as a consequence, the working class of the advanced imperialist nations should struggle against the colonialist-imperialist forces.[40]

In a notable interview that Sartre gave in 1975, his basic anarchism was clearly affirmed. He was unalterably opposed to the power of elites and their oppression, remaining in solidarity with the masses. Because he saw all philosophical systems to be in a state of flux, he was against any set system of analysis. He was suspicious of all political organisations, but held the Italian Communist Party as the least evil of all the various parties. For human freedom, he asserted his anarchism.[41]

The 1968 May Events were heavily influenced by anarchist ideas and activities. To be sure, contemporary anarchists differed from their progenitors in some respects. For example, they recognised the important libertarian elements in Marxism and respected its social analysis. After a brief presentation of the background that led to the May 1968 upheaval, we shall comment on its essential developments and why it failed, then offer a basically anarchist analysis of the events and hopes that it engendered through the eyes of one of its most active militants and theoreticians, Daniel Cohn-Bendit ("Danny the Red").

From 1967 to the spring of 1968, a veritable student explosion occurred in various universities over sexual liberation, specifically the right of dormitory students to have members of the opposite sex in their rooms, and other student concerns, like overcrowded classes and opposition to US involvement in Vietnam. On March 22, students at the Nanterre campus, demanding the release of friends recently arrested in Paris for demonstrating against the war, occupied the administration building for two days. (Hence the Twenty-Second of March Movement.) On May 3, Cohn-Bendit's speech at the Sorbonne (both the Sorbonne and Nanterre are part of the University of Paris) on the Twenty-Second of March Movement before a large student crowd was broken up by police who arrested several students. Soon afterward, students battled the police. When on May 5, the government announced that the baccalaureate degree did not automatically admit one to college, this was the last straw for students at the Sorbonne who fought special police units from May 6 to 11. A conciliatory speech by Premier Pompidou seemed to calm the storm, but on May 13 the Communists and the CGT called for a nation-wide general strike for May 14, which saw hundreds of thousands of students and workers marching in the streets of Paris. It was at this time that students seized the Sorbonne and workers at Nantes occupied the Sud Aviation factory. Other plant seizures soon followed, notably that of Boulogne-Billancourt Renault near Paris on May 18. These sparks soon led to ten million workers participating in the most extensive general strike in French history. The strikes were characterised by a general spontaneity: The rank and file initiated them, the union bureaucrats followed. The sit-in strikers generally made the following proposals: (1) the unity of all workers; (2) participatory democracy, usually in a workers' assembly in plant or office; (3) worker control of the factories/offices in varying degree; (4) discussions involving the full range of socio-economic and cultural problems that confront workers.

On May 25, the De Gaulle government signed an agreement with leading representatives of French labour which granted substantial wage increases primarily to end the general strike. Workers at Renault promptly rejected the package on the grounds that economic gains were no longer sufficient; younger workers in particular insisted that the Gaullist government be replaced by a popular one that would accept worker control of industry, not to be realised because, although the government was scarcely in control of events at the end of May, it had sufficiently recovered by the middle of June to beat its opponents decisively.

Why did the May Events fail? First, the left was not only hesitant in exploiting the general strike, but was divided on whether its Communist and non-Communist elements should collaborate. Second, the bureaucratic inertia that characterised left parties and unions prevented decisive action. Third, the government had the support of the bourgeoisie and the loyalty of at least the military officers. Basically for revolutionary success, prolonged economic crisis or defeat in war seemed to be essential preconditions, not the case in 1968.⁴²

The preparatory stage for the 1968 May Events was ensconced in the intellectual ferment of university students and teachers who, increasingly alienated by a conformist and restrictive bourgeois society, organised groups that proposed anarchist solutions. One of the more important, the *Enragés*, founded in 1957, was particularly active at the Universities of Bordeaux, Nantes, and at the Nanterre Campus. The major themes of their thought included critiques of: (1) capitalist and Communist authoritarianism related to economic exploitation and hierarchical organisation; (2) capitalist technology which not only dehumanised workers, but was part and parcel of a capitalist ethos that promoted false material needs; (3) reformist-bureaucratised unionism that had become part of the governing apparatus, to be swept away by revolutionary worker councils based on participatory democracy. As intellectual sources, the Situationists often cited Kropotkin and especially Bakunin. Their ideal society was based on a liberating spontaneity and the Gravian-Kropotkian view of work.⁴³

The Twenty-Second of March Movement was heavily influenced by anarchist conceptions. Their best-known spokesperson was Daniel Cohn-Bendit, a sociology student at Nanterre whose views were a composite of Marxist and anarchist thought. His *Obsolete Communism* followed the thought of Marx, Bakunin, Rosa Luxemburg, Makhno (an anarchist revolutionary), and Claude Lefort, the leading figure of *Socialisme ou Barbarie* (a theoretical journal of the fifties and early sixties which argued that Marxism was caricatured by Communist bureaucrats in the Soviet Union).

Cohn-Bendit asserted that the May Events were made by students and workers, but did not succeed because of the timidity and intransigence of the Communist and socialist parties whose influence in the trade unions contributed to stopping its momentum. In particular, he accused the French Communist Party and its union arm, the CGT, supposedly the most revolutionary party and union respectively, of betraying the students and workers because their authoritarian and bureaucratic power structures, interlocked with those of the bourgeois state and those of the counterrevolutionary Soviet Communists, were ultimately fearful of change.⁴⁴

EXAMPLES OF THE ANARCHIST TEMPERAMENT

His views of the March and November 1917 Russian Revolutions, further revealing his anarchist beliefs, held that the Russian proletariat spontaneously (although cognizant of their prior socialist orientation) made the first and forced the Bolsheviks to make the second or be bypassed by events. Once in power, however, the Bolsheviks undermined the soviets of workers, peasants, and military that had made the second revolution.[45]

For Cohn-Bendit, the spontaneously formed strike and action committees of 1968, which disdained authority and bureaucracy in the revolutionary anarchist tradition, had a possibility of toppling the bourgeois state along with the bureaucracies of the various left-wing parties and unions. These committees, for him, which embodied the revolutionary élan of large sections of the proletariat, were based on a non-hierarchical order that erased distinctions between leaders and followers. All local decisions were made by locally based general assemblies and delegates to higher assemblies were rotated to prevent the rise of a permanent revolutionary elite.

The revolutionary model of Cohn-Bendit was greatly indebted to Bakunin, Kropotkin, Grave and Pelloutier who theorized that the bourgeois state can be overthrown through a series of popular confrontations and strikes leading to a general one.[46] In this schema of imminent revolution, the proletariat would act on the assumption or Sorelian "myth" that the revolution could occur at any time despite such innumerable difficulties as division between skilled and unskilled workers and the "complex set of bureaucratic pyramids of society that reinforce apartness or seriality."[47]

In a distinctly anarchist analysis, Cohn-Bendit realised that the abolition of bourgeois property or nationalisation of the means of production and exchange were not in themselves sufficient to ensure socialism. Indeed, the revolution had to smash all forms of hierarchical organisation through the medium of participatory democracy. In addition, cognisant of the traditional insistence of Marx and anarchists on resolving the dichotomy between mental and manual labour as quickly as possible, he asked for its rapid and expeditious resolution because failing to do so would prevent the attainment of equality and even under socialism restore the expert and the bureaucrat. In following the anarchist and the libertarian Marxist patterns, he insisted that socialism should encompass economic, social, and cultural equality in a political setting of participatory democracy.[48]

For Cohn-Bendit, the critical date of the 1968 May Events was May 24, when the revolutionary crowds in Paris, having already burned the Stock Exchange, abandoned their revolutionary instincts by heeding the advice of the bureaucrats of the Parti Socialite Unifié and other parties not to seize key government buildings. Thus, they lost the opportunity to effect a socialist revolution.[49]

Notes

1. On Simone Weil's life, see Simone Pétrement, *La Vie de Simone Weil* (2 volumes, Paris: Fayard, 1973). This is the definitive work. Another excellent work on Weil is by E. Piccard, *Simone Weil* (Paris: Presses Universitaires de France, 1960). On Weil's final reflections, many of which are concerned with Christ and Christianity, see her *La Connaissance surnaturelle*, ed. Albert Camus (Paris: Gallimard, 1950). Camus chose the title.
2. Simone Weil, *Oppression et Liberté* (Paris: Gallimard, 1955). 1 am using the English version, *Oppression and Liberty*, trans. by Arthur Wills and John Petrie (Amherst: Univ. of Mass. Press, 1973), pp. 83ff and pp 1-24; the quote is on p 19.
3. Simone Weil, *La Condition Ouvrière* (Paris: Gallimard, 1951), especially pp 21ff, 72ff, and 113ff.
4. Simone Weil, *The Need for Roots: Prelude to a Declaration of Duties toward Mankind*, trans. by Arthur Wills, with a Preface by T. S. Eliot (Boston: The Beacon Press, 1955), pp 13-15 and p 19.
5. *Ibid.*, p. 44.
6. *Ibid.*, pp. 35ff and pp. 74F.
7. On Camus, see Germaine Brée, *Camus* (New Brunswick NJ.: Rutgers University Press, 1959). On Camus' work, see the analysis by Lev Braun, *Witness of Decline, Albert Camus: Moralist of the Absurd* (Rutherford, NJ: Fairleigh Dickinson University Press, 1974). Also, see Philip Thody, *Albert Camus: A Study of His Work* (New York: Grove Press, 1959).
8. On Camus' novels, see Albert Maquet, *Albert Camus: The Invincible Summer* (London: John Calder, 1958); and, Conor Cruise O'Brien, *Albert Camus of Europe and Africa* (New York: Viking Press, 1970).
9. Albert Camus, *The Rebel: An Essay on Man in Revolt (L'Homme révolté)*, trans. by Anthony Bower, Foreword by Sir Herbert Read (New York: Vintage Books, 1956), p viii has Read stating that Camus is close to the anarchist position.
10. *Ibid.*, pp 156-60 on Bakunin; pp 164-73 on anarchist and other revolutionary terror. Camus discusses the Russian anarchists at length, but scarcely mentions French anarchists.

EXAMPLES OF THE ANARCHIST TEMPERAMENT

11. *Ibid.*, p 208 on Godwin.
12. *Ibid.*, pp 217-18 on socialist elites; pp 125-32 on state revolutionary terror.
13. *Ibid.*, p 218.
14. *Ibid.*, p 22 for both quotes.
15. *Ibid.*, p 217.
16. *Ibid.*, pp 297-98.
17. *Ibid.*, p 298.
18. *Ibid.*
19. *Ibid.*
20. *Ibid.*
21. *Ibid.*
22. *Ibid.* On the quarrel between Camus and Sartre which was sparked by *The Rebel*, see Bernard Murchland, "Sartre and Camus—The Anatomy of a Quarrel," in Michel-Antoine Burnier, *Choice of Action: The French Existentialists on the Political Front Line* (New York: Random House, 1968), pp 175-94.
23. Albert Camus, *Resistance, Rebellion, and Death*, trans. and intro. by Justin O'Brien (New York: Alfred A. Knopf, 1961), pp 87-97.
24. *Ibid.*, pp 237-48.
25. On Sartre's early life, see his autobiographical *Les Mots* (Paris: Gallimard, 1964). On Sartre's involvement in various causes and so forth, see Michel Contat and Michel Ryblaka, *Les Ecrits de Sartre: Chronologie, bibliographie commentée* (Paris: 1970).
26. The best source for Sartre's opinions is in his monthly *Les Temps Modernes*.
27. On Sartre's philosophy and politics, see Anthony Manser, *Sartre: A Philosophic Study* (London: Athlone Press, 1966); Marjorie Grene, *Sartre* (New York: New Viewpoints, 1973); Hazel E. Barnes, *Sartre* (Philadelphia: J. B. Lippincott, 1973); Pietro Chiodi, *Sartre and Marxism* (Hassocks, Sussex: The Harvester Press, 1976); Mark Poster, *Existential Marxism in Postwar France: From Sartre to Althusser* (Princeton: Princeton University Press, 1975).
28. Jean-Paul Sartre, *L'Etre et le néant: essai d'ontologie phéneménologique (Being and Nothingness)* (Paris: Gallimard, 1943).
29. Jean-Paul Sartre, *L'Existentialisme est un humanisme* (Paris: Nagel, 1946).
30. Jean-Paul Sartre, *Critique de la raison dialectique* (Paris: Gallimard, 1960). For the English edition, which I am using, see *Critique of Dialectical Reason*, trans. Alan Sheridan-Smith (London: NLB, 1976), p 822.
31. *Ibid.*, pp 123, 131, 148-49.
32. *Ibid.*, p 37.
33. *Ibid.*, pp 260-504 on various human ensembles and associations and their evolvement. On institutions, see pp 576-663; on a pledged group evolving into an institution, see p 608; on "opposite of freedom" see p 638; on the new bureaucratic state and Nazi anti-Semitism, see pp 642ff.; on "other-direction," see p 650.

34. An important argument of the work.
35. Sartre, *Critique*, pp 638-40. Italics not mine in the quote. On p 608 Sartre states: "This permanent living structure of coercion is a necessary determination of sovereignty as authority." This is pure Gravian.
36. *Ibid.*, p 699; pp 781-94; p 241 for "damned of the earth," p 325 on the long quote. On institutional inertia and "obligations," see *ibid.*, pp 606.
37. Sartre, *ibid.*, pp 240ff.
38. *Ibid.*, pp 351-404; pp 687ff.
39. *Ibid.*, pp 661-62.
40. Cf. *ibid.*, pp 716-34 with Grave's *Société mourante*, pp 171-98. There is essential agreement.
41. *New York Review of Books*, August 7, 1975, p 14.
42. On the 1968 French May Events, the following works should be consulted: Adrien Dansette, *Mai, 1968* (Paris: Pilon, 1971). Christian Charrière, *Le Printemps des enragés* (Paris: Fayard, 1968). Alan Priaulx and Sanford J. Ungar, *The Almost Revolution: France 1968* (New York: Dell Books, 1969). Henri Lefebvre, *The Explosion: Marxism and the French Upheaval* (New York: Monthly Review Press, 1969). Bernard E. Brown, *Protest in Paris: Anatomy of a Revolt* (Morristown, NJ: General Learning Press, 1974).
43. On the Enragés, see R. Vinet, *Enragés et situationistes dans le mouvement des occupations* (Paris: Gallimard, 1968).
44. On the Twenty-Second of March Movement and its ideas, see Daniel Cohn-Bendit and Gabriel Cohn-Bendit, *Obsolete Communism: The Left-Wing Alternative*, trans. Arnold Pomerans (New York: McGraw-Hill, 1968). On the intellectual influences, see p 133 on Lefort; pp 215-17 on Luxemburg; and pp 220ff on Makhno. For a critique of Soviet Communism, see pp 199-219, on leftist bureaucrats cooperating with the bourgeoisie, see pp 170-94.
45. *Ibid.*, pp 202-03.
46. *Ibid.*, pp 78-81 on action committees.
47. *Ibid.*, pp 14ff., p 63, and p 108 for "complex set of bureaucratic pyramids."
48. *Ibid.*, p 19, p 90, pp 105-06, p 255.
49. *Ibid.*, pp 70-71, pp 124ff.

16

POSTSCRIPT, 2002

ANARCHISTS THROUGHOUT THE WORLD today are faced by many unpleasant realities, but also with hopeful ones, reflecting the state of the class struggle between left and right. Today, global capitalism led by the United States, through its institutions, like the International Monetary Fund (IMF) and its cohort World Bank (WB) and now the World Trade Organization (WTO), in the service of large transnational corporations (TNCs) girdling the globe, commands the heights of the world economy. Indeed, these manifestations of capitalism's power are now leading the world to ecological disaster and to its twin of a nuclear holocaust; the implosion of Communism in the Soviet Union has impoverished Russia, basically destroying its infrastructure, exposing the world to its nuclear arsenal of approximately 6,000 bombs. The U.S. has 7,200 aimed at Russia.

Grave's views on a bureaucratic Soviet Communism have proved to be correct, i.e., a "socialism" without democracy and civil liberties (Camus' "Caesarean and military socialism"), leads to the return of capitalism. Communist China is now also becoming capitalist. The Communist elites in these nations were instrumental in restoring capitalism and in squelching the socialism of their workers, peasants, and progressive mental labourers.[1] But popular socialist forces, including left-wing socialism comprising traditional anarchism and libertarian Marxism will not go away, and popular forces have brought some reform in the advanced capitalist nations. But living standards in the First World are now threatened by rising pollution and the TNCs, while the Third World is sinking ever more into poverty. We first observe the rise of capitalism through its institutions in the service of the oligopolistic TNCs and then proceed to reforms brought about by the left.

THE ANARCHISM OF JEAN GRAVE

The dominance of capitalism over Communism has been largely fashioned by U.S. actions, such as rebuilding a war-torn Western Europe through the Marshall Plan and aiding in the construction of the European Economic Community becoming the European Union (EU) in 1991.

In tandem with these and other trade blocs was the fostering of international "free" trade. Its first step was the Bretton Woods Conference in 1944 that established the IMF and WB to lend money, the former to debt-ridden nations, the latter for long-term development—both under the auspices of the United Nations (UN), with the U.S. playing the primary role. In 1948, the UN, again under U.S. leadership, founded the General Agreement on Tariffs and Trade (GATT), which through various rounds has greatly reduced tariffs worldwide to where in 2000, the average for farm products is 50 percent, but for manufactured goods only from 4 to 10 percent.

In the early 1980s, following the lead of the U.S., most trade and financial barriers among nations were removed, by Germany in 1981, France in 1984, and the EU in 1998. Only Japan and the East Asian nations imposed severe trade restrictions as they remained in a more traditional mercantilist mode, but are now relenting towards more free trade with the economic crises of the late nineties. In 1995, GATT set up the WTO, which, along with the IMF and WB, is now the principal capitalist weapon enforcing privatisation and free trade or rule of the TNCs.

(The WTO, which in 2002 includes 130 nations and all the major economic powers, has wide authority to allow the unfettered rule of TNCs against national impediments to markets, granting its members "most favoured nation" status, all having equal egress to entrance.)

With the end of World War II, capitalism in the West (U.S. and Western Europe) and Japan experienced a period of unparalleled economic growth from 1947 to 1973, a "Golden Age" for the historian Eric Hobsbawm. In this picture, a partial socialism is important only in Western Europe which saw high economic growth rates outside of Great Britain, of 5 percent annually, partly fueled by the Marshall Plan, mass production methods, new technologies, and economic integration.

This rapid growth literally changed the nature of much of the Western European labour force, while creating a labour shortage. Its large agricultural labour component for instance, in France and Italy, shrank from a third and two fifths just after the war to 5 and 7 percent respectively, while the number of industrial, service, and white-collar workers increased correspondingly. The labour shortage itself was overcome by more women entering the paid work force and immigrants from Southern Europe, Turkey, and North Africa.

As living standards rose, mass consumerism became widespread in the advanced capitalist world as average working-class families now purchased automobiles, and so forth.

The golden years of capitalist growth, however, were followed by relative economic stagnation to the present, with recessions in the U.S. for instance, in 1974-75, 1979-82, and early 90s. In the 1997-2001 period, outside the U.S., much of capitalism was or is in a severe economic slump, especially Japan, Russia, Argentina, Brasil, Mexico, Turkey, and much of East Asia outside China, with EU nations having an average unemployment rate of more than 10 percent, while Third World nations in the last twenty-five years have had zero or negative economic growth.[2]

The hallmark of this capitalism is increasing capital concentration of capital/technology nationally and internationally through mergers. The U.S. will be taken as a national example: The largest 600 corporations generate 80 percent of sales revenue and the Standard and Poor's 500 (the leading 500 corporations) has 85 percent of market value of publicly traded companies. These phenomena are also related to the 10 trillion dollars in the value of leveraged buyouts and acquisitions in the last twenty years.

Several of only many examples of this concentration by sales in selected areas: In the mass retail field, Wal-Mart alone has half; four drugstore chains, almost half; four airlines, two-thirds; two grain exporters, half; five automobile companies, most; two grain exporters, half. In assets, twenty insurance companies have half; in banking, less than fifteen, half, but by 2005, nine-tenths.[3]

Globally, increasing capital concentration is through the aegis of TNCs and international banking, stock, bond, and currency markets. TNCs are the unifying productive element here, having plants in two or more nations, with a fourth to a third of their profits coming from outside the parent location.

THE ANARCHISM OF JEAN GRAVE

The international economic giants are the largest five hundred TNCs, which, in 1998, for instance, conduct 70 percent—40 percent of it intra-firm—of the 3.2-trillion-dollar world trade. Indeed, the leading 350 alone have more than a fourth of the world's productive assets and comprise a third of the GDP of economically advanced nations. In 1999, of the top five hundred, 244 are from the U.S., 173 from the EU, and 46 from Japan; and of the top hundred, 70 are from the U.S., 26 from the EU, and 4 from Japan. Three-fourths of TNC investment is in the First World, the remainder in developing nations, but now new capital flows to the latter are 40 percent of foreign direct investment.

These developments are related to imports and exports and large global stock and bond flows: for the former, a large part of many national GDPs—a fourth for the U.S. and half for France, Germany, and the UK; for the latter, in the U.S., for instance, in early 2000, foreigners bought 30 percent of new stock purchases (7 percent in 1998) and 40 percent of new bonds including federal (20 percent in 1998). Another instance of this is the French stock market, in which American and British investors through pension funds own between 30 and 40 percent of it. In the realm of industrial stock alone, foreigners own a fourth of the French and up to two-fifths of the British.

In plant and other installations, U.S. and EU TNCs have now invested approximately a trillion dollars in each other's markets. The TNCs are now so large that the largest ones have sales exceeding that of many nations; the leading twenty-five alone have annual sales topping 25 billion dollars or more by the early nineties. The largest five in percentage of sales in these critical economic areas have a monopoly advantage (internationally five corporations having half the market) in the nineties: in consumer durables (70), automobiles and trucks (60), airlines (55), aerospace (55), electrical/electronic components (50 plus), and steel (50); and not far from it in oil (40 plus), personal computers (40 plus), the media (40 plus), chemicals (35), and insurance (25).

The power of the TNCs and large banks is so pronounced over national governments that the last shred of national sovereignty over TNCs is now proposed by the Organisation for Economic Cooperation and De-

POSTSCRIPT

velopment (OECD), made up of the leading twenty-nine nations. Its economic package, the Multilateral Agreement on Investment (MAI), would offer a *carte blanche* to TNCs in purchasing, selling, and moving companies without regard to national laws. Furthermore, under MAI rules, nations would neither subsidise their domestic industries nor demand that foreign corporations abide by national guidelines for economic development. Capital now would be truly globalised, making national boundaries largely superfluous. Near-term consequences of this would include weakening of labour unions and environmental protection. Because of socialist and other opposition, MAI talks have stalled, but for how long?

Indeed, Chapter 11 of the North American Free Trade Agreement allows corporations to sue nations for "damages from governments" when their laws impinge on "future profits" (seventeen or so cases now basically involving environmental laws) which may be expanded in the future to attack public services which compete with private firms; this is undermining the democratic processes of the nations involved, allowing a MAI-like solution.

In 2001, more than three trillion dollars daily circles the globe, of which 15 percent is in the form of capital funds and commodity trading, the remainder in currency and other complex forms of speculation, like hedge funds. Trading is conducted through giant computer networks, the largest being the New York Clearing House Interbank Payment System (CHIPS), made up of eleven private banks that offer their services to 142 other banks globally; it interacts with smaller similar networks, like the Society of Worldwide Interbank Financial Communications (SWIFT) in Belgium, linking a thousand or so banks, and a few other smaller computer complexes.

This almost uncontrolled computer/electronic system has encouraged tax havens in the Bahamas, Cayman Islands, Bermuda, Hong Kong, Isle of Man, and elsewhere; in the Grand Cayman Island alone, 575 banks and trust companies handle 500 billion dollars in assets. But, of course, laws permit this squirrelling away of money. It is estimated by Merrill Lynch that in 1998, six trillion dollars is deposited by the world's wealthy (two-fifths held by U.S. citizens) in these offshore tax havens, U.S. tax losses alone at 70 billion dollars annually.

THE ANARCHISM OF JEAN GRAVE

One expert on money movements, Anthony Ginsberg, estimated that about half the stock of the industrialised world was associated with tax havens. William Mulholland, the CEO of the Bank of Montreal, informed a Canadian parliamentary committee that "I can hide money in the twinkling of an eye from all the bloodhounds that could be put on the case." (Some of the 200 billion dollars annually made from illegal drugs is part of this money laundering.) The Securities and Exchange Commission, in a well-known finding, itself allowed that "off-the books transactions, bogus transfers, and double sets of accounts"—all standard routines of New York's Citibank—were consistent with "reasonable and standard business judgement," that circumvent "currency regulation" and "tax laws." Obviously, the line between the legal and illegal is so blurred here that normal law is almost inoperative as it has been transcended by secrecy and speed; recent revelations of Russian money laundering in the many billions of dollars by government officials and criminals is an instance of this.

Today, in the U.S., for instance, TNCs conduct much of their production in low-wage nations like China, Mexico, and Indonesia. By the eighties, 38 percent of all manufactured goods consumed in America, as opposed to 14 percent in 1969, came from abroad. This relative deindustrialisation is related to various factors, such as a strong dollar, less expensive foreign goods relatively high wages (lower than that of many European nations), and lack of an industrial policy to protect domestic industry.

Some perspective on globalisation of capital: In the 1860s and 70s, the world witnessed much free trade, high tariffs coming later. Too, capital movements abroad as percentage of GDP are in the 1990s lower than those in the late nineteenth century when the wealthy of England and France heavily invested in Australia, Canada, New Zealand, and the U.S.

After World War I and during the Great Depression, international investment and trade dropped drastically as autarky reigned, but after World War II they rose again. But, while international investment before was of the long-range variety, as in railroads and manufacturing, today much of it is in international assembly lines making manufactured goods and in short-term stock, bond, and currency funds, highly leveraged and speculative. Indeed, with the instant electronic technology of today, the herd mentality easily leads to economic crises. Worldwide, in the last twenty years, there were ninety major bank crises, while from 1870 to 1913, five, only one leading to a crisis in currency exchange rates.

With increasing importance of global mutual funds in stocks and bonds, in conjunction with the new powers of the GATT/WTO complex, any democratic socialist success, as in France, is hostage to international capital and to regional economic integration requirements, like those of the EU. Indeed, global monopolisation of the TNCs, and their attendant economic and political power, is forcing nations and various states in the U.S. to grant them favourable subsidies and tax breaks simply to operate there. This development also compels smaller companies beholden to TNCs economically to ruthlessly compete with one another for their contracts, either lowering wages and benefits for workers or causing higher unemployment, thus the race to the economic bottom for workers, including the savaging of unions.

These economic phenomena, of an ever more internationalised capitalism, have made for the lessening of trade wars among nations, although they still persist, as by the U.S. recently to force Russia, Japan, and others to curtail steel exports to it, and by the EU's preventing U.S. TNCs from being subsidised with offshore tax havens.[4]

This globalisation of capital is not all, for nations in competing with one another to attract plants and installations of TNCs, in addition to the inordinate power of capital to influence tax law, has resulted in subsidies/lower taxes for corporations: In the mid-nineties for the U.S., Nader's Centre for the Study of Responsive Law estimates them at 167 billion dollars annually through tax abatements, increased depreciation allowances, tax write-offs for acquisitions and mergers, industrial revenue bonds, and so forth.[5]

An ominous development now is the spectre of ever-increasing industrial pollution adversely affecting the atmosphere and the quality of water and soil, in which the very survival of humanity is involved. To be sure, the scientific community is in the forefront to alert humanity of this danger. The "World Scientists' Warning to Humanity," a 1992 position paper inaugurated by the Union of Concerned Scientists and endorsed by 1,575 of the world's leading scientists, admonished that "human beings and the natural world are on a collision course," and "if this is not checked...the living world...will be unable to sustain life in the manner that we know," thus "need to avoid the collision our present course will bring."

The Kyoto, Japan, December 1997 Conference in which representatives of the world's nations met to discuss controlling greenhouse emissions and consequent climatic warming underscored the seriousness of the problem, but their tentative agreements to lessen carbon dioxide levels to below those of 1990 were inadequate; indeed, no major nation as of 2001 has ratified them; the U.S. itself disavowing its modest proposals.

Now, the October 2000 report of the United Nations' Intergovernmental Panel on Climate and Change (IPCC), composed of hundreds of scientists, has warned that the threat of greenhouse gases/warming is increasing to the point that its 1995 estimate of a rise from 1.8 to 6.3 degrees Fahrenheit by the end of the 21st century is now from 2.7 to almost 11 degrees Fahrenheit.

Pollution today is a way of life, intimately involved with technology. Now annually, almost 7 billion tons of carbon dioxide from use of fossil fuels (coal, oil, and gas, a fifth from the U.S.), become part of the atmosphere (from the beginning of the Industrial Revolution to the present, many hundreds of billions of tons), adding to the greenhouse effect, warming the planet's atmosphere by 1° Fahrenheit in the 20th century.

According to the IPCC and others, the consequences of this warming of air also warms the oceans, leading to the rise of sea levels in the 21st century from 20 to 30 inches as polar and other glaciers melt, flooding low-lying areas. In addition, there will be changes in weather patterns, already noticeable, including more droughts in some regions, but more rain in others. As usual, poor nations will have greater difficulties in coping with these changes than wealthy ones.

There is also the annual environmental damage to land, forest, and water. For the first two in hectares (2.47 acres), 11 million of forest is destroyed, 6 million of land lost to desert, and 1.5 million saturated with salt; and 26 billion tons of top soil is washed away. Then, there are the many tens of billions of pounds of waste, from fossil fuels, pesticides, heavy met-

POSTSCRIPT

als, radiation form nuclear-bomb testing and nuclear-power plants, and other toxic material, inevitably spilling into lakes, seas, and oceans. Over-fishing, in combination with toxic waste, has also greatly reduced fishing yields in nine of the world's seventeen major fishing grounds, four no longer economically viable.

The noxious combination of ozone and particulates (minute particles from combustion emitted by automobiles, power plants, and factories) heavily pollutes the air in half of American cities, and of many others, especially in poorer nations industrialising rapidly, like China and India.

Then, too, there is severe ozone depletion—ozone protects life on earth from the harmful ultraviolet rays of the sun—in the upper atmosphere, in Antarctica at times, and its thinning in the rest of the planet, caused by chlorofluorocarbons (CFCs) used in refrigeration and other products; a million tons of it was produced annually by the 1970s, not only increasing skin cancer, but attacking micro-organisms on land essential to life. Production of CFCs is now being phased out, but it will take at least a century for the ozone layer to return to its former state.

Some specificity in pollution adversely affecting human food consumption: Coal-burning power plants emit mercury into the air/water system, particularly endangering the health of pregnant women and children. About 50 million people in the U.S. alone drink tap water infested with fecal bacteria, lead, and other toxic matter. Fertilisers in the U.S. are still scarcely regulated, unlike in Europe and Canada, invariably made from the wastes of steel, wood, paper, and petroleum products that have dioxin (a particularly deadly substance), lead, mercury, cadmium, and arsenic, among other harmful substances. Cadmium itself is readily absorbed by plants in the food chain, like wheat, rice, and corn. Dioxin is ingested by cattle (5 percent of their diet is soil), then passed on to meat eaters. Add to this, cattle and poultry that are fed poultry droppings and carcasses of other animals and hides. As for fish, more than half are contaminated by heavy metals and PCBs, two-fifths sold not even edible. Yet another form of pollution, a most insidious one, is of antibiotics fed to poultry, cattle, and pigs to prevent illness, passed on to humans in the food chain, who when ill are less likely to respond favourably to treatment employing antibiotics. Not surprisingly, health-food stores focusing on vitamins and organically grown food are proliferating in wealthier neighbourhoods.

The environmental crisis, involving both the capitalist and Communist worlds—in China 8 percent of its GDP is devoted to immediate cleanup of pollution—is deepening as polluting technology, related to obsessive corporate economic growth in both camps, continues to proliferate. For instance, the bureaucratic/technical elites of the so-called Communist nations, in constantly imitating their capitalist counterparts, contribute to the pollution problem as they rush to industrialise along Western-capitalist lines, thereby reinforcing their power over the working class and peasantry.

There are now a myriad of problems to be rapidly resolved to control pollution. A cardinal one is how to quickly change present polluting technologies with non-polluting ones, while keeping people employed and maintaining present living standards in the First World, which, of course, does not have to include much of the present junk consumerism: but this proposal itself entails convincing the more affluent sectors of society, including most of mental labour, to change it.

Of course, there is a possibility that capitalist elites may partially solve the pollution problem with new technologies, like oil-ingesting micro-organisms to clean oil spills and new hybrid cars employing the standard gas combustion engine and electricity stored in batteries; also, within twenty years, fuel cells, which change liquid hydrogen into electricity to power automobiles, with water as their only by-product, may be mass produced.

The pollution crisis is now part of the mix that pits two ethics against one another, of capitalism and a proper socialist one. The former operates on assumptions of great socio-economic inequality, with its exploitative relations, and a consumerist technology whose end is continual growth and profit now (without them, capitalism dies), with scant regard for the welfare of future generations. The latter formulates a world of general socio-economic equality with non-exploitative relations whose economic planning, focusing on the importance of technicity and rationality over false economic needs and planned obsolescence, should save humanity.[6]

POSTSCRIPT

In the aftermath of World War II, bureaucratic/authoritarian socialism rapidly increased its influence. The Soviet Union imposed a harsh Stalinism on Eastern Europe. In the West, the war's end brought about the rise of large socialist and Communist parties (the latter especially in France and Italy), which pushed for extensive nationalisation of basic industry and banking, along with much-needed social welfarism.

In West Germany, nationalisations were not encouraged, although an advanced social-welfare system which dated to the Bismarck period continued. To be sure, traditionally conservative parties, like the Christian Democrats in Germany and Italy, went along with the reforms; the collectivism of war and shared hardships experienced during it undoubtedly aided the socialist project, as did the rise of Soviet power.

A brief examination of the French post-war experience follows: In addition to the nationalisations of the railroads and armaments industry in the 1930s, the 1944-48 ones encompassed the coal mines, gas, electricity, Renault auto works, large banks/insurance, and Air France was established. Workers through work committees also had input into management decisions. Further nationalisations followed in the 1980s, but since then, some privatisation has taken place.

In the French social-legislative arena, there are now in place a well-regarded (the best in the world according to the World Health Organization) national health-insurance system, excellent children's allowances and day-care program, government-subsidised low-rent housing, rather adequate unemployment insurance (58 percent of the average wage for two years, versus 48 percent for six months in the U.S.) fairly adequate old-age pensions, minimum wages, and aid to the indigent (all higher than those in the U.S. relative to median income) five weeks of annual pay with vacation for workers, and free tuition, with heavily subsidised room and board, in higher education. This French example is largely representative of other EU nations.

Today, under the thumb of a neoliberalism, spearheaded by TNCs and unregulated capital flows circling the globe, there is widespread unemployment in France and the rest of the EU. There are two avenues open for resolving this problem: (1) To reduce the substantial social-welfare expenditures, including less protection for labour, thus lowering labour costs to increase capitalist profits; or (2) to move to the left by raising taxes on the wealthy, curbing their wasteful "conspicuous consumption," reducing, if not eliminating, military outlays, increasing the nationalised economic sector, and democratising the workplace through worker participation in the decision-making process.

In France, under the Socialist François Mitterand in the eighties, who led a Popular Front government of Socialists and Communists, there was an attempt to more fully realise socialism through more nationalisations and more social welfare; in the latter sphere, vacations were extended from four to five weeks and the retirement age with full pension reduced to age sixty. But this government neither democratised the workplace, nor greatly raised taxes on the wealthy, nor reduced military expenditures: A critical reason for this was ferocious capitalist opposition to them, including the threat of capital flight to seriously destabilise an economy in which imports/exports accounted for almost half of its economic activity. Furthermore, as France was in the EU, its economic policies were to a large degree part of the larger EU economic wheel.

The partly failed Mitterand experiment now reveals that an opening to socialism is limited for a medium-size economy like the French. The way out for socialism is to coordinate the activities of many socialist parties, including national labour unions becoming intimately involved with those of nearby nations to co-ordinate common policies and goals. In short, socialism can become viable only internationally in Europe.

In the meantime, with France as an example, Socialists, with communist and green allies, in 1997 defeated the Centre and Right on the promise to lower the workweek to thirty-five hours, and to institute a public works program, both to lower high unemployment. Significantly, the former is now a reality, and despite the latter, unemployment is still more than 10 percent.[7]

But socialists in general and the socialist left in which anarchists are situated should not be discouraged by the many difficulties they face. The urban working class is relatively young, first emerging from the Industrial Revolution in England in the middle of the eighteenth century, a phenomenon now engulfing the world's poorer nations. Furthermore, most of the working class in 2002 is still only several generations from the traditional/repressive/parochial countryside, and, although the continual influx of rural immigrants destabilises working-class unity, it constantly enlarges the working class itself. Indeed, despite the advantages, of the bourgeoisie and traditional power structures over urban and rural workers, the twentieth century witnessed many socialist and Communist revolutions, and the rise of democratic socialist parties.

To be sure, social democracy, especially where unions are strong, has given workers some power in controlling the workplace and even the direction of economic development. This is most advanced in Germany, in which half the workers are in unions and in which co-determination is operative in plants employing more than a thousand workers, ordaining that half the supervisory board members of a corporation represent the workers, the other half, owners, with management having no vote on the board. Management itself is appointed jointly by owners and workers. In this configuration, worker councils have jurisdiction over working conditions, including work shifts, and participate with owners in determining corporate economic strategy, including allocation of jobs and layoffs/cutbacks. The power of workers here is, of course, still limited, but incomparably higher than that of their American and other counterparts.

Socialism has already nationalised much of banking, utilities, transport, and industry. As percentage of national investment, for instance, the public sector share in selected key nations is: France, 55; Italy, 45; Norway, 40; Sweden, 30; and, Germany, 20, the last in the form of stocks. In addition, half of the top fifty EU corporations in auto, steel, aerospace, electronics, and computers are partly or fully state-owned. In banking, French banks are largely government-owned, as is the Bank of England, among others.

But there is a successful capitalist counter-offensive to privatise nationalised industries. For instance, Great Britain under Margaret Thatcher has privatised many formerly nationalised sectors, such as British Airways, gas, railroads, electricity, water (but not British Petroleum), and the former Communist nations are also engaged in massive privatisation, as are heavily indebted nations, like Mexico, Argentina, and Brasil, dictated to by the IMF and WB. Indeed, in poor nations today, any nationalized industry has scarcely any prospect to remain so under the new international capitalist hegemony.

Large denationalizations in Great Britain and the slight one in France, for instance, have nothing to do with efficiency of operation. Since large, nationalized, semi-nationalized and privately-owned companies have autonomous managers supported by the usual panoply of experts and bureaucrats, the nationalization/privatization issue is basically related to the ongoing struggle between labor and capital. The wages of nationalized companies may be slightly higher than those of comparable private-sector industries, but the amount is negligible from a larger economic perspective. But in the developing nations, where nationalized firms have been closely allied to political parties in power, some economic inefficiencies occur, and privatization there results in higher profit margins as labor loses social benefits and is more exploited.[8]

In addition to the parliamentary left—Communists, Socialists, and Greens—there is now a plethora of left-wing socialist groups, particularly active in university settings and their periphery, usually made up of students and former ones, many economically marginal and alienated from bourgeois society and the reformist politics of the parliamentary left.

The university, no longer the preserve of the elite, is now a revolutionary engine for social change as the progressive ideas of the past and present have great attraction for students, especially in the liberal arts and social sciences. Millions of students have been exposed to and influenced by socialist conceptions, many becoming socialist activists during their university years, only to drop out when they enter the deadening world of conformity and routine of job, family and ambition.

The New Left is basically an updated amalgam of Marxism and anarchism, in which Trotsky, Mao, Bakunin, Kropotkin and Marcuse are some of the leading characters (Grave should be also). It opposes the contemporary bourgeois system, of the large corporation, with its impersonal nature based on profit, and its supposed rational technological efficiency and social hierarchy. This not only includes capitalist corporations but big government, along with their military industrial complexes, and big labor unions and socialist parties whose bureaucracies largely favour the status quo.

To counter this unholy combination of power and inertia stifling the individual, the New Left emphasizes individual autonomy and spontaneity as against institutional authority, with its manipulative aspects, rejecting the consumerist throw-away ethic, itself related to capitalist alienation and classism, to be replaced by an aesthetic utilitarianism allowing for more free time to engage in self-development and social/community activities. Too, the abolition of any form of racism or ethnic prejudice is upheld and the working- and lower-middle classes are not perceived as inherently stupid or unimaginative, but alienated by capitalist oppression, thus not to be led by so-called enlightened socialist elites. To let the individual flourish in freedom, the aim is to decentralize decision-making with extensive participatory democracy in a socialist milieu.

Principal groups having such ideas or variations of them are the Students for a Democratic Society in the U.S. and the *Il Manifesto* group in Italy and the French student movement spearheading the 1968 revolt.

To be sure, there also exist direct action groups, a small minority of the New Left, impatient with slow change, essentially urban guerillas engaged in combat against leading conservative politicians, banks (robbing them), police stations, and even military installations. They include the Red Brigades in Italy (they murdered Aldo Moro, the Italian Prime Minister, in 1978) and their supportive networks lodged in *Autonomia* chapters, the anarchist Baader-Meinhoff gang in Germany, and the Weatherpeople (changed from the sexist Weathermen) in the U.S. Today, anarchists are also in the forefront in demonstrations against the IMF and WB.[9]

Perhaps we have now reached a stage of historical development where capitalist power unifies globally to better control labor and prevent imperialist rivalry leading to world war and socialist revolution. This development now favors capitalism in the short run, but peace among the great powers should strengthen socialism in the future because of these contradictions/problems:

THE ANARCHISM OF JEAN GRAVE

- The continuing globalization of capital in financial markets (stocks and bonds in mutual funds and currency) and credit system or borrowing, with accompanying imbalances, is leading to wild swings of their valuations, exacerbated by speculative hedge and other funds, threatening to bring about financial and accompanying economic chaos. This itself is related to capitalism's inherently uneven development, resulting from imbalances in investment/profit/production/consumption complex.

- The countryside is now emptying rapidly under the impetus of the "green revolution," including new genetically engineered seeds by Monsanto, DuPont, and others, and the continuing spread of capitalism, with its insatiable need for inexpensive labor. In 1950, 70 percent of the world's population lived in rural areas; today it is just over half. For instance, under NAFTA, inexpensive U.S. corn is destroying a rural corn-based way of life in Mexico, displacing small subsistence farmers economically forced to migrate to the cities as a large reserve labor army for capital; invariably unemployed/underemployed, their human situation is tragic as the mutual aid of family/village is destroyed by the urban slum. In Mexico and other poor nations, these usually "unofficial" new residents live in indescribably primitive conditions of poverty and squalor, lacking even minimal housing, health care, sanitation, food, schooling, and transportation. The estimated population of selected cities in millions in 2000, including their outer slums, Mexico City, 16.4, Sao Paolo, 17.8, Bombay, 18.1. By 1990, fifty-four city complexes worldwide had populations of more than five million people. Wherever international capital penetrates poorer nations, its market relations make ever more of their people superfluous, resulting in a socioeconomic imbalance between the minority tied to international capital and the majority who are left out.

- The communications revolution—inexpensive newspapers, radio and television, videos, movies, and even computers—allows the peasantry and working-class to become ever more aware of conditions outside of their immediate environment/locality and nation, of the ongoing class struggle. Even if most of the media are capitalist-controlled, replete with diversions, the main thrust of their message, the glamour of West-

POSTSCRIPT

ern consumerism/high living standards now enjoyed by the bourgeoisie, alone greatly exacerbates class struggle, as most of the population cannot feast on the consumerist cornucopia.

- The continuing waste of the military-industrial complex (800 trillion dollars worldwide in 2000) which eats into the scarce resources of social welfare
- Increased social tensions should arise favouring socialist solutions as a result of growing populations, especially concentrated in urban areas, although the birth rate (births per woman) is itself declining rapidly, from six to three in poor nations and from three to generally under two in rich ones from 1950 to 1995. But with the declining birth rate, an ageing population requires higher economic surpluses for support, either to come by taxing the wealthy more or raising taxes on workers, or higher productivity, the last a long-term solution. The degree of social welfare now divides European socialism, favouring slight increases, and European conservatism, proposing cuts on the basis of free-market "competitiveness."
- With lower birth rates and women increasingly working outside the home, the traditional patriarchal family will progressively lose its influence.
- Spreading pollution, with accompanying lower living standards.
- Since the rise of neo-liberalism (the IMF/WTO combination) income and wealth gaps between the rich and others, especially the poor, is rising in both developed and poor nations. For instance, in the U.S., the wealthiest 1 percent has 40 percent of wealth and 15 percent of income, while the bottom 40 percent have no net wealth and 13 percent of income; real median wages have also declined by 10 percent from 1973 to 2000. In many poorer nations, there is even more inequality. In Brazil, for instance, the richest fifth has almost two-thirds of the income and almost all the wealth, typical for Latin America. But some areas of inequality, like income differentials between the average and that of the bottom fifth, are just as large in the U.S. and Britain as in poorer nations like Brasil and Guatemala, in which the income of the bottom

fifth is only a fourth that of the average one. In fact, globally, class polarity widened from 1960 to 2000 as the richest 20 percent increased its share of income from 70 to 85 percent.

From a worldwide perspective, inequality among nations now continues to the point where in the mid-nineties, in respective percentages, the economically advanced nations, with 20 percent of the population, have 84.7% of the GNP, 84.2% of trade, 85.5% of domestic savings, and 85% of domestic investment; those in the 2nd, 3rd, 4th quintiles, 13.9%, 14.9%, 13.8% and 14.1%; and for the bottom quintile, 1.4%, 0.9%, 0.7% and 0.9%.

Today, almost half the world's six billion people live on less than two dollars a day, with almost half of this segment subsisting on less than a dollar a day, while the wealth of Earth's richest 200 families—all billionaires—at a trillion dollars equals the annual income of the world's poorest two-fifths.

Some specificity now on the horrendous poverty in selected nations, obviously exacerbated by very sharp class polarities; one of which, Brazil, has a relatively high per-càpita GDP ($6,200 in 1999). In Brasil, out of 160 million people, 108 million are considered poor by Brasilian standards, 40 million extremely so, including 12 million *abandonados*, children without parents roaming the streets, while the richest 10 percent have about half the income and more than seven-tenths of the wealthy. In India, with a population of a billion, two-fifths subsist below the poverty line, half in abject poverty, not able to eat a full meal daily; a seventh of the families own up to 80 percent of the land, while three-tenths do not have any—this in a society that is predominantly rural, with half the people illiterate. In Indonesia, out of its 220 million population, half the children are malnourished. In Pakistan, with a population of 140 million, the poverty rate is 40 percent, with an illiteracy rate of 80 percent. In Sub-Saharan Africa—it does not include the Republic of South Africa—most of its more than half billion people are in dire poverty. To be sure, Communist North Korea has recently experienced famine, and more than 40 percent of its people are poverty-stricken, and in Communist China, the partial return to capitalism has caused much socioeconomic hardship, as has the collapse of Communism in Eastern Europe and the former Soviet Union.

- The working class in both the economically advanced and poorer nations expects higher living standards from capitalism, but downsizing, seeking ever less expensive wage-platforms and employing technology to cheapen and make labor ever more redundant, is savaging labor generally through lower real wages, speed-ups and higher unemployment-variants exist, like less unemployment with lower wages (the U.S. model), or higher unemployment with wages still lagging somewhat (the EU model). Official unemployment in the U.S. in 2002 is in the 6 percent range, but 10 percent in the EU.

Thus it is that the increasing exploitation of labor has resulted in rising working class activity: Since 1995, general strikes have erupted in France, Italy, Spain, Belgium, Greece, Canada, South Korea, Argentina, Brasil, and Colombia, among other places, more so than in any other time. Also, two recent polls in Britain, on whether the class struggle exists, had the affirmative answer at 45% in 1964 and 81% in 1995. In the U.S., the "yes" on supporting strikes in 1984 was 34 percent and 46 percent in 1996.[10]

That living standards are falling while the GDP is rising because of ever scarcer natural resources, more pollution, and other infirmities of modern capitalism is the thesis of progressive economists.

In one such recent work, *For the Common Good*, Herman E. Daly and John B. Cobb Jr. affirm that after factoring in the cost of economic growth/pollution—advertising, air and water pollution, long-term environmental illness to human beings, noise, loss of topsoil and non-renewable natural resources, time lost in commuting, automobile accidents, and so forth—which they deduct from the accepted GDP, the standard of life actually drops in recent times: In the U.S., from 1950 to 1986, in 1972 dollars, per capita income more than doubles, but in their "index of sustainable economic welfare," which takes into account the above rising costs, the real standard of life increased a fourth, reaching its peak years from 1968 to 1979, then declining a tenth.[11]

THE ANARCHISM OF JEAN GRAVE

These figures do not include the expensive social alienations with great loss of life of class-exploitative societies, such as the ravages of obesity, smoking tobacco, alcohol, and other drugs, crime, individual and corporate, military expenditures, and wealthy lifestyle of the wealthy and upper-middle classes, with most of the others, like the lower-middle class and workers attempting to imitate them as much as possible, and monopolistic overcharging (a ninth of GDP) when five corporations have at least two-fifths of the domestic market. Examples of these costs and deaths where applicable in the nineties in annual dollars for the U.S.: obesity, 200 billion and 300,000 deaths; gambling profits at 50 billion; alienation at work in the form of absenteeism and psychosomatic/psychological illness, 200 billion; smoking tobacco, 100 billion and more than 430,000 deaths; alcoholic drinks, almost 200 billion and 12,000 deaths; illegal drugs like heroin and cocaine, 200 billion and 16,000 deaths; the prison industry with 2 million persons incarcerated and crime in general, including costs to victims and so forth, almost 500 billion; the military and intelligence agencies, 300 billion dollars; wasteful personal expenditures, including planned obsolescence, based on status and class, at least a fifth, if not much more, of GDP; tax cheating, mostly by the wealthy and business, 300 billion—these in a 6 to 9 trillion dollar GDP.[12]

They have been joined in their critique of neo-liberalism and its mantra of corporate growth at the expense of the environment and working/lower-middle classes by Richard Douthwaite (*The Growth Illusion*), David C. Korten (*When Corporations Rule the World*), Bookchin (*Post-Scarcity Anarchism*), a leading American ecologist/anarchist, founder of the Institute for Social Ecology at Goddard College, Barry Commoner (*Making Peace with the Planet*), and others. Their alternative is to break up the TNCs with locally based economies under quasi-socialist or socialist arrangements.[13]

The specific plans of Bookchin will be presented on solving the pollution/social problems, whose vision of future society is similar in many respects to those of Grave.

They principally include: the employment of solar, wind, and water power (it should also include nuclear fusion, hydrogen, and biomass) as

POSTSCRIPT

sources of energy, replacing oil, gas, and thermonuclear fission, in conjunction with new technologies, like electronics/computers, to allow for dispersal of production in small workplaces. This combination should help resolve the vexing problem of the dichotomy between manual and mental labor, for that of the integrated variety, ending, for all practical purposes, this divisive nightmare, contributing to ever more social solidarity. To this ensemble, he adds a pervasive participatory democracy lodged in local assemblies appointing members to coordinating bodies continuously responsible to them, the ultimate objective being a "community in which the social environment is decentralized into rounded, ecologically balanced communes," of cooperative/community-owned property, bringing about the "harmonization of nature and man" worldwide.

Another partial solution to pollution is to construct near-space stations, and colonise the moon and Mars for conducting polluting technologies.[14] There is, of course, a problem to be faced by socialists opting for this course. Can they maintain high living standards in the economically advanced nations with the new proposed technologies to overcome waste and pollution? Perhaps.

But this assumes that a concerted effort be made now! Even so, it may be too late because the tasks involved to fully implement the new technologies may take a generation. Indeed, because there is a time lag for a build-up of carbon dioxide in the atmosphere, climate warming or the rise of the oceans may not be preventable, the richer nations better able to deal with this catastrophe than the poorer ones. In this vein, half measure to abate pollution are simply false hopes. We may add here Grave's notion that anarchism or approximate human equality requires the continued expansion of the forces of production to end scarcity and allow the good life for all. But with the coming ecological crisis, this may not occur and humanity may regress to some form of fascism.

Nevertheless, in a utopian spirit, given the expected catastrophe awaiting humanity, we present a brief view of a preferred possible "socialism" and "communism" in the spirit of Grave and other socialists. Socialism progressively diminishes the dichotomy between manual and mental labor, favors participatory democracy in the workplace, guarantees full employment and comprehensive social services (daycare for children, old age and disability pensions, and comprehensive medical and other insurance), and human rights (customary civil liberties, like freedom of speech, press, assembly, and elimination of sexual, ethnic, and religious discrimination). The workday itself is not neglected, of not many hours, allowing individuals the necessary time to develop their interests/talents, participate in civic affairs, and enjoy themselves.

Gradually, these elements should expand to further approximating anarcho-communist free distribution of goods and of services—in addition to the other services provided, such common basic needs should be assured to all on demand as food, clothing, transportation, and so forth.

As already mentioned by Grave, economic statisticians working in various "political" levels—in the communes, locally, nationally and internationally—would presumably coordinate their activities to provide society with various planning options to now also reduce pollution and traditionally correct economic imbalances among the various regions. For instance, they can present various economic models, final decisions being made through the aegis of democratic voting.

This economic coordination/planning should be aided by the new technology. There are now in place high-speed computers that digest almost instantaneously almost innumerable amounts of information to follow consumer preferences and draw intricate economic models. The 1990 IBM Option Blue computer, for instance, can perform a trillion calculations a second, and by 2004 a projected computer will do a hundred trillion ones a second. (Computers already do some creative reasoning, i.e., one not associated with any specific problem or sets of them, as in chess.)

Computerization in steel, machine-building, service and other industries, is now advancing rapidly. Furthermore, robots are now becoming ever more common, Japanese industry leading the way, invading not only the manufacturing sector, but also the service one. In 2000, there are 950,000 robots worldwide, each replacing four workers on average. Automated assembly lines in industry are now also becoming ever more common and electronics are now employed in work formerly done by receptionists, bank tellers, and others. These and other new technologies at once allow for the possible return of the small-scale utopian socialist vision to be combined with large-scale enterprise.

POSTSCRIPT

One may ask if scientific/technological dynamism would be impaired under a relatively egalitarian socialism? I would think not. Even in capitalist America, for instance, most of the advanced research is conducted with public monies, by the military-industrial complex and universities, then presented gratis or almost so to business to develop for commercial purposes for profit. Scientific discoveries are now highly socialized, involving a largely cooperative effort, unthinkable without the contributions of past generations and the now-prevalent team approach, often interdisciplinary, in the face of complexity.

On the matter of property the new socialist/anarchist-inspired society in its socialist or first phase would have in a mixed Proudhonian-Mutualist and Bakuninist manner three forms of property—private, collective and public: Private property in the form of personal belongings and housing is allowed, but private profit-making enterprises are either limited or eliminated. Thus it is that private enterprise of a small nature, like a family business, is permitted, as are private collectives (where workers are more or less equal stockholders) having up to a hundred or so members.

As long as a private bourgeois sector exists, larger socialized enterprises, in the hands of both regional/national or even international associations, should include worker ownership to balance it in the form of various regional/national or other stock funds coming from the "profit" or efficiencies after other needs are met, as in development and infrastructure. Management itself, depending on socialist sophistication/education, is either elected by workers or composed of them, including mixtures of both.

Within the enterprises themselves, decision making on everyday and longer affairs is through affinity groups, meeting in *ad hoc* primary assemblies. Since the collectives are part of larger economic networks, associated with local/regional ones, including "governmental bodies," and even national/international ones, participatory democracy is mediated by various groups, facilitated by the electronics/computer revolution. In these workplace arrangements, workers are not necessarily tied to one work site, but to many, labor as mobile as capital, always in the economic loop, usually on the local/regional level, not interfering with any existing salary differentials or causing unemployment or any undue friction between various economic sectors, some expanding, others contracting.

THE ANARCHISM OF JEAN GRAVE

Democratic decision-making itself should be progressively economically rational as the socioeconomic whip dividing individuals and status groups diminishes with socialist solidarity/technology ending traditional scarcity/insecurity. Parallel to this development would be the increasing realization by everyone of their interdependence in developing technologies to aid their self-realization and personhood, while protecting the Earth's environment.

As for consumer goods, free choice prevails as individual interests in art, recreation and other areas varies; Socialism here expands individuality from its restrictive capitalist horizon bounded by status and class or the myth of the present "free market" under oligopolistic restrictive advertising. The last employs the conditioning techniques of the psychologists John B. Watson and Edward Bernays and utilizes the social-psychological insights of Thorstein Veblen as depicted in *The Theory of the Leisure Class*, emphasizing "invidious distinction," of identifying the buyer with the "better people" who set the standards of "excellence," itself tied to planned obsolescence for profit. It is, thus, a myth that consumers today have free choice. A socialist market transcends these class parameters/criteria for those of technological excellence and utilitarianism, combined with a proper aestheticism.

To be sure, in this society, prices for goods exist for the sake of economic efficiency or as yardsticks in relationship to such criteria as protecting the environment and in reducing alienation at work. In the first phase, some socioeconomic inequality exists in these forms:

- Salary differentials based on skills, not too steep with the rapid increase of more education;
- Savings accounts exist, but pay no interest;
- High death taxes prevail, especially on those who have accumulated much private property, as in the private cooperative sector.

Finally, with the rise of an ever-more sophisticated technology, along with the growth of a socialist consciousness in society, salary and other economic differences will be progressively erased, and property as now conceived will no longer be significant in human affairs, anarcho-communism.[14]

POSTSCRIPT

Notes

1. On the monstrosity of Stalinism and its deformation of socialism, see Roy A. Medvedev, *Let History Judge: The Origins and Consequences of Stalinism* (New York: Alfred A. Knopf, 1971), pp 152-257, for instance. Roy A. Medvedev, *On Socialist Democracy* (New York: Alfred A. Knopf, 1975), pp 108-47, on the lack of democracy within the Communist party; pp 225-26, on the steep salary differentials between workers and elite, including perquisites, on the order of 50/100 to 1; pp 227-28, on the special privileges of the elite; pp 164-209, on the lack of speech and press freedoms. Moshe Levin, *Russia/USSR/Russia: The Drive and Drift of a Superstate* (New York: The New Press, 1995), p 73, by 1928, the Bolsheviks become a bureaucratic-hierarchical-administrative party; pp 185-208 on the rise of the Stalinist bureaucracy which in the course of industrialization subordinated the workers to it; pp 311-32, on Stalinism being replaced by "bureaucratic absolutism." On Soviet society, see Moshe Levin, *The Gorbachev Phenomenon: An Historical Interpretation* (Berkeley, CA: Univ. of CA. Press, 1988), pp 43-56, on urbanization and new work force. On the dissolution of the Soviet Union, including causes of, as hierarchical and authoritarian work relations, steep labor division, and lack of democracy: see David Kotz with Fred Weir, *Revolution from Above: The Demise of the Soviet System* (London: Routledge, 1997), pp 34-61, on perestroika and fall of communism; pp 63-72, on the intelligentsia; pp 109-55, on the party-state elite and political struggles; pp 157-99, on shock therapy and its aftermath. Also on privatization: Rose Brady (a *Business Week* editor), *Kapitalizm: Russia's Struggle to Free Its Economy* (New Haven: Yale Univ. Press, 1999), pp 44-154 and 212-16. Although supporting Russian capitalism, she presents many of its unsavory aspects. Stanislov Menshikov (a Russian economist), "A Ruling Class Destroys its Own Regime," *Monthly Review Press*, Vol. 49, No. 5, Oct. 1997, pp 49-57; he also presents much material on the social origins of the new rich and avers that most of mental labor (university and other teachers, engineers, and so forth) supports socialism. On China, see Jasper Becker, *The Chinese* (New York: The Free Press, 2000), pp. 65-86, "Getting Rich is Glorious."

2. On general economic and other developments discussed in this section, see Eric Hobsbawm, *The Age of Extremes: A History of the World, 1914-1991* (New York: Pantheon Books, 1995), pp 257-319. For an excellent economic history of this period, focusing on the U.S., Germany, and Japan, see Robert Brenner, "The Economics of Turbulence: A Special Report on the World Economy, 1950-98," *New Left Review*, No. 229, May/June 1998, entire issue.

3. On economic concentration, see Adolf A. Berle Jr. and Gardiner C. Means, *The Modern Corporation and Private Property*, Revised Edition, (New York: Harcourt, Brace, and World, 1968), pp ix-x and 18-46. (First published in 1933.) For ever more economic concentration in the 1980s and after, see William H. Dugger, *Corporate Hegemony* (New York: Greenwood Press, 1989), p 17. Steven Brouwer, *Sharing the Pie: A Disturbing Picture of the U.S. Economy* (Carlisle, PA: Big Picture Books, 1991), pp 14-16. Bennett Harrison, *Lean and Mean: The Changing Landscape of Corporate*

THE ANARCHISM OF JEAN GRAVE

Power In America (New York: Basic Books, 1994), pp 19 and 64. Paul Hawken, *The Ecology of Commerce: A Declaration of Sustainability* (New York: Harper Collins, 1993), p 8. Walter Adams and James B. Brock, *Dangerous Pursuits: Mergers and Acquisitions In the Age of Wall Street* (New York: Pantheon Books, 1989), pp 12-15 ff. David Korten, *When Corporations Rule the World* (West Hartford, CT: Kumarian Press, 1995), pp 221 ff. On bank concentration, see *Consumer Reports*, March 1996, pp 10-15. On public utilities concentration, see *New York Times*, Dec. 18, 2000, p C6. On interlocking directorates, see Domhoff, *Who Rules America?*, pp 33-49. On the Pujo Subcommittee, see Arthur S. Link, *American Epoch: A History of the United States Since the 1890s*, (New York: Alfred A. Knopf, 1958), pp 51-52.

4. On TNCs, see Korten, *Corporations*, pp 163-77 and 187. On their economic importance, with scarcely any national regulation, see De Anne Julius, *Global Companies and Public Policy: The Growing Challenge of Foreign Direct Investment* (New York: Council of Foreign Relations Press, 1990), pp 6-121. William Greider, *One World Ready or Not: The Manic Logic Of Global Capitalism* (New York: Simon and Schuster, 1997), pp 211-22, on the top TNCs whose sales have risen from 721 billion dollars in 1971 to 5.2 trillion dollars in 1991. Barnet and Cavanaugh, *Global Dreams*, pp 385-402, on the globalization of trading stocks, bands, and currency, with scant or non-existent government supervision, resulting in widespread tax fraud/evasion. Edward S. Herman, "Globalization in Question," *Z Magazine*, April, 1997, pp 8-11, affirms that under present arrangements, any single national control of these money movements is impossible as it simply exposes it to international capital flight. William K. Tabb, "Are New Trade Wars Looming?" *Monthly Review*, Nov. 1999, pp 22-34, asserts that although there may be a few trade wars in the future in selected areas, the power of the TNCs and other international capital is simply too strong to permit any general ones. On the six trillion dollars in off-shore tax havens, see Alan Cowell and Edmund L. Andrews, "Undercurrents at a Safe Harbor," *New York Times*, Sept. 24, 1999, pp C1 and C14. On holdings by Americans abroad and foreigners in the U.S., see Doug Henwood, *Wall Street: How it Works and for Whom* (London: Verso, 1998), p 61. On foreign stock ownership in France, see Craig R. Whitney, "Anxious French Mutter as U.S. Envoy Tries to Sell Globalism," *New York Times*, Dec. 2, 1999, p A10. On U.S. stocks and bonds owned by foreigners in early 2000, see Robert Brenner, "The Boom and the Bubble," *New Left Review*, Nov./Dec., 2000, pp 28-29. Doug Henwood, "The Nation Indicators," *The Nation*, July 19, 1999, p 12, *Akron Beacon Journal*, June 29, 1995, p B6, on inequality. On the greater internationalization of capital in the late 19th century as opposed to the 1990s, see Nicholas D. Kristoff, "At This Rate, We'll Be Global in Another Hundred Years," *New York Times*, "Week in Review" Section, May 23, 1999, p 5.

5. On government giveaways to corporations, see *Common Cause Newletter*, March 1996. Ralph Nader, "Nader's Nineties," *Mother Jones*, July/Aug., 1990, pp 24-27. Robert L. Borosage, "The Politics of Austerity," *Nation*, May 27, 1996, pp 22-24. Neil deMause, "To the Highest Bidder," *In These Times*, May 31, 1998, pp 11-13. Noam

POSTSCRIPT

Chomsky, "Power in the Global Arena," *New Left Review*, No. 230, July/Aug., 1998, pp 13-18.

6. On this statement by the world's leading scientists, see Paul R. Ehrlich and Anne H. Ehrlich, *Betrayal of Science and Reason: How Anti-Environmental Rhetoric Threatens Our Future* (Washington, DC: Island Press, 1996), pp 242-50. Also, see the debate on Pollution and the socialist response in the *Monthly Review*, April, 1998, by two leading American Marxists, John Bellamy Foster, "The Scale of Our Ecological Crisis," pp 5-16, and "Rejoinder to Harvey," pp 31-36, and David Harvey, "Marxism, Metaphors, and Ecological Politics," pp 17-31. On the Kyoto Conference, two articles on its eve in the *Akron Beacon Journal*, Nov. 30, 1997, p A12, outlining the problems faced and probable lack of resolution, contained much pertinent information and were prophetic: Robert S. Boyd, "Climate meeting aims at elusive target," and Robert Rankin, "Deal on global warming fight is called unlikely." On the IPCC report, see H. Josef Hebert, "UN panel warns of global warming," *ibid.*, Oct. 26, 2000, p A3. On the deteriorating eco-structure, see Tom Athanasiou, *Divided Planet: The Ecology of Rich and Poor* (Boston: Little, Brown, and Co., 1996), pp 163-226 focuses on the culpability of global capitalism. Geoffrey Lean and Don Hinrichsen, *Atlas on the Environment* (New York; Harper Perennial, 1994), pp 61-64 and 89-92, for instance, on "freshwater pollution" and "urban air pollution." On practical technology to end much of pollution rapidly, see Barry Commoner, *Making Peace with the Planet* (New York: Pantheon Books, 1990), pp 41-140. On this also see, Lester R. Brown, *et al.*, *State of the World 1994* (New York: W.W. Norton, 1994), pp 81-98, for instance, is on transportation. This series begins in 1984.

7. On France, see, for instance, Daniel Singer, *Is Socialism Doomed? The Meaning of Mitterand* (New York: Oxford Univ. Press, 1988), pp 97-152 and 251-95.

8. On nationalizations, see, for instance R. Joseph Monsen and Kenneth D. Walters, *Nationalized Companies: A Threat to American Business* (New York: McGraw Hill, 1983), p 17, on the percentages of nationalization for many nations; pp 1-51 are very informative. M.V. Posner and S.J. Woolf, *Italian Public Enterprise* (London: Gerald Duckworth, 1967), pp 1-70. On recent privatizations, see Simon Jenkins, *Accountable to None: The Tory Nationalization of Britain* (London: Hamish Hamilton, 1995), pp 23-40, for an overview of recent denationalizations. Thomas Clarke and Christos Pitelis, eds., *The Political Economy of Privatization* (London: Routledge, 1993), has twenty-one articles on the subject. Ferdinando Targetti, ed., *Privatization in Europe: West and East Experiences* (Brookfield, VT: Dartmouth, 1992), has fifteen articles on the subject.

9. On the New Left in America and Europe, see: Theodore Rozak, *The Making of a Counter-Culture* (Garden City, NY: Doubleday, 1969). Lawrence Lader, *Power on the Left: American Radical Movements Since 1946* (New York: W.W. Norton, 1979). Carl Boggs, *The Socialist Tradition: From Crisis to Decline*, (New York: Routledge, 1995), especially pp 181-220.

10. On future conditions for socialist activity, see Immanuel Wallerstein, "The Agonies of Liberalism: what Hope Progress?" *New Left Review*, No. 24, March/April, 1994, pp 3-17. On the superior social safety nets constructed by European Social Democracy relative to the U.S. one, see Robert Kuttner, *The Economic Illusion* (Boston: Houghton Mifflin, 1984), pp 229-63. On the two United Nations' reports, see *U.S. News and World Report*, March 6, 1995, p 68; and Barbara Crosette, "U.N. Survey Finds Rich-Poor Gap widening," *The New York Times*, July, 15, 1996, p A3; and David Harvey, "The Geography of Class Power," in Leo Pantich and Colin Leys (eds.), *The Communist Manifesto Now: Socialist Register 1999* (New York: Monthly Review Press, 1998), p 66; this article has a plethora of information on today's international working class and its many problems. On rising working-class activity in the 1990s, see Sheila Cohen and Kim Moody, "Unions, Strikes and Class Consciousness Today," in Pantich and Leys, *Communist Manifesto*, pp 102-23. On the existence of a capitalist worldwide elite scarcely concerned with the social problems of their "home" nations, see Christopher Lasch, *The Revolt of the Elites and the Betrayal of Democracy*, (New York: W.W. Norton, 1995), pp 25-49. On the horrendous poverty in the various nations, I culled most of it from the *New York Times*. On declining birthrates, see, for instance, Michael Specter (*New York Times*), "Falling Birth Rates Raise Alarms," *Akron Beacon Journal*, Aug. 9, 1998, pp A1 and A6.

11. Herman Daly and John B. Cobb, Jr., *For the Common Good; Redirecting the Economy Toward Community, the Environment and a Sustainable Future* (Boston: Beacon Press, 1989), pp 1-84 and 401-54.

12. These statistics have been culled from the press, the local newspaper, *Akron Beacon Journal* and the *New York Times*, as well as such journals as *The Nation, In These Times, Mother Jones, New Left Review*, and *Z Magazine*. On wasteful expenditures, I am most indebted to Thorstein Veblen, *The Theory of the Leisure Class* and other works. On monopolistic overcharging, the Philip A. Hart (Democratic Senator from Michigan) Senate Committee on monopolies in the 1970s estimated that their pricing practices consumed a sixth of what consumers pay.

13. Richard Douthwaite, *The Growth Illusion: How Economic Growth Has Enriched the Few, Impoverished the Many, and Endangered the Planet* (Tulsa, OK: Council Oaks Books, 1993), pp 4-50, 284-323. Korten, *When Corporations Rule the World*, pp 25-50 and 229-47.

14. In addition to the views of Proudhon, Bakunin, Kropotkin, and Grave, see Murray Bookchin, *Post-Scarcity Anarchism*, pp. 41 and 106 on the quotations. Also, Murray Bookchin, *Remaking Society: Pathways to a Green Future* (Boston: South End Press, 1990), pp 185ff. On "Decentralization and Technology," presents a well-reasoned anarchist case for a sane society without pollution. I am also indebted to Thorstein Veblen, *The Engineers and the Price System* (B.W. Huebsch, 1921), pp 52-107.

INDEX

A

A New Discovery of Terra Incognita Australis (de Foigny) 121
Adam, Paul 31,37,39,50,63,70,87, 123,197
Ajalbert, Jean 40,45,93,96
Albert, Charles (Charles Albert Daudet) 11,61-62,70,80,89-90,95,106,155, 161,170-171
alienation 23,25,129,157,163-164, 187,191-192,196
Allonier 6
Alphonso XIII (Spain) 64
Amos 118
Anarchism and Socialism (Plekhanov) 116,147,150
Anarchistes de Gouvernements (Malatesta) 100
anarcho-communism 22-23,31, 73-75,124,133,142,144,147-148
anarcho-syndicalism 23,61,73-74, 85,142
Andrea, Johann 26,121
Andrieux, Louis 29,33
Angrand, Charles 94,96
Aristotle 118-119,123
Armand, Ernest 80,82-83,85-86
art and anarchism 87-88
atheism 127
authority 7,14,29,49,54,65,76,89-90,98, 102,123-128,131,134-135,140-141,145, 147,163,169,172,174,187
Autonomia 187
Aux jeunes gens (Kropotkin) 63
Aviño (Farras A.) 64
Axa, Zo d' 39,86

B

Baader-Meinhoff gang 187
Babeuf, Gracchus 122-123,159
Bakunin, Michael 15,19-23,26,28,31,39, 42,73-74,82,89,93,122,124,126,130-131, 136,159,165,168-170,186,195,200
Balzac, Honoré de 45,89
Barbusse, Henri 40,45,112,114
Barotte, Madame 113
Barrès, Maurice 37,43,72
Beauvoir, Simone de 149,159
Benoît, Charles 61,69-70
Benoît, Clotilde Thérèse 35
Benoît, Madame Joseph 47
Benoît, Joseph 36,47
Berkman, Alexander 110
Bernays, Edward 196
Bismarck, Otto von 13,183
Blanqui, Louis-Auguste 10,12-15,42
Bookchin, Murray 70,144-145, 149,192,200
bourgeoisie 5,10,20,24,27,34,62,74-75, 77,88,112,120,122,127-128,130-131,133-134,152,157,164,167,172,185,188
Bourses du Travail 74,76,84
Breton, Jules L. 55
Bretton Woods Conference 174
Brothers of Mary 6
Brothers of the Christian Doctrine 6
Bulot 52-53,57

C

Caesar, Julius 1,160,173
Cafiero, Carlo 26
Campanella, Tommaso 121,123

Camus, Albert 155,158-160, 170-171,173
Capital (Marx) 84,106,110, 135,138,198
capitalism 21,25,28,38,73-74,77,84,88,
  114,126,130-132,134,136,138,142,
  156-157,159-160,173-175,179,182,
  187-188,190-191,197
Carnot, Sadi 51
Caserio, Santo-Jeronimo 51,56-57
Casimir-Perier, Jean 55
Chatel, Charles 52
Christianapolis (Amdrea) 121
ciompi 120
City of the Sun (Campanella) 121,145
Civil Disobedience (Thoreau) 39
Clairvaux Prison 55
Clemenceau, Georges 70,72,85
Clichy 46-47
co-determination 185
Coeurderoy, Ernest 38,44
Cohn-Bendit, Daniel 166,168-170, 172
colonialism 97,106,128,161,165-166
Combat (newspaper) 158-159
Communist 1,5,97,101,104-105,111,133,
  137,155,159,161,166-168,173,182-186,
  190,196,200
Communist parties 133,183
computers 150,176,185,188,192,194
Confédération Générale du Travail
  (CGT) 74
Costa, Andrea 26
Courbet, Gustave 15
Critique de la raison dialectique (Sartre)
  135,162,171
Cross, Henri-Edmond 94,96

D
Daedalus 119
Darwin, Charles 39,44,82,86,151,
  153,162
Dash, Comtesse 6
De Gaulle 161,167
De la capacité politique des classes ouvrières
  (Proudhon) 20,133

Décembre 6
Déclaration (Manifeste des Seize) (Grave et
  al.) 107
Delompré 8
Demain (journal) 160
Democracy in America (de Tocqueville)
  122,132,138
Descaves, Lucien 39,44,51,87,93,96
Diderot, Denis 39,121,124
Dreyfus Affair 78
Dreyfus, Alfred 66
Drumont, Edouard 37,39,43-44, 51,57
Dubois, Félix 36,43
Dumartheray, François 22
Dumas, Alexandre (the elder) 6
Dumoulin, Georges 84
Dunois, Amédée 71,74,76,84
Duval, Clément 40

E
Ecole Normale Supérieure 155,161
Economic and Philosophical Manuscripts
  (Marx) 136
education 2,6,10,12,21,62,65,71,77,
  88,121,131,140,150,156,160,165,
  183,195-196
Eltzbacher, Paul 71,112,114
Emerson, Ralph Waldo 93
Engels, Friedrich 1,21,122,125,
  135-138,148
Entre Paysans (Malatesta) 63
Erikson, Erik 12
Eros and Civilization (Marcuse) 123,150
Escape from Freedom (Fromm) 12,136
Essay on Population (Malthus) 126
European Union (EU) 174-176,
  179,183-185,191
Exceptional Laws 48,51,53,55-56

F
Faure, Félix 52,54-55,61,67-69,
  72,75,83,86,101
Fédération des Bourses du Travail 74

INDEX

Fénéon, Felix 52,87
Finet 35
First International 14,19,21,31,34
Flaubert, Gustave 50,95
Foigny, Gabriel de 121
For the Common Good 191,200
France, Anatole 37,63,99
Frantz-Jourdain 53
Freedom (periodical) 12,32,102, 107-108,121,136,144,149,160
French Revolution, 1789-94 1,3,66,88,96,121-122,131,137,159
Fromm, Erich 12,123,136

G
Gambetta, Léon 13-14
Gargantua and Pantagruel (Rabelais) 38
Garibaldi, Guiseppe 78
Gaugin, Paul 51
General Agreement on Tariffs and Trade 174
Germinal (Zola) 88,137
Girard, André 61-62,69,71,101,106,109
Godwin, William 121,159,171 133,138
Grave, Jean 11,17-18,33,36,42-43,45, 49-51,57,66,70-72,82-86,95,106-109, 112-114,135,137-138
Guesde 26,32,39,74
Guérin, Daniel 79,85
Guérin, Jacques 102

H
Hegel, Georg, W. F. 20,136,151,153
Henry, Emile 48
Henry, Fortuné 55
Hephaestus 119
Hermann-Paul 63,71,94,99
Hervé, Gustave 61,69
Hobsbawm, Eric 45,174,197
Holbach, Baron d' 121
Homage to Catalonia (Orwell) 117,123
Hugo, Victor 45,50

I
Ibsen, Henrik 93
Ideology and Utopia (Mannheim) 122-123
Industrial Workers of the World 23
integrated labor 148
International Monetary Fund (IMF) 173-174,186-187,189
International Social Democratic Alliance 21
Iribe, Paul 98
Isaiah 71,118

J
Jaurès, Jean 57,72,97-99,106
Jean Christophe (Rolland) 101
Jefferson, Thomas 121
Jesus of Nazareth 119
Jouhaux, Léon 103
July 1830 Revolution 10
Jura Federation 23,32

K
Kelly, Aileen 31,147,150
Kerensky, Alexander F. 104
Keynes, John Maynard 129
Kilbatchiche, Victor (Le Rétif, Victor Serge) 80-81,85
Koeningstein, François (Ravachol) 47
Kropotkin, Peter 22,31,35,95, 135,137,148

L
La Bataille 18,100,103,107-109
La Bataille Syndicaliste 103,107-109
La Chute (Camus) 158
La Colonisation (Grave) 63,106
La Condition Ouvrière (Weil) 170
La Grande famille (Sous l'uniforme) (Grave) 12,16,18,25,32,47,87,89,129
La Libre Fédération 102,107-108
La Lutte universelle (Félix Le Dantec) 80,86
La Paix par les Peuples (Faure et al.) 101
La Peste (Camus) 158

203

La Plume 38
La Révolte 18,36-37,41,43-47,51-53,55-57, 61-62,70,82,92,110-111,113
La Révolution Prolétarienne 70,155
La Révolution Sociale 29,33
La Société au lendemain de la révolution (Grave) 29,33,71,124,136-138, 141,147-149
La Société future (Grave) 16,18,55,71,75,84,95,124,132-133, 135,137-138,141,148-149
La Voix du Peuple 75
labor division 197
Labori, Fernand 11,32,45,48
Law of Freedom (Winstanley) 121
Law of Maturities 14
Lazare, Bernard 37,41,48,50,63,67,70,72,87
Le Bulletin des Groupes Anarchistes 27
Le Cri du Peuple 39
Le Dantec, Félix 80,86
Le Feu (Barbusse) 40
Le Journal 51,68,72
Le Journal du Peuple 68,72
Le Libertaire 61,75
Le Matin 134,138
Le Prolétaire 25,32
Le Révolté 33,35-37,42-43
Le Vengeur 13
Lenin, V.I. 12,104-107,109, 132,137-140,148,165
Les Aventures de Nono (Grave) 91,95
Les Conquérants (Malraux) 112,114
Les Entretiens Politiques et Littéraires 87
Les Temps Nouveaux 18,33,36,42-43,60-63,67,69-72,74,76, 78-79,82-86,89,92-96,98-99,101-102, 105-106,109-111,135,137-138,149
Libertad, Albert 80-81,85-86
Lichtheim, George 138,140,148
Lombroso, Césare 134,138
London International Congress (anarchist) 28,33

Longuet, Charles 15
Loubet, Emile 64,68
Luce, Maximilien 37,63,87,93-96,103,107,111,113
Lyons 14,19,26,28,30,34,42,51,134

M
Multilateral Agreement on Investment (MAI) 177
Maitron, Jean 11,17,32,56,84-85,114,116,134
Making Peace with the Planet 192
Malatesta, Errico 26-29,32,63-64,78-79, 82,85,100-101,107,110,137,145,149
Mallarmé, Stephane 37
Malraux, André 112,114,138
Malthus, Thomas Robert 126
Manouvrier, Professor 53
Marcuse, Herbert 122-123,132,138, 145-147,149-150,153-154,186
Marseilles Labor Congress 32
Marx, Karl 1,15,17-19,21-22,24-27,31,64, 72,84,89,110,119,122,124-125,127,129-131,133,135-141,145-150,153-154,156, 162-163,165-166,168-169,171-173,186
Marxism 1,17-18,21,122,124-125,127, 145,149,162,166,168,171-173,186
Maupassant, Guy de 39-40,45
May Events 155,166-168,170,172
Merrill, Stuart 51,60,69,87,177
Micah 118
Michel, Louise 12,15,29,32-34,64, 82,87,96,152-154,171
Michels, Robert 12,152-154
Mill, John Stuart 31,45,56,93,123, 135-136,138,186
Minville 25-26,32
Mirbeau, Octave 37,39,45,47,49-51, 55-57,68,72,93,99,116,135
Mitterand, François 184,199
Monatte, Pierre 74,78-79,85,103-105,155
More, Sir Thomas 16,22,24,31,38,66, 119-121,123,138,157,159
Morelly 121,123,159

INDEX

Moro, Aldo 97,187
Mosca, Gaetano 151-154
Mulholland, William 178
Müntzer, Thomas 120
Mussolini, Benito 152
mutual aid 3,65,73,79,91,98,112, 117,125-127,135,141,147,154,188
Mutual Aid (Kropotkin) 39,135
Mutualism 19-20,73,81,158

N
Napoleon I 1-2,10-11,13
Napoleon III 1-2,11,13
nationalisations 183-184
Nettlau, Max 32,106,112,114,138,148
New Left 145,186-187,197-200
New York Clearing House Interbank Payment System (CHIPS) 177
New York Review of Books 147,150,172
Nietzsche, Friedrich 80
1984 (Orwell) 163,174,191,199

O
Oppression et liberté (Weil) 156
Organisation for Economic Cooperation and Development (OECD) 177
Organisation, initiative, cohesion (Grave) 72
Ortiz, Léon 41,45,52,54
Orwell, George 117,123,163
Owen, Robert 19

P
Paine, Thomas 121
Paolidès, Apostol 27
Pareto, Vilfredo 151-154
Paris 2-6,8-14,17-20,23,25-26,28,30-36, 38,41-48,51-53,55-57,60,64,68-73,78-80, 82-87,89,91,94-96,99-101,105-109,112- 114,116,123,130,134-138,149,154-155, 159,166-167,170-172
Paris Commune 3,9,14,17,20,73,130,159
Parti des Travailleurs Socialistes de France 25-26

Parti Ouvrier Français 74
peasantry 1-2,10,130-131,137,158,182,188
Pelloutier, Fernand 61,64,74-77, 83-84,160,169
Père Duchêne (newspaper) 13
Père Peinard (newspaper) 51,61,69,75
Phaleas of Chalcedon 119
Pierrot, Marc 61-62,70,76,84,105
Pini 37,53
Pissarro, Camille 87,93-94
Pissarro, Lucien 60,87,94
Plato 118-119,149
Plekhanov, George 116,147,150
Poincaré, Raymond 98
Polish uprisings 10
Political Parties 12,152,154
pollution 147,173,179,181-182,189, 191-194,199-200
Pompidou, Georges 167
Popular Front 157,161,184
Post-Scarcity Anarchism (Bookchin) 144,149,192,200
Pottier, Eugène 39,44
Pouget, Emile 29,34,37,50-52,54, 56-57,61,64,67,69,75,83
Prague Spring of 1968 161
private property 19,28,75,117-118,121, 127,131,136,149,152,158,196
propaganda by deed 21,28-30,33, 41,47-49,51-54,57,63,131
Protestant Reformation 120
Proudhon, Pierre-Joseph 1,15,19-22,30,39,54,73-74,81,88,93,95, 122,124,127,132-133,138,141,157-158, 160,162,195,200
Publications des Temps Nouveau (monthly bulletin) 108
Pyat, Félix 13
Pythagoras 22,31,118

Q
Quarante ans de propagande anarchiste (Grave) 2,11,112

R

Rabelais, François 38
racism 97,125,128,136,163,165-166,187
Rassemblement Démocratique Révolutionnaire (RDR) 159,161
Rauschenbusch, Walter 128,136
Read, Sir Herbert 6,79,85,170,198
Reclus, Elie 15,41
Reclus, Elisée 15,22,31,35-37,41-42,45, 47,49,53,55,57,60-62,65,69-70,87,95, 116,124,136-137,145,149
Reclus, Paul 31,41,45,52,57,100,103
Réflexions sur la violence (Sorel) 75
Reid, Mayne 6,96
religion 12,70,75,122,124,127-128, 136,141,156
Renaissance 88,120
Responsabilités (Grave) 91,95
Resurrection (Tolstoy) 66
Retté, Adolphe 51,61-62,70
revolution 2-3,7,10-11,13-14,16-17, 20-21,23-24,26-27,29,33-35,40-42,47,52, 54,56,61,64,71,73-79,81-84,88-90,93,99, 103-105,109,111-112,117-118,120-121, 124-126,129-134,137-141,148-150,152-153,155-157,159-160,164-165,167-171, 185-188,195
Revolution 1848 1,10,20-21,38
revolutionary collectivism 20
revolutionary syndicalism 76,78-79,109,157,164
Richepin, Jean 37,39,51,93,96
Roads to Freedom (Russell) 144,149
Rolland, Romain 101,108-109
Rousseau, Jean-Jacques 65,71,121,136
Roux, Jacques 122
Russell, Bertrand 144,149
Rysselberghe, Theo van 94-96

S

Sacco, Nicola 110,113-114
Saint-Auban, Emile de 49-50,53-54,56-57
Sainte-Croix 92
Saint-Prix, Jean de 109
Saint-Simon, Claude-Henri de 2,11
Sartre, Jean-Paul 113,125,135,155, 159,161-166,171-172
scarcity 125,135,162,193,195
Schmidt, Johann Kasper (Max Stirner) 80,86
Schweitzer, Albert 161
Schweitzer, Charles 161
Securities and Exchange Commission (SEC) 139,178
Shaw, George Bernard 147,150
Signac, Paul 37,60,62,93-94,96,101,107,111
Situationists 168
Sixth Section Group of Paris 28
Smith, Adam 123,129,138,171
Social Darwinism 39,44,162
Social Revolutionary Group of Lyons 28
Social Study Group of the Fifth and Thirteenth Wards of Paris 26
Socialist Revolutionary Party (Russia) 23
Société des Gens de Lettres 39,45
Society of the Seasons 10
Sorel, Georges 75,83-84,157,160,169
Soviet Communism 172-173
Soviet Union 80,110,168,173, 183,190,197
Spencer, Herbert 39,44
Spilleux, Egide (Serraux) 29
Stalinism 156,159-160,183,196-197
State 5,7,9,11-12,14-17,29,39,42,45,47, 54,56-57,63,66,72,75,80,84,88-89,99-102,107,111-114,118,121-123,126-128, 130-131,134,136,139-140,145-147,149, 151-152,156-159,162-163,166,168-169, 171-173,179,181,185,197-198
State and Revolution (Lenin) 105,109,137,140,148
stateless 145-146
Steinlen, Alexandre 63,93-94,96,111
Stendhal (Marie Henri Beyle) 89
Stirner, Max. *See* Schmidt, Johann Kaspar 80,86

INDEX

Stock, P.V. 12,17-18,33,56,71, 84,95,149,170
strikes 34,62,74,77-78,83,104,167,169,191
Sumner, William Graham 151-154
SWIFT 177

T
Tailhade, Laurent 51,68,72
Tawney, R.H. 10,12,149
Tcherkesoff, Warlaan 26,62,70
Terre Libre (Grave) 84,89-90, 141,143,148-149
Thatcher, Margaret 185
The Civil War in France (Marx) 140,148
The Communist Manifesto (Marx and Engels) 1,200
The Descent of Man (Darwin) 151,153
The Impossibilities of Anarchism (Shaw) 147,150
The Philosophy of Right and Law (Hegel) 151,153
The Politics (Aristotle) 119,123,198
The Republic (Plato) 118
The Ruling Class (Mosca) 152-154
The Theory of the Leisure Class 136,196,200
Thierry, Augustin 6
Thiers, Louis Adolphe 14-15
Thirion 4,9
Thomas, Mabel Holland (Mrs. Jean Grave) 31,33,38,65,71, 79,84,120-121,138,199
Thoreau, Henry David 39,44,93
Tocqueville, Alexis de 122,138
Tolain 160
Tolstoy, Leo 29,39,44,65-66,71,89,93
transnational corporations 173
Trial of the Thirty (Paris) 46,52,57
Trotsky, Leon (Lev Davidovich Bronstein) 12,80,104,186

U
Utopia (More) 22,31,38,112,120-123,136,148,150

utopia 1,31,38,90-91,112,120-124, 126,134,139,141-142,145-148,150, 159,193-194

V
Vaillant, Auguste 48,56
Vallès, Jules 13,17,39
Valloton, Felix 94,96
Vanzetti, Bartolomeo 110,113-114
Varlin, Eugéne 15
Veblen, Thorstein 136,196,200
Vergnolles 9
Verhaeren, Emile 93
Vermersch 13
Vielé-Griffin, Francis 87

W
Wagner, Richard 20,89,93,95
Walden (Thoreau) 39
War and Peace (Tolstoy) 66
War Communism 140
Watson, John B 196
Weatherpeople 187
Weber, Max 151-154
Weil, Simone 148,155,170
Weill, Georges 5,11-12,116
Wells, H. G. 112,114
When Corporations Rule the World 192,197,200
Whitman, Walt 93
Winstanley, Gerrard 121,136
Wintsch, Jean 102
working class 3,14,32,39,48,76,103,112, 130,157,164-166,182,184,190-191,200
World Bank (WB) 173-174,186-187
World Trade Organisation (WTO) 173-174,179,189

Y
Yvetot, Georges 76

Z
Zimmerwald Conference 100-101,107
Zola, Emile 4,39-40,44-45,51,57, 67-68,72,88,93

ALSO PUBLISHED BY BLACK ROSE BOOKS

The history of anarchism in Portugal.

FREEDOM FIGHTERS
Anarchist Intellectuals, Workers, and Soldiers in Portugal's History
João Freire

translated by Maria Fernanda Noronha da Costa e Sousa

Some eighty years ago, Portugese libertarians were organized under the banner of syndicalism. This movement deeply marked the history of Portugal.

Freedom Fighters examines anarchist ideas and how these arrived in Portugal, and how the anarchist program gained popularity with both the working class and intellectuals, people who believed in the slogan 'with neither God nor master.'

This fascinating history is traced from the beginning of the 20th century through the Spanish Civil War and the Second World War. The role of the anarchists during Salazer's dictatorship is examined with much previously unknown documentation. Of particular interest is the history of the anarchists during the 1974 'Carnation Revolution' and during Portugal's emergence as a contemporary liberal democracy.

> *Freedom Fighters* is now, and will remain for a long time, a necessary book to any who look to do new research on the subject.
> —Miguel Serras Pereira, *Público*, Lisbon

Freedom Fighters fills a large gap in the history and sociology of Portugal. Much of the analysis and documentation presented in this important work will help the contemporary reader to understand Portugal today.

João Freire is a professor of Sociology at the University of Lisbon.

216 pages, photographs
Paperback ISBN:1-55164-138-0 $24.99
Hardcover ISBN:1-55164-139-9 $53.99

ALSO PUBLISHED BY BLACK ROSE BOOKS

Bookchin's books are classic statements of contemporary anarchism.

MURRAY BOOKCHIN READER
Janet Biehl, editor

This collection provides an overview of the thought of the foremost social theorist and political philosopher of the libertarian left today. His writings span five decades, and subject matter of remarkable breadth. Bookchin's writings on revolutionary philosophy, politics, and history are far less known than the specific controversies that have surrounded him, but they are deserving of far greater attention.

Consistent throughout his work is a search for ways to replace today's capitalist society with a more rational and humane alternative. The selections in this reader constitute a sampling from the writings of one of the pivotal thinkers of our era.

> A major American political philosopher. —*San Francisco Chronicle*

> Murray Bookchin stands at the pinnacle of the genre of utopian social criticism. —*The Village Voice*

> Murray Bookchin's books are of critical importance. —*New Scientist*

Janet Biehl is also the author of *Finding Our Way: Rethinking Ecofeminist Politics*, and, with Murray Bookchin, *Politics of Social Ecology*, both published by Black Rose Books. She lectures at the Institute of Social Ecology in Plainfield, Vermont. Murray Bookchin, Professor Emeritus at the School of Environmental Studies, Ramapo College and Director Emeritus of the Institute of Social Ecology, has authored more than a dozen books on urbanism, ecology, technology and philosophy.

288 pages, bibliography, index
Paperback ISBN: 1-55164-118-6 $24.99
Hardcover ISBN: 1-55164-119-4 $53.99

BOOKS OF RELATED INTEREST FROM

WORDS OF A REBEL
Peter Kropotkin
This collection contains articles written between 1879 and 1882, and thereby includes his earliest material. This is the first complete English version.
229 pages ✻ Paper 1-895431-04-2 $24.99 ✻ Cloth 1-895431-05-0 $53.99

BAKUNIN The Philosophy of Freedom
Brian Morris
Bakunin was a holistic thinker whose anarchism fully deserves to be recognized... an extraordinary man full of a primitive exuberance and strength.
159 pages ✻ Paper 1-895431-66-2 $18.99 ✻ Cloth 1-895431-67-0 $47.99

MANUFACTURING CONSENT Noam Chomsky and the Media
Mark Achbar
Charts the life of America's most famous dissident, from his boyhood days to his current role as outspoken social critic.
264 pages ✻ Paper 1-55164-002-3 $26.99 ✻ Cloth 1-55164-003-1 $55.99

send for a free catalogue of all our titles
BLACK ROSE BOOKS
C.P. 1258, Succ. Place du Parc
Montréal, Québec
H2X 4A7 Canada
or visit our web site at: http://www.web.net/blackrosebooks

To order books:
In Canada: (phone) 1-800-565-9523 (fax) 1-800-221-9985
email: utpbooks@utpress.utoronto.ca
In United States: (phone) 1-800-283-3572 (fax) 1-651-917-6406
In UK & Europe: (phone) London 44 (0)20 8986-4854 (fax) 44 (0)20 8533-5821
email: order@centralbooks.com

Printed by the workers of
MARC VEILLEUX IMPRIMEUR INC.
Boucherville, Québec
for Black Rose Books Ltd.